Bad Boys

Bad
Boys

$\mathcal{W}$HY
WE LOVE THEM,
HOW TO LIVE WITH
THEM, AND WHEN
TO LEAVE THEM

Carole Lieberman, M.D.,
and
Lisa Collier Cool

A DUTTON BOOK

DUTTON
Published by the Penguin Group
Penguin Books USA Inc., 375 Hudson Street, New York, New York 10014, U.S.A.
Penguin Books Ltd, 27 Wrights Lane, London W8 5TZ, England
Penguin Books Australia Ltd, Ringwood, Victoria, Australia
Penguin Books Canada Ltd, 10 Alcorn Avenue, Toronto, Ontario, Canada M4V 3B2
Penguin Books (N.Z.) Ltd, 182–190 Wairau Road, Auckland 10, New Zealand

Penguin Books Ltd, Registered Offices:
Harmondsworth, Middlesex, England

First published by Dutton, an imprint of Dutton Signet, a division
of Penguin Books USA Inc.
Distributed in Canada by McClelland & Stewart Inc.

First Printing, April, 1997
1   3   5   7   9   10   8   6   4   2

Grateful acknowledgment is made to the following for permission to reprint
copyrighted song lyrics: "The Leader of the Pack." Words and music by George
Morton, Jeff Barry, and Ellie Greenwich. © 1964 (Renewed 1992) EMI MUSIC
PUBLISHING LTD. and TENDER TUNES MUSIC CO. All rights controlled
and administered by SCREEN GEMS-EMI MUSIC INC. All rights reserved.
International Copyright secured. Used by permission.

 REGISTERED TRADEMARK—MARCA REGISTRADA

LIBRARY OF CONGRESS CATALOGING-IN-PUBLICATION DATA:
Lieberman, Carole.
Bad Boys : why we love them, how to live with them, and when to leave them /
Carole Lieberman and Lisa Collier Cool.
p.   cm.
ISBN 0-525-94116-9
1. Man-woman relationships.   2. Women—Psychology.
I. Cool, Lisa Collier.   II. Title
HQ801.L457   1997
306.7—dc21   96-49710
CIP
Printed in the United States of America
Set in Sabon
Designed by Jesse Cohen

This book is printed on acid-free paper. ∞

This book is dedicated to all the women who are still hoping for a Prince Charming to make their fairy-tale fantasies come true, and especially to four very lovely princesses—Tiffany, Alison, Georgia, and Rosalie.

ACKNOWLEDGMENTS

We gratefully acknowledge the invaluable contributions of:

Our editors at Dutton: Audrey LaFehr, who shared our vision of what this book would become, and Leah Bassoff and Julia Serebrinsky, who helped us polish and shape our manuscript with their insightful suggestions.

Our agent, Jimmy Vines, who, from the start believed in the heat and light that this book would generate.

All our girlfriends and other women who have whispered their bad-boy secrets to us over the years. We honor your privacy by changing your names and identifying circumstances, but each of you knows how special you really are to us.

Dr. Carole Lieberman also acknowledges:

My parents, Sylvia and Sidney Lieberman, who made all this possible. Your devotion has always been my source of strength.

The bad boys I've known and loved, most especially M. M., B. T., H. L., J. B., and R. W. Without your love, laughter, and tears, I would not have obtained the wisdom I can now share with other princesses.

Those who have, with encouragement and conviviality, accompanied me along this journey: Trish Alexander, Dr. Mari Edelman, Dr. Claudie Lannoy, Dr. Maimon Leavitt, Gayle Singer, and Ginny Weissman.

Lisa Collier Cool also acknowledges:

John Cool, my husband, sweetheart, and friend. With you, I've truly found the prince of my dreams.

Oscar Collier, my father and former literary agent, for his advice, patience, and loving encouragement during the writing of this book.

My friends and colleagues in the publishing world: Sue Benson, Peter Bloch, Helen Gurley Brown, Denise Brodey, Guy Flatley, Nancy Kalish, and Linda Murray for all their support, enthusiasm, and inspiration.

CONTENTS

My folks were always putting him down.
They said he came from the wrong side of town.
They told me he was bad, but I know he was sad.
That's why I fell for The Leader of the Pack.

— "The Leader of the Pack"

INTRODUCTION

What *is* a bad boy? He's a rebel without a cause, a cool dude in a motorcycle jacket, a real-life Huckleberry Finn who wants to take you on a wild river ride to adventure. He's wounded, moody, misunderstood—a dreamer, a seducer, a daredevil. He is a man of mystery and a fascinating paradox. He's both a lost little boy and a man with a dark side. He breaks your heart with his wicked ways, but whether he's a wanton wolf or a dangerous desperado, he makes you long to rescue him from *his* pain. He's hurtful, cruel, or simply careless and self-absorbed, but you can't resist jumping on his motorcycle and roaring off into the steamy night with him. And once you've given him your heart forever . . . he's gone with the wind!

He is someone who sets off throbbing sexual and aggressive passions within you. Because he's aloof and elusive, you get caught up in the challenge and excitement of the chase—though he's not always someone you'd really want even if you did capture him. A bad boy may tell you he's not good enough for you or not what you deserve—and heartbreakingly, he's generally right. He's a frog you hope to turn into a fairy-tale prince with the magic of your kiss, a theme I'll explore in greater depth along with a variety of other fairy tales and fantasies that may be fueling your bad-boy attraction.

From pianists to professors, surgeons to sportscasters, film actors to foreign tour guides, my past is littered with enough bad boys to last a lifetime. My affinity for romantic rogues became evident in early childhood. One summer, the other kids at camp warned me about a guy—let's call him Jack—who had a pattern of giving a girl his letter sweater as a sign that the two of them were going together, then asking for it back the next week. That intrigued me because it created a challenge: Jack may reject *other* girls after a week, I thought, but he's going to love *me* forever.

Before long I was wearing that coveted sweater. All too soon, however, a chill had set in—literally, since Jack repossessed his seductive sweater, then draped it over a different girl's shoulders a few days later. I was left to shiver alone, but I was also hooked on the wild, thrilling ride of loving a bad boy. After all, not only did I win the sweater and his fickle heart—if only for a while—but my reign as his favorite lasted longer than any of my predecessors' had . . . at least *two* weeks!

It wasn't long until another bad boy caught my eye. I was thirteen, and "Noel" was an exciting older man of 18. He soon gave me his ID bracelet, and I felt like Cinderella when she found the handsome prince who would bring magic to her life. As the romance progressed, however, my prince started showing a darker side—by becoming increasingly jealous, possessive, and controlling. He insisted that I wear the ID bracelet every moment, but each time I walked inside my front door, I had to quickly stash it away. My mother was horrified at the idea of me making a commitment at such a tender age—especially to a bad boy. Instead of twinkling with the silvery glow of young romance, the ID bracelet soon began looking and feeling more like a handcuff.

By the time I finished high school, my parents' disapproval couldn't keep me away from "Rocky"—in fact, it was part of the attraction that drew me to this sexy stud in a black leather jacket who roared around on a high-powered motorcycle. One look told me that I'd found a real-life "Leader of the Pack," because he fit that classic rock song's lyrics perfectly. Now I can look back and see that this was his unconscious hold on me. He was bad, sad, and from the wrong side of the tracks, a rebel with a reputation—and not for making the honor roll. He was everything that spells heart-stopping danger, the kind of guy who lives fast, dies young, and leaves a good-looking corpse. Our relationship also burned out fast, but to this day whenever I pass a jukebox playing "Leader of the Pack," I can't help wondering whether Rocky's "song" ended with screeching brakes and a fiery crash.

Those were the first bad boys I was involved with, but they certainly weren't the last. In both my personal life and my career as a psychiatrist, psychiatric script consultant to Hollywood writers and producers, courtroom expert witness, and talk show guest and host, I've met just about every variety of seductive scoundrel there is. In here, I'll be drawing upon my own experiences of love, laughter, and tears and the experiences other women have shared with me, to help you understand the secrets of your own heart and the secret psyche of the seductive, moody, misunderstood, passionate, dangerous, and ultimately elusive man you love.

Join me for an intimate look at the twelve types of bad boys—the dark dozen—and why you find yourself irresistibly drawn to the same impossible type of man over and over again. You're in for some surprising insights as to how your romances with bad boys may be more like fairy tales than you think.

We can't help tenaciously clinging to the romantic notion that we'll find our Prince Charming and ride off into the sunset to live out a perfect fairy-tale ending. But sometimes the realities of our lives make it hard for the perfect world of our dreams and fairy tales to survive. It is my fondest hope that this book will *illustrate how to turn a frog into a prince* and bring you closer to the *happy ending* that you deserve.

—Carole Lieberman, M.D.
Beverly Hills, California

1

OUR LOVE AFFAIR
WITH BAD BOYS

Once upon a time there was a woman who wanted to find a handsome prince and live happily ever after. Unfortunately, the men this Beauty fell in love with turned out to be real Beasts. They sulked, broke her belongings during their tantrums, cheated on her, borrowed money that they never repaid, or vanished for weeks on end. During each of these upsetting episodes, she'd swear that she was done with that man forever—but just when she thought she'd gotten up enough nerve to say, "It's over," somehow it always came out as, "Call me tomorrow, *please.*"

Whenever she told friends about her latest horror story, she always began the same way: "He actually thinks . . ." One of her beastly boyfriends actually thought she'd wire him a thousand dollars in Mexico after he hadn't called her for a month, and another that she would rush to his apartment at 3:00 A.M. for sex with him—and to her eternal embarrassment, both were *right.*

Are you also living a fractured fairy tale, where none of the frogs you kiss ever prove to be the prince of your dreams? If so, you're in good company. Throughout history, women have been attracted—and intrigued—by men who are "mad, bad, and dangerous to know," as Lady Caroline Lamb, a great beauty of her day, once described her lover, nineteenth-century Romantic poet Lord Byron. Meanwhile the nice guys sat in their garrets, eating their solitary meals and wondering why they couldn't get a date. Though they can be maddeningly unpredictable, dishonest, or downright mean, scoundrels have always had an undeniable appeal to many of us—an erotic edge of danger that's hard to resist.

Today, most of us share Lady Caroline's obsession, as we relish all of the delicious details about the bad boys of our age: President Clinton, William Kennedy Smith or the other Kennedy men, Ted Bundy, Mike Tyson, Joey Buttafuoco, Prince Charles, Sean Penn, John Wayne Bobbitt, Tupac Shakur, the Menendez brothers, and of course, the most infamous rogue of all, O. J. Simpson. We even get swept away by bad boys of the screen— from the dashing and demanding Victor Newman on the TV soap opera *The Young and the Restless* to the recent swarm of movie vampires, who literally leave women swooning in the aisles.

What's the mysterious spell that men who mistreat women cast over so many of us? And what's *really* behind all that masculine misbehavior that enthralls and appalls us? Here is a closer look at these intriguing rogues, and why we keep hooking up with such heartbreakers.

Seductive Fantasies

Our fascination with bad boys begins long before we are old enough to look lustfully at a sexy rebel in a leather jacket who roars recklessly through life on his motorcycle, or feel our heart beat faster when we see Wanted posters of dangerous criminals at the post office. It starts when we are approximately two to seven years old—the age at which we form our "love map," an unconscious image of our idealized lover, and how we'd treat each other in a relationship.

Whether we melt for wounded poets, melodramatic daredevils, or charming con men depends on what kind of masculine role models we were exposed to during this crucial stage in our psychological development. If the men we encountered then—either in real life or in favorite storybooks—were bad boys, they become the amorous archetype that gets imprinted in our mind and heart. When we feel a sudden chemical click with a particular rogue we meet as an adult, it's because he fits the romantic fantasies we formed as children, and, therefore, feels psychologically "right" for us.

Some of the fantasies now etched on our love map spring from the fairy tales and classics of children's literature our parents read to us when we were young. Though they may seem like simple tales of magic, adventure, and romance, these stories are actually filled with hidden psychological messages that have resonated with generations of girls. By glamorizing male characters who are dishonest, daring, defiant, or even dangerous to women, they teach us to love bad boys, and to identify with the damsels in distress who get hurt by them.

What we discover as we delve into the fantasy world of fairy tales is that there are hardly any good boys in these stories, and all of them are dreadfully dull. Instead, most male characters get women and wealth by stealing magic lamps, telling clever lies, and chasing every path to pleasure that they come across. Since there's always a tenderhearted princess to rescue them when they get into real trouble, they're free to be as wild and impulsive as they want to be. We quickly see that bad boys have the power to make exciting things happen—and to take women along on their roller-coaster ride to adventure.

Later chapters of this book will explore twelve fairy tales about bad boys—and good girls—that may play a much larger role in your romances than you realize, or explain why you never find the prince who will make you happy ever after. Many women are drawn to the same impossible man over and over because they secretly view themselves as a Beauty, Cinderella, or Little Mermaid, and have embarked on a lifelong quest for their fairy-tale costar.

If your dream lover is a heartless prince, a brooding beast, or a wanton wolf, you may be surprised what these stories reveal about you, and the men that you're attracted to. You may also recognize some of your ex-lovers, friends, relatives, or even your boss when you read this rogues' gallery of the twelve most seductive scoundrels. These "Terrible Twelve" span the whole bad-boy spectrum from the fixer-uppers to the misunderstood, from married men to lethal lovers. You'll get a glimpse into the secret psyche of commitment phobes, grandiose dreamers, compulsive flirts, power-mad princes, self-absorbed seducers, mystery men, passionately possessive—and potentially *abusive*—men, dangerous desperadoes, and lovers with a dark side.

Naturally, fairy tales aren't the only media that advise girls that, when it comes to boys, badder is *better*. They are just the first of countless glamorized images of exciting, sexy, and deliciously *wicked* men that girls are barraged with, ranging from melodramas that make the mustache-twirling villains who tie damsels to railroad tracks seem much more intriguing than the boring good guys who save them, to the romantic outlaws of the Old West who lure innocent schoolteachers into danger, to the darkly passionate vampires who sneak into women's beds at night and suck the blood out of them.

During our erotically charged adolescent years, when we reevaluate our love maps, we're besieged by words and pictures that explicitly reveal what an outlaw's real allure to women is: He's defiantly *sexual*. To make sure we get the message about how bad and dangerously erotic they are, male gangsta rap and rock stars grab their leather-covered crotches and simulate sado-masochistic sex acts on stage; while female singers bewail the painful passions that "The Leader of the Pack" arouses in them, or that their bad-boy lover is "Killing Me Softly With His Song." Music videos are a breeding ground for bad boy–good girl relationships. The heroes in black leather, chains, and whips teach guys that girls love to be tied up, raped, and brutalized; while female viewers learn that this is what you need to do to get or keep such *cool studs*.

Through novels like *Gone With the Wind*, the "bodice ripper" romances sold at every drugstore, or the "rape" comic books that are now popular with some teenage girls, who devour the dark erotic adventures of characters like "Rapeman," we find out that bad boys don't just promise dangerous sex—they *deliver* it. Who can forget Scarlett O'Hara pounding her fists in vain protest on Rhett Butler's back as he began to make violent love to her, and how she purred with rapturous delight the next morning? In these more recent fairy tales, we also read about maidens who are ravished by arrogant aristocrats, enslaved by sultry sultans, or kidnapped by impassioned pirates—and love every sexy second of it.

Bad boys of the screen have been enticing us to drool over them or be in awe of them ever since movies and television began. From *Rebel Without a Cause* to *Cape Fear*, from Ralph Kramden's threats to send Alice "to the moon" to *Melrose Place*," some of today's baddest boys in Hollywood reflect their feelings about the women in their life in the movies and TV shows that they make. These modern tales fuel our fantasies and lure us to continue the search for love in a bad boy's arms.

This overlap of sex and aggression—two potent, inborn drives that are very closely linked—is a major part of what makes bad boys so *addictive*. They give us a high like no other: an intoxicating brew of physical and emotional extremes—pleasure and pain, romance and rape, eroticism and danger. Even though we know these glamorized men are hazardous to our psychological health, we may be powerless to resist them because we've bought the biggest fairy tale of all—that these high-risk relationships are the *ultimate* in passion.

Daddy—The Original Bad Boy

The more the fairy-tale fantasies and media images that you are exposed to as a child match your childhood *reality*, the more powerfully they will be imprinted on your love map. Because the relationship that you had with your father when you were young—and how you saw him treat your mother—serves as a model for your adult romances, this book also examines some hidden psychological reasons why you find scoundrels so seductive. Among the most significant factors that may play a role in your bad-boy fascination are:

The Allure of the Unattainable

If you're drawn to rogues you sense you can never have—perhaps because they're married or emotionally unavailable—you could still be stuck in a childhood stage all girls go through. Lusting after these men echoes your longing to steal Dad away from Mom, and have him all to yourself. This forbidden wish may have sparked an unconscious conflict you have yet to resolve: On the one hand, you feel secretly intrigued by the challenge of winning your father—or lovers who seem just as unattainable as he was; on the other hand, you feel threatened by it. That could make men who are impossible to get seem like the perfect solution—you get the thrills of the chase, with no fear that you'll ever actually *capture* them.

A Compulsion to Repeat Painful Events from Your Past

Bad boys may hold a fatal attraction to you because you have an overpowering need to replay a disturbing drama from your childhood in your adult love affairs. Consciously, you want to pick a partner who won't hurt you in the ways your father did, but unconsciously you're on a quest to find somebody just like the original bad boy in your life—Daddy. Even though you risk excruciating pain from these relationships, you secretly hope that by reliving the trauma that wounded you as a girl—over and over, if necessary—you will eventually figure out how to give the story a happy ending. Your fantasy is that, with the right rogue, you'll finally heal, and be able to move on. Jocelyn found herself increasingly attracted to Chaz and eventually realized that part of his allure was that he had the same Dr. Jekyll and Mr. Hyde personality that her father did: Usually a gentle soul, he would suddenly explode into unpredictable outbursts of rage. Her efforts to coax him to calm down were just as unsuccessful as they'd been with her father. Though neither of them hurt her physically, she perceived their rage as a painful withdrawal of love and felt like a vulnerable child.

The Rescue Fantasy

Even though these heartbreakers are often very hurtful and destructive to women, there's also a lost, fragile, and troubled side to them that's extremely seductive. Paradoxically, we may get hooked on a man who causes *us* pain because we want to save him from *his* pain, and be rewarded with his undying love. This scenario can be especially appealing if we felt our father needed rescuing—from an addiction or emotional or financial problems that overwhelmed him, or from our mother, who just didn't love and appreciate him the way that we did. He may have been hurtful, neglectful, or even abusive, but to us, he was a tragically misunderstood outcast who could be healed of his pain if we only loved him enough. We don't want to abandon our father or our lover, no matter how destructive he is to us, for fear that he'll then crash and burn like "The Leader of the Pack."

An Abusive Childhood

Tragically, the ultimate "bad boy" is a father who was sexually seductive or physically violent when you were growing up. Not only can these painful experiences leave you with a compulsion to replay your girlhood traumas by unconsciously picking partners who are abusive, but they can etch an association between sex and violence, or love and danger, into your adult love map. Chrissy trembles with excitement and fear every time she hears her beau whip his belt out of his pants as he undresses. That sound used to warn her that her father was about to beat her. To this day it makes her feel a mixture of eroticism and danger.

A girl who is mistreated by her father may feel so worthless that she believes a bad boy is all she deserves, or that her father was right—she's such a bad girl that she *should* be punished and mistreated by men.

A Hidden Desire to Avoid Intimacy

Selecting boyfriends who are wildly unsuitable, or phobic about commitment, can be a way to avoid confronting our own anxieties about getting too close to the men in our lives. After all, we can always blame it on him if our romance turns out to be an exciting roller coaster that ultimately leads nowhere, or lament to our friends that we're just unlucky in love, as Kristin does. They believed her—until one of them saw a handsome, single, and obviously successful attorney try to pick her up at a party. She rudely rejected him, and spent the evening trying to get the attention of an out-of-work actor who was sullenly knocking back tequila shots at the bar. We avoid intimacy to escape the pain of being spurned, which stirs up memories of early rejections from our dad.

Your Parents' Marital Relationship

Erin speaks scornfully about how her mother put up with her father's philandering, lying, and drinking—yet she repeatedly forgave her last several lovers for these exact flaws. Seeing her mother treated badly by her father taught her this is what women have to take if they want love, sex, companionship, and financial security. Our parents' marriage may be more of a model for our love affairs than we realize, because we're all subtly influenced by the interactions we see between the two most important people in our lives as we grow up.

A Secret Desire to Rebel

Sometimes what makes bad boys seem utterly irresistible isn't how right they are for us, but how *wrong* they are for our parents, as Mia recently realized when her latest lover, who has a cocaine habit—and a wife—looked up at her after sex and said, "You must *really* hate your parents."

(Mothers are often more intolerant of bad boys than fathers are. And revenge is sweet when we flaunt these men as if to say, "It's all your fault, Mom, for not having surrendered Daddy to me.")

An Attraction to Melodrama

Bad men may lie, cheat, or break your heart, but at least they're never boring! For some women, who secretly prefer to *avoid* a permanent entanglement, the challenge of trying to win these lovers' unpredictable affections gives an air of delicious excitement and mystery to life. Others, who feel deprived of the power and freedom men enjoy to act on their darker impulses, may embrace the perilous passion of a bad-boy relationship as the only great quest and adventure that's available for women. But we often get caught up in a Cinderella fantasy and stay too long at the ball—wasting time in a bad relationship.

Vicarious Pleasure

One reason radio bad boy Howard Stern is so wildly popular is that he says all the dirty, rude, or shocking things that we'd love to say ourselves—if we only had the nerve. Similarly, we may take secret pleasure in a lover's naughty antics because we have a hidden, wild streak we don't dare express. Because many of us grow up feeling constrained by society's rules—or our parents'—and believe we aren't as free to live out adventures in real life as men are, we may unconsciously identify with male anti-heroes of fiction or fact. We get a voyeuristic thrill from seeing them do what we only dream of—act on our dark, repressed desire to be bad, defiant, or even *dangerous*!

The Power of Taming the Lion

A very bad boy is like a raging lion with a thorn in his paw, who circles the village looking for prey and frightening the villagers. If you're the one to take the thorn out of the lion's paw, you will have tamed him by healing his wounds. Though there's always the potential for his ferocity to break loose, you hope his devotion to you will keep him under your spell. This makes you—not him—the most powerful one in the village.

Anatomy of a Bad Boy

Was your lover born to be wild, or did his childhood make him that way? Actually, it's a bit of both. While later chapters of the book will probe the hidden reasons for your man's wicked ways in more detail, here's a brief overview of some of the major ones:

A Defiant Streak

If your boyfriend shows a total disregard for the rules, morality, or laws the rest of us live by, he may be driven by an unconscious need to rebel against the *first* authority figure in his life—Mommy. The more that he felt smothered and trapped by the power and control she had over him then, the more strenuously he'll resist any restriction that other people—especially women—try to impose on him now. Breaking the rules is his way of breaking free of his mother and asserting his independence. Ironically, when he acts like a naughty little boy, what your lover is actually trying to prove to you—and most of all, to himself—is that he's a *man*.

Unresolved Anger

Is your man needy, excessively demanding, and ensnared in constant crises that he expects *you* to extricate him from? His voracious appetite for attention could spring from a childhood that was the opposite of a rebel's. Instead of having a relentlessly controlling mother who never left him alone, he had one who was never there for him, because she was physically absent from his early life due to death or divorce, or emotionally ill-equipped to be a warm, nurturing mother. That's left him both hungry and hostile: He's angry with his mother—and all women—for not meeting his needs. Exhausting you with his demands, and hurting you if he feels you haven't done enough for him, is his way of getting revenge on a mother who forced him to grow up too soon.

A Desire for Discipline

If your mate is always looking for trouble—and usually finds it—he may have an unconscious wish for *punishment*. As a boy, he may have realized that being bad was the best way to get attention from a mother who otherwise ignored him, or favored one of his siblings. Every time he did something wrong, he saw she'd immediately react with an exciting display of emotion, turn her entire focus on him, and grow intensely involved with him. Being able to produce such a strong effect on his mother made your boyfriend feel powerful, and encouraged him to act even more provocatively the next time—a pattern he may repeat with you.

There's also another secret pleasure his mother's punishments may have held for your beau when he was a boy. Being put over her lap for a good spanking, or getting other physical discipline from her, could have triggered an association in his mind between violence and sex, pain and passion, and danger and sensual arousal—giving him a compulsion to endlessly replay these psychologically potent themes in his relationships with women.

His Male Role Models

Should you blame your man's mother for all his naughty habits? Not at all. The original bad influence in his life could have been an utterly incorrigible rascal of a father who, though he may have had a lovable side, modeled misbehavior for him. Even as your partner does his best to live up—or *down*—to Dad's image, he may deny that his treatment of you and other women echoes in any way his father's treatment of his mother. Jeffrey, for example, thinks it's just an odd coincidence that he and his father both cheat on their spouses, not an obvious case of like father, like son. But no son wants to seem like a sissy in his father's eyes, so Jeffrey unconsciously wants to be at least as bad as Dad.

Biological Imprinting

Part of your lover's drive to be bad might be encoded in his genes, a legacy from primordial times when being aggressive, selfish, and sexual were traits that enhanced our odds of *survival*. Since the dawn of human civilization, there has always been a need for rebels, risk takers, and rogues to break the rules and constraints that hold the rest of us back, and boldly rush into danger as they explore new frontiers of adventure. Much as we love to hate bad boys, we also admire the bold, untamed, and defiantly uninhibited side of their nature that's helped keep our species full of lusty vitality.

Media Influences

The same storybooks, TV shows, and movies that made you feel there's something glamorous and seductive about a scoundrel could be what influenced your lover to become one. As a boy, he may have longed to be like the alluring adventurers that romped through his favorite fairy tales, slaying ferocious dragons, outwitting witches, and charming the panties off pretty princesses. But with so many romantic outlaws to choose from, how did your man decide which fantasy to act out? In the next chapter, you'll find a detailed quiz that will reveal *exactly* what kind of rogue you've lost your heart to—and give you the key to understanding the dark secrets of his soul.

2

*W*HAT'S HIS PROBLEM ANYWAY?

*S*amantha thought she'd dated every type of bad boy there is—until she met her latest lover. "I can't figure Brent out at all. On our first date, he was incredibly attentive, and acted as if he was really hot for me. Not only did he hang on my every word, but he actually knelt down and wiped off my boots when I spilled something on them. He kissed me good-bye and promised that we'd see each other again next week. When I called a few days later to ask him to a party, however, he barely gave me the time of day and mumbled that he'd get back to me. When I didn't hear from him, I went with another guy, only to find Brent's apologetic message on my machine imploring me to see him again as soon as possible. I've gone out with him several times since then, and although I find him charming, he seems strangely unavailable. I just don't know what to make of his hot-and-cold feelings for me."

Now Samantha is calling up her girlfriends, hoping that someone can answer a question every woman in a difficult love affair has asked: "What's his problem anyway?" If you are equally bewildered by your boyfriend's behavior—or want to find out exactly what's behind his wicked ways—this quiz can help you diagnose what kind of rogue has stolen your heart, and direct you to the portions of this book that explore his secret psychology in depth.

Look at the personality traits listed under each of the twelve quiz categories, and check the space for Always if the trait is typical of your man, Sometimes if it is partly true, or Never if it doesn't describe him at all.

1. Is He a Frazzled Frog?

<u>Always</u> <u>Sometimes</u> <u>Never</u>

Always	Sometimes	Never	
_____	_____	_____	A) He wants you to take care of him by being the cuddly, nurturing mother he never had.
_____	_____	_____	B) He's a perpetual little boy who refuses to grow up—and he's proud of it.
_____	_____	_____	C) He warns women not to expect too much of him by flaunting his neediness.
_____	_____	_____	D) Besides his addiction to you, he has at least one other addiction.
_____	_____	_____	E) You feel you're really too good for him because he, his possessions, and his life are in such disrepair.

2. Is He a Wanton Wolf?

<u>Always</u> <u>Sometimes</u> <u>Never</u>

Always	Sometimes	Never	
_____	_____	_____	A) He looks at women hungrily— as if he were eating them up with his eyes.
_____	_____	_____	B) Having mastered the game of seduction, he knows how to size women up quickly and make strategic moves.

_____ _____ _____ C) When he flaunts his smooth lines, money, or power, he may seem too slick.

_____ _____ _____ D) He's always trying to carve more notches in his belt: from just winning women with his eyes to actually seducing them into his bed.

_____ _____ _____ E) He uses you as "home base" while he's out flirting and prowling for conquests.

3. Is He a Would-be Wizard?

<u>Always</u> <u>Sometimes</u> <u>Never</u>

_____ _____ _____ A) He makes extravagant promises to you but doesn't deliver.

_____ _____ _____ B) He's a dazzling and incurable show-off.

_____ _____ _____ C) He dreams big, but his life is littered with false starts, discarded jobs, and girlfriends.

_____ _____ _____ D) He has episodes of intense self-doubt when he feels like an imposter and wonders if he only has delusions of grandeur.

_____ _____ _____ E) He's a fast talker, thinker, and spender, and a high-energy lover.

4. Is He a Philandering Prince?

<u>Always</u> <u>Sometimes</u> <u>Never</u>

_____ _____ _____ A) He hides or flaunts his marital status.

_____ _____ _____ B) He'll tell you his wife is either a bitch or a saint—definitely someone who doesn't understand him.

_____ _____ _____ C) While dutifully taking out the trash, he's fantasizing about trashy lingerie.

_____ _____ _____ D) He doesn't necessarily want a divorce, but he gives you just enough hope to keep you hanging on.

_____ _____ _____ E) He feels he deserves two women competing for him.

5. Is He an Autocratic Aristocrat?

<u>Always</u> <u>Sometimes</u> <u>Never</u>

_____ _____ _____ A) He wants to control you.

_____ _____ _____ B) He withholds his affections and is stingy with his money or possessions.

_____ _____ _____ C) He's a perfectionist who wants to fix your flaws.

_____ _____ _____ D) His fear of being overwhelmed by his emotions makes him keep you at a distance.

_____ _____ _____ E) He's compulsive about details to keep his life in order.

6. Is He a Marriage-shy Monarch?

<u>Always</u> <u>Sometimes</u> <u>Never</u>

_____ _____ _____ A) No one measures up to the detailed checklist that describes his dream girl.

_____ _____ _____ B) He looks for something wrong with every woman he dates—so he can drop her.

_____ _____ _____ C) He delays or avoids any move toward emotional intimacy.

_____ _____ _____ D) He wants to keep his erotic and romantic options open.

<table>
<tr><td>_____</td><td>_____</td><td>_____</td><td>E) He's wary of signs you're moving in on him—if the relationship heats up, his sex drive cools down.</td></tr>
</table>

7. Is He a Brooding Beast?

<u>Always</u> <u>Sometimes</u> <u>Never</u>

Always	Sometimes	Never	
_____	_____	_____	A) Underneath his moodiness, he's a sensitive, artistic soul.
_____	_____	_____	B) He's perpetually complaining about his talents not being appreciated.
_____	_____	_____	C) He yearns for you to rescue him from his wounded existence.
_____	_____	_____	D) His conflicts about success and failure cause him to sabotage himself.
_____	_____	_____	E) He's highly attuned to his inner state and may be hypochondriacal.

8. Is He a Pert Puppet?

<u>Always</u> <u>Sometimes</u> <u>Never</u>

Always	Sometimes	Never	
_____	_____	_____	A) Basically a spoiled brat, he feels entitled to VIP treatment.
_____	_____	_____	B) He lies to get his way or to avoid conflicts with you.
_____	_____	_____	C) He's his own first love, and neglects your needs.
_____	_____	_____	D) He's a master at manipulating you into doing what he wants.
_____	_____	_____	E) His impulsiveness gets him into mischief, while he flees from responsibility.

9. Is He a Bewildering Bluebeard?

<u>Always</u> <u>Sometimes</u> <u>Never</u>

———   ———   ———   A) He shrouds himself with an air of mystery.

———   ———   ———   B) There's a particular part of his life marked "hands off."

———   ———   ———   C) You wonder about the skeletons in his closet and are tempted to snoop around.

———   ———   ———   D) He stops you from unlocking his secrets by dodging questions, giving you gifts, or distracting you with sex.

———   ———   ———   E) If you corner him with the truth, he may bite his lip, play innocent, or feign hurt.

10. Is He an Adventurous Aladdin?

<u>Always</u> <u>Sometimes</u> <u>Never</u>

———   ———   ———   A) He has an insatiable need for thrills (from speeding on his motorcycle to scaling cliffs).

———   ———   ———   B) He takes you on a bumpy, high-speed ride of emotional ups and downs.

———   ———   ———   C) He seductively draws attention to himself by his flamboyant and fearless style.

———   ———   ———   D) He relies on his magical sexual talents to keep you addicted to him.

———   ———   ———   E) His melodramatic ways convince you that he's more in love with you than he really is.

11. Is He a Voracious Vampire?

<u>Always</u> <u>Sometimes</u> <u>Never</u>

_____	_____	_____	A) He mesmerizes you with a whirlwind courtship and instant devotion.
_____	_____	_____	B) He's irrationally jealous and may stalk you to see if you're cheating.
_____	_____	_____	C) He's passionately possessive and wants you to be constantly available.
_____	_____	_____	D) He enthralls and overpowers you with his sexual charisma.
_____	_____	_____	E) His volatile emotions may erupt into verbal, physical, or sexual abuse.

12. Is He a Ruthless Robber?

<u>Always</u> <u>Sometimes</u> <u>Never</u>

_____	_____	_____	A) A dangerously charming con man, he lies, cheats, steals, or worse—without remorse.
_____	_____	_____	B) He's obsessed with violence and pornography.
_____	_____	_____	C) He's aloof—except when his aggressive impulses explode.
_____	_____	_____	D) He has a history of antisocial behavior from truancy to drug trafficking, hubcap thefts to homicide.
_____	_____	_____	E) You suspect he has erotic fantasies of hurting or humiliating you in bed.

Scoring

Count each Always as 2, each Sometimes as 1, and each Never as 0. Add up the scores for the five traits listed under each category. You will have twelve separate scores (one for each category), which will range from 0 to 10.

Now, create "His Bad Boy Profile" by turning to the drawing

below and listing on the lines provided each category (such as "Pert Puppet" or "Wanton Wolf") where you gave your man a score of 1 or more. Write down the highest-scoring category first, the second highest (if any) next, and the lowest last.

To find out what kind of rogue you're involved with, and learn which sections of this book feature the full psychological scoop on his wicked ways, consult the chart at the end of the chapter.

His Bad Boy Profile

Chart: Who's That Bad Boy in Your Bed?

Here's what the quiz scores mean, and where you can find out more about the man in your life. The category (or categories, if he tied in two or more) he scored highest in is the key to understanding him, while categories he scored lower in are additional features of his psychological makeup that you need to be aware of.

If he scored in:	Then he's:	Read:
Frazzled Frog	A Fixer-Upper Lover	Chapter 3
Wanton Wolf	A Compulsive Flirt	Chapter 4
Would-be Wizard	A Grandiose Dreamer	Chapter 5
Philandering Prince	Misunderstood—and Married	Chapter 6
Autocratic Aristocrat	Mr. Power Mad	Chapter 7
Marriage-shy Monarch	A Commitment Phobe	Chapter 8
Brooding Beast	A Wounded Poet	Chapter 9
Pert Puppet	A Self-Absorbed Seducer	Chapter 10
Bewildering Bluebeard	A Man of Mystery	Chapter 11
Adventurous Aladdin	A Dramatic Daredevil	Chapter 12
Voracious Vampire	A Prince of Darkness	Chapter 13
Ruthless Robber	A Lethal Lover	Chapter 14

3

THE FIXER-UPPER
LOVER

Long ago there was a king whose youngest daughter was very lovely, but lonely. On hot summer afternoons, she'd go into the dark wood near the castle and sit beside a cool well. To amuse herself, she had a solid gold heart she loved to toss in the air and catch.

One day, she tossed it a little too far, and watched helplessly as it fell into the deep water of the well. She began to sob as if her heart were broken. Sensing opportunity, a Frog who was lurking in the slimy depths of the well swam eagerly to the surface. Smiling ingratiatingly, he asked, "What's wrong, sweet Princess? Your tears could fill a well."

The princess looked up and saw the Frog lifting his ugly head out of the dark water. "Oh, is it you, old wart-face? I weep because I've lost my golden heart. It has fallen into the well."

"I'll help you," replied the Frog. "But what will you give me if I bring it back for you?"

"Anything you like, my dear Frog," she said tearfully. "You can have any of my dresses, my jewels, or even the gold crown I have on my head."

"*Those would be nice,*" he croaked. "*But what I'd really like is for you to love me, and let me be your playmate. I want you to feed me from your little golden plate, and give me drinks from your little golden cup, and take me to sleep in your little silken bed. If you promise me all this, then I'll find your heart.*"

Too distraught to think clearly, she replied, "*I'll promise anything you want, if you just bring my heart back.*"

As soon as he heard her promise, the Frog dove deep into the well and soon paddled back to the surface with the gold heart in his mouth. He tossed it on the grass, and the princess grabbed her pretty plaything and ran off.

"*Wait!*" *cried the Frog.* "*Carry me with you. I can't run as fast as you!*"

The princess paid no attention, and soon forgot all about the Frog, who slipped sadly back down into his well. That night, as she was having dinner, there was a knock on the door. When she saw the Frog sitting on the castle doorstep, she quickly slammed the door in his face.

There was a second knock at the door. The Frog could be heard splashing about and crying piteously:

> "*Princess, please don't shut me out!*
> *It's your promise I've come about!*
> *Remember me from the deep well?*
> *I was there when your poor heart fell!*"

Have you lost your heart to a man who is more of a frog than a prince? Tess says her lover definitely has a few psychological warts. "He's thirty-one, but he's never really found himself, or figured out what he wants to be when—or if—he grows up. One week he'll think he wants to be a computer programmer, and the next, he'll talk about becoming a stockbroker. Meanwhile, he's driving a cab, and living like a starving student—in a fifth-floor walk-up apartment that's knee-deep in dirty laundry, moldy pizza boxes, and old beer cans."

Despite these unappetizing characteristics, she considers him an intriguing repair project. "He's like a jigsaw puzzle—all the right pieces are there—but jumbled up, so the challenge is trying to put them back together. Since Artie is smart, good-looking, and energetic, I'm confident that if he could just find the right job, and cut down on his drinking, he could make something of himself."

Sarah's lover is equally unlucky, in her opinion, since he is constantly beset by one problem after another. "Sometimes I feel like his personal crisis hot line. Two or three times a day, he'll call for advice, sympathy, and general stroking. It's gotten to a point where I almost hate to answer the phone, because he's always complaining about something. But if I'm not in when he calls, he leaves a guilt-inducing message on my voice mail and makes me feel awful about not being around in his hour of need. My friends have nicknamed him 'the telephone terrorist.' "

His Telltale Traits

In one of his comedy routines, Woody Allen joked about having such impoverished parents that they bought his dog from a store that sold "slightly damaged pets." If your boyfriend reminds you of a pathetic puppy, or a frayed frog who croaks at your door for help, you may have fallen for a fixer-upper lover. Here is how you recognize these fascinating—but extremely frustrating—creatures.

He's a Perpetual Tadpole—and Proud of It

While your lover is happy to try new academic, psychological, or work-related "growth experiences"—he has a boyish love of exploration—he's not really willing to change or mature. Instead, he clings to all the childlike, undeveloped parts of himself, and rejects everything he associates with being a grown man. Like the fairy-tale Frog, he yearns to be your playmate—not your husband. He may parade his immature interests, like Danielle's boyfriend, who collects Superman comic books and spends hours playing video games.

He Doesn't Have a Well of His Own

When your boyfriend takes you home with him, don't expect much, since he probably rents a makeshift little place, leaps from one temporary sublet to another, or lives in other people's homes. His possessions are meager, boyish, and in bad repair, like those of a struggling student. He's the kind of guy who uses a coat hanger as a TV antenna and keeps his beat-up books in orange crates. Most of his windows are painted closed, and his sink leaks. Predictably, his car is also a piece of junk, with one headlight bashed in and a malfunctioning heater. What he's telling the world isn't just that he can't afford much, but also that women in particular shouldn't *expect* too much from him, because he feels as broken-down on the inside as his belongings are on the outside.

What He Lacks in Success, He Makes Up for in Excuses

It's not your lover's fault that he's stuck on the bottom rung of the corporate ladder, is running a business that is always on the brink of bankruptcy, or has spent years languishing on the fringe of a glamorous field where others have gained riches and success. According to him, the obstacle is his ogre of a boss, unscrupulous competitors or backstabbing coworkers, unimaginative clients, or in the case of Krista's boyfriend, just plain bad luck. "To hear him tell it, he has a Midas touch in reverse, since everything he touches seems to turn to slime. The reason is always vague, maybe a mysterious marketplace force that even a top economist couldn't have anticipated in advance." But no matter what excuse your man uses, it's really his lack of confidence that keeps your Frog from standing on his own two webbed feet.

He's Uncomfortable or Helpless When He's Alone

Since your Frog finds it extremely frightening to take care of himself, he's devastated if a love affair—or even a close friendship—ends, and urgently seeks a new relationship to replace the one that's lost. Like the Frog, he may go to great lengths to secure the nurturing he thirsts for, even if he has to volunteer to do some unpleasant task, like diving into dirty water to fetch the princess's heart. He may try to conceal his desperate neediness at first—so as not to scare prospective friends or lovers off—and frequently starts relationships by seeming to focus on the other person's needs. A woman who has kissed more than a few frogs points out, "These men are like ingratiating parasites: First they make sure to position themselves securely, *then* they eat away at you."

He Wears a Flashing Neon Sign That Says, "Take Care of Me!"

Even if he does you a favor or two at first, it doesn't take your lover long to reveal his real agenda—getting you to take responsibility for his needs. He *flaunts* his dilapidated hovel and his pitiful excuse for a career, well aware that they are an irresistible invitation for someone competent—like you—to step in and shore up his crumbling existence before it collapses completely. Soon after he's got you hooked, he'll display a ravenous need for reassurance and advice, even on the most mundane daily decisions you'd make without a moment's hesitation. Sometimes your Frog's constant croaking for attention reminds you of a baby who frantically wails, "Pick me up! Feed me! Love me and hold me . . . but don't expect me to be a man."

You Secretly Feel You're Too Good for Him

At the start of the romance, you were probably as disdainful of your lover as the princess was of her Frog. Perhaps his personality grated on your nerves at first—you hated his helplessness, or were irritated by his constant complaining. Or perhaps you found his appearance off-putting, as Sherry does with her new boyfriend, whom she describes as a small squirrelly man with terrible taste in clothes. Yet, despite your conviction that this man is totally beneath you, you can't resist him—which is a paradox that has still got you puzzled. "Why am I with this loser anyway?" you ask yourself, as you try to figure out how this guy ever managed to worm his way into your heart—or your bed.

He Has Current or Past Addictions

Since your lover feels empty inside, he is drawn to the *quick fix* that alcohol, drugs, gambling, food, sex, or shopping (a compulsion he's probably too poor to indulge in all that often) seem to promise. Whether the man in your life is hooked on a self-destructive habit right now, or was treated for one in the past, he's extremely susceptible to developing a new addiction—*you*. This flattering fixation may be one of the hidden seductions he holds for you, since it is an ego boost to have a lover who desires you so desperately.

He Wants You to Always Be Available to Him

If your man didn't think you'd expect something in return—like a commitment, which is one of the emblems of adulthood that he shuns—he'd wear you around his neck like a pacifier, and comfort himself with you all day long. Since a fixer-upper lover knows he can't stay at your side all of the time, he's likely to use the telephone as an umbilical cord that keeps him attached to you. He may call you six times a day, just to check in and make sure you're still there. Or, like Sarah's lover, the telephone terrorist, he may sulk if he gets an answering machine instead of you—even if he just spoke to you an hour ago. To him, being out of touch, even for a short while, is like having his pacifier snatched away—it's too much to endure.

To satisfy his constant craving for a connection, your lover may also manufacture minor crises, as Sarah's does, so he'll have an excuse to call you; or he'll frequently ask you to do small—or large—favors for him. That way, even when he can't see or talk to you, there's still a link, because he knows you're doing something for him. It's another way of always having you at his beck and call, without seeming so relentlessly demanding that you are tempted to leave him.

He's the Cuddliest Lover You Ever Had

Along with wanting to reach out and touch you by telephone, he is just as snuggly in person. He may be partial to public displays of affection—it doesn't embarrass your lover in the least to have the whole world see him kissing you on a street corner, because he *wants* everyone to know you're his girlfriend. In private, he loves you just as tenderly. Though his erotic moves may not be particularly polished or practiced, he writhes with raw sensuality and is incomparably thrilled to be with you. Because he's sexually undemanding and puts no pressure on you to have an orgasm, you can let go of your inhibitions and be as wild as you wish. Afterward, he doesn't just roll over and fall asleep like your previous lovers did—instead, he endearingly fits himself to your body like a sweet little spoon, and holds you all night long.

His Fixations and Fantasies

What's the high that your lover keeps looking for—but never seems to find—as he drains his whisky glass, snorts his cocaine, feeds his coins into the slot machine, or succumbs to a consuming passion for *you*? It's an unconscious quest for the ultimate fix: the euphoria of infancy, where he is nestled at his mother's warm breast as she nourishes him with her inexhaustible love. To him, nothing could be more deliciously intoxicating than this blissful dependency. Since that's not what he got from Mother as a baby, he's been left feeling perpetually empty, craving "fixes" to fill him up.

His mother was probably nearly as inadequate as Timmy's was: "You know the famous experiment where they took baby monkeys away from their real mothers, and gave them 'mother' monkeys made of rigid wires? Well, my mother was like that." In the experiment that Timmy's referring to, the baby monkeys who were raised by the metallic mothers holding milk bottles were traumatized because they didn't get the affection and attention they needed. Deep down, your guy feels like those baby monkeys—and wants you to be the warm, fuzzy mother he never had.

While you might expect that being forced to fend for himself at an early age would turn your lover into a self-reliant person, actually the opposite is true. He is still indignant about being robbed of his childhood by his mother, who not only wasn't there for him, but may have expected him to take care of his siblings . . . or her. As an adult, he continues to vehemently reject the independence she thrust upon him before he was ready. That's why he takes such spectacularly poor care of himself now: He's trying to show her—and everyone else—how ill-equipped he is to be sent out into the adult world.

Don't make the mistake of believing that your boyfriend is as helpless as he pretends to be, as Paulette did with her ex-fiancé. "It wasn't until after we broke up that I realized how cleverly he used his apparent weakness to control me. After all, you'd hardly suspect somebody who can barely get dressed in the morning of being a master of manipulation, but that's just what Luke was. He had me so busy extricating him from one crisis after another that it never dawned on me that he was *preying* on my sympathy and insecurities. Even though I was working non-stop to fill the bottomless well of his needs, he always made me feel I wasn't doing *enough* for him. His constant guilt trip worked to keep me in an incredibly draining, one-sided relationship because I was so afraid he'd leave. Now that I've stopped buying into it, I keep thinking, 'If he can't live without me, why isn't he dead yet?' "

Some clingy men have another covert weapon to gain control: their past history of addictions. Their unspoken, but still very potent, threat is that if you're not there for them, they will go back to their bottle, their needle, or their roulette wheel to fill the void that's inside of them. That, of course, would be *your* fault, according to their twisted logic, since they absolutely refuse to accept any responsibility for their self-destructive choices.

As Paulette has found out, overly dependent men like Luke can have a lot of covert hostility toward the women they date. Their hunger for attention doesn't just spring from their yearning for a softer, cuddlier mother who will fill them with good food and good feelings about themselves. They also want her—or women they see as substitutes for her—to pay for the disappointment she caused them. Like the Frog, who demands to eat from the princess's plate, drink from her cup, and sleep with her in her silken bed, they are needy *and* greedy. They're not interested in just sharing what you have; secretly, they want to have it all for themselves, as a symbolic vengeance against their depriving mother, who left them so thirsty for love.

If this makes your lover sound like a bit of a leech, there's a good reason. He's stuck in an early stage of development, where it's normal for babies to have a symbiotic relationship with their mothers. When he calls you six times a day just to check in, he's reenacting the separation anxiety that still plagues him. He's like a toddler who wanders briefly away from his mom at the beach, then runs back to her to reassure himself she's still there. Because your boyfriend's mother didn't pay enough attention to him back then, he's learned that independence can be hazardous— you could get knocked down by the big waves and drown before anyone notices. Understandably, he feels it is safest to cling as tightly as he can, and to throw a tantrum at the slightest sign that you're not available on demand.

Your Frog's father may have given him another powerful motive to want to stay a tadpole forever. His dad may have been an addict himself, or in such obvious distress from other woes that your boyfriend concluded as a child that growing up was both dangerous and depressing. Watching his incompetent dad's struggles to be a man—he didn't earn enough to provide well for his family, couldn't keep his wife satisfied (she may have had extramarital affairs), or constantly got into predicaments—made your partner anxious about how well *he'd* cope with the burdens of adulthood. Why should he be any better at it than his father was? he asked himself.

To avoid failing as a man—and ultimately as a husband and a father—your lover feels it is best to stick to something easy to succeed at: being a little boy. That's why he wants you to agree to take care of him: It diffuses any expectation you may have that he will take care of *you*, either now or in the future.

Why You're Kissing a Frog

What's the strange fascination a fixer-upper lover can hold for us, as he simultaneously attracts and repels us? Very often, he'll seduce us into a relationship with a covert promise similar to the one that the princess's Frog made: that he *won't* steal our heart—or break it—as a partner who has more to offer might. As long as we agree to take care of him, he assures us that he won't leave us.

That can be the siren song that induces you to accept a lover you initially consider to be far beneath you. It is an especially attractive bargain if you've been hurt by other men in the past or are afraid of being abandoned. Having a slightly damaged pet as a partner takes a lot of the risk out of romance; you can escape the loneliness of being without a lover without having to worry about being swept away by an out-of-control passion that would leave you vulnerable to rejection. Even if you accidentally lost your heart, as the princess did, your Frog reassures you that he'd hand it back to you intact, because he is so harmless he couldn't possibly hurt you.

Not seeming very dangerous is what gives a needy, dependent man a certain *erotic* allure. Even though your partner may not do anything special in bed, knowing that he won't abandon you frees you to abandon *yourself* to sexual pleasure and soar to new heights of ecstasy. Seeing how appreciative he is of your every touch—and how he gives you a *beatific* smile afterward, like a satisfied baby who has just finished his bottle—is a real ego boost: You think if you've pleased him that much, you must be a real tigress in bed, no matter what your previous boyfriend said in his nastier moments.

Having a lover who is a bit broken-down can also be gratifying in other ways as well. A man who always cries for help lets us feel like heroines who can solve his problems, and be artists who paint him into whatever we want. Consider Judith, who claims to be trying to help her man battle the bottle, yet is so sympathetic when he falls off the wagon—again—that he has little real impetus to attack his drinking problem effectively.

That's because whenever he yields to his habit, she seems like a saint in comparison, which enhances her self-esteem. The weaker he proves himself to be, the more powerful she feels—since she's in control of herself, and he's not.

Codependent women like Judith are often acting out the secret ambivalence most of us feel toward a fixer-upper lover, whether he is addicted to a substance, or just to us for the nurture we offer him. On one level, we'd like to repair our perpetual tadpole into a prince and be with a partner who is worthier of our love; but on another, we see advantages to keeping him just as he is—dependent and unable to function well without us. This unconscious conflict explains why we might launch a campaign to get our partner to lose weight, quit drinking, or find a better job, then sabotage it by bringing him a box of chocolates, keeping wine in our cupboard, or forgetting to set the alarm clock the night before he has a job interview.

It's a dilemma that's hard to solve, since there are powerful reasons why you've picked a frog in the first place: You feel safe with a man who says he's happy to hop along at your heels, and let *you* control the relationship. Unfortunately, the price he charges is your self-respect. Helping him to grow up could be hazardous, you feel, because he may break his implicit promise to stay with you forever, and run off with your golden heart.

Can You Live Happily Ever After?

Reluctantly, the king's daughter went to the door to keep her promise. She had barely opened it a crack before the Frog pushed his way in. He hopped along at her heels until she got to the dining table and then said, "I am very hungry. Now lift me up so we can eat together from your golden plate."

Wrinkling her nose, the princess lifted the Frog onto the table, holding him as far away from her as possible. The Frog ate greedily, leaving nothing on the plate for the princess. Then he took her golden cup and drank all her wine, complaining afterward that it was an inferior vintage. Finally, the Frog looked up expectantly and said, "I've eaten enough for now. Carry me to your soft, silken bed so we can sleep together."

She wept at the idea of letting the moist, slippery Frog into her bed, but picked him up with two fingers and carried him to a corner of her room. As she got into her bed, he came creeping over and croaked, "Now you must kiss me, just as you promised." She shivered with revulsion, sighed deeply, and closed her eyes so she wouldn't have to see the Frog, who had already puckered his lips expectantly. Grudgingly, she gave him a light peck.

"You're quite a kisser," he remarked, giving her the once-over with his bulging eyes. "Let's try out those silken sheets now."

"Aren't you ever satisfied, you warty lowlife?" the princess yelled in fury when the Frog slid his hand up her nightgown. She flung him out her bedroom door as forcefully as she could. But as soon as he left her hand, he turned into a handsome prince, and landed solidly on his feet.

What are the prospects for changing your frog into a prince? The first thing to realize about a fixer-upper lover is that he is like a fixer-upper house: He may seem like a bargain at first, but there are always some hidden problems that take more time, energy, or money to solve than you'd expected. If you're still determined to take on the job, this handy guide could speed up the repairs.

Fix Your Own House First

Nourish yourself, and you may find you no longer need to settle for a fixer-upper lover. If you build yourself a cozy psychological home, the attraction of being with a man you secretly consider to be beneath you—but who will never leave you—may vanish. Convince yourself that you are such a hot property that any man would be proud to be your partner, and you will discover the world's full of princes who are fixed up already.

Even if you decide you'd rather stick with your Frog, there's still a crucial reason to attend to your own growth as well as his: The more you fix your Frog and nurture his self-confidence, the more he may eventually conclude that he can do a lot better than a woman who was willing to accept him warts and all. It's like the Groucho Marx joke: He doesn't want to belong to any country club that would allow him to be a member. Once he's out of the tadpole phase, your lover may not want to be around anybody who reminds him of it—like you. By changing and developing along with your mate, however, you may be able to negotiate past this danger point, since you can shed your psychological warts too.

⇀ Recognize That Repairing Him Can Be an Ongoing, Even Endless Project

Don't get so optimistic at the first sign of improvement that you set yourself up for disappointment, as Maggie did. "When my boyfriend finally broke down and got some decent furniture—and a lavishly equipped tank full of exotic fish—I was thrilled, since he used to be so indifferent to his surroundings that his apartment was one step up from a shed. Perhaps I should have recognized it as a warning when I saw he'd deliberately bought fish that kept eating each other, but I was so sure everything would be okay now that I ignored this red flag.

"Then he did something that sent a cold shiver down my spine. Soon after he got a new job that required frequent travel, he said that his fancy fish were too much trouble to maintain now, so he'd flushed them all down the toilet. Every hope that I'd had for him was destroyed with that one flush, because a guy who could so easily break his commitment to his pampered pets could similarly abandon plans to settle down or have a family."

Instead of Trying to Feed All His Insatiable Demands Yourself, Steer Him to Outside Resources

Recognize that it is not your failing if you are unable to anticipate and satisfy his every whim. It will only lower your self-esteem if you blame yourself for not having enough, or not being enough to fill his bottomless well. Why spend your evenings anguishing with him over what job would be right for him or how he could move off the bottom rung of the corporate ladder when a career counselor or headhunter can give him much more useful and professional advice than you could? Similarly, instead of just commiserating with him about his emotional problems— a draining, often thankless task—steer him toward appropriate self-help books, support groups, or a psychotherapist. Since he craves and devours attention, your man should secretly welcome the opportunity to have *more* people working on his problems, while you'll welcome having the pressure and guilt of being his sole caretaker lifted from your shoulders.

If You Pamper Him, Do It Out of Love, Not Desperation

Don't try to keep your lover hooked by catering to his every whim. Doing too much for him makes *you* seem needy—a trait that, ironically, in view of his own insatiable hunger, he's secretly contemptuous of in others. It also can invite, or even provoke, him to victimize you: Like a voracious parasite, he'll devour all the food, love, energy, money, sex, and emotional support that you have to offer, but once he's drained you dry, he may move on to eat from someone else's plate—which, of course, was what you were trying to avoid by being overaccommodating.

That doesn't mean that you can't indulge a maternal side of your nature from time to time—just that you should do it when you *sincerely* want to, not because you feel he expects it or will leave if you don't. Lucy was understandably sympathetic when her lover came down with the flu the night before he was scheduled to give a speech. "I decided to surprise him with a goodie basket—and bought out half the drugstore. When I got home and looked at the ridiculous quantities of herbal tea, cough drops, and over-the-counter flu remedies I'd bought, I knew that I was going way over the top, and pared it down to a *small* assortment, plus a few homemade cookies."

If He Has an Active Addiction, Refuse to Be an Accomplice in It

If your lover has an uncontrolled addiction, it will inevitably poison your love affair and destroy any hopes that you may have of a future with him. As long as he is enslaved by a self-destructive habit, he isn't free to give his heart to you. Worse still, he may project the loathing and repulsion that he feels toward himself for continuing to abuse a substance that's injuring his body and spirit onto you—and hate *you* for tolerating his toxic habit.

While there are plenty of drug rehabilitation programs, detox centers, psychotherapists, and twelve-step programs that could aid him with his addiction, the catch is that your lover has to *want* their help—not just out of fear that you'll leave him, but because he's genuinely committed to overcoming it. If he denies that he has an alcohol or drug problem when you confront him about it, there's an approach that's often remarkably effective: an *intervention*, where you assemble his friends and relatives to sit with him and talk to him about how concerned *they* feel about his addiction. Having all the people he trusts most give him the same message is a powerful, and potentially *sobering*, experience that could turn your addict's life around.

If an intervention fails, you must give him the ultimate—and most painful—form of help: leaving him. Your refusal to put up with his self-abusive behavior could be the shock that breaks the spirit-deadening spell that drugs, alcohol, or another addiction holds for him. If so, your Frog may finally find the inner resources to turn *himself* into a clean, sober prince.

Be Ready to Fling Your Frog Out Your Bedroom Door If He Takes Too Much from You

While you don't want to cut the umbilical cord too suddenly—or he'll look around for someone more sympathetic—it is important to discourage overdependency. If he's ever to grow up and become a prince, your lover has to learn how to make a healthy separation from his mother—or you. Encourage him to start making his own repairs, by showing him what steps to take and then standing back so he can do them on his own.

Expect him to keep running to you for reassurance for a while, with his frequent phone calls and cries for help, however. Just as he used to keep checking in with his mother—and clung more tightly after she ignored him—he'll have periods when he expects an almost claustrophobic closeness, as well as times when his self-confidence surges, and he's able to do more for himself. It's all part of the inevitable ebbs and flows that you should anticipate as your little tadpole cautiously swims toward manhood.

4

THE COMPULSIVE FLIRT

*O*nce upon a time, there was a little country girl, who always wore a bright red cape with a hood that her doting grandmother had knitted for her. One day, her mother gave her a basket of pastries she'd baked, and asked Little Red Riding Hood to bring them to her grandmother, who was ill. "Be careful as you cross the woods," her mother said. "Don't stray from the path, and don't speak to anyone you might meet there."

Off the little girl went, skipping along the path through the woods. Soon she met a handsome Wolf, with gleaming, dark eyes and a long, pointy nose. "Good morning, my pretty little damsel," he said, thinking what a tasty morsel she'd make for his lunch. "Where are you going on this beautiful summer day?" Forgetting her mother's warning, she replied, "To the house next to the mill across the woods, where my grandmother lives."

"I must act craftily, so as to catch them both," the Wolf thought as a cunning look came over his face. "Why not pick some of those lovely flowers for your grandmother?" he smoothly suggested to Little Red Riding Hood, pointing to a spot far from

*the path and deeper into the woods. With these words, he
started racing down a shortcut as fast as he could, as Little Red
Riding Hood wandered off the path, stopping frequently to
gather flowers and chase butterflies.*

*Minutes later, the Wolf was at Grandmother's door. Imi-
tating a child's voice, he said, "Granny, it's me, Little Red
Riding Hood. I've come to bring you treats my mother baked for
you." The grandmother opened the latch. The Wolf gobbled her
up in one gulp, then dressed himself in the old woman's night-
clothes and climbed in her bed. Pulling the covers to his chin, he
lay in wait for Little Red Riding Hood. . . .*

Is your boyfriend a wolf who views any female he meets—
whether she's a pretty little schoolgirl or a gray-haired granny—
as fair prey for his charms? Ellen's lover has a way with women,
she says, with a mix of pride and petulance in her tone. "That's
fine when he is making nice to my mother, but not so terrific
when he's so busy bantering with the waitress who is taking his
order that I wonder if he even remembers I'm at the table. At
parties, he is always trying to win some woman's attention, with
little jokes, compliments, or just batting his luscious lashes at
her. Then I'm on the edge of my chair—even if she's one of my
friends—for fear she will start batting *back*. I keep telling myself
I shouldn't be so insecure, because in my heart, I know that he's
just a harmless flirt, and would never actually *cheat*."

Michele, on the other hand, worries that her sweetheart is up
to more than playing eye games at parties, or a little flirtatious
talk—she suspects he's on the prowl for *sexual* conquests. "Since
he's in advertising, it didn't surprise me he was always going out
to dinner or drinks with clients—until I noticed he wasn't wining
and dining the bald-headed brand manager of his new cereal
account at night, but any remotely good-looking woman who
crossed his line of sight at work. I might believe that he was only
devoted to his career if it weren't for the hungry way he looks at
women, as if he were eating them up with his eyes. Then I have
to wonder, if he's mentally undressing them right in front of me,
what's he doing when I'm not around?"

What makes a flirt so infuriatingly attractive to us, even if he's directing his seductive signals at someone else? And can you ever *really* capture a restless Romeo's heart and keep his affection firmly fixed on you, and you alone? That challenge could be a bigger part of his intrigue than you realize. . . .

His Telltale Traits

Before delving deeper into why you might be drawn to a flirt, however, let's make sure your boyfriend really is one. After all, even the most devoted of boyfriends might feel a crackle of erotic electricity if a pretty woman started coming on to *him*, or sneak a quick peek at that blonde on the beach who is overflowing her bikini top. Here's how to spot a real wolf.

He Gets Along Better with Women Than with Men

Francesca says that her lover actively avoids male company, even at social gatherings where men and women split into separate groups. "All the other guys will be swilling beer and gabbing about sports, but Mike claims he hates that macho bullshit, so he's always with the women, even when we're talking about leg waxing. Most men would rather die than listen to such excruciatingly feminine stuff—but he's never happier than when he is the only male in a crowd of women. It's sort of like having his own private harem—and besides, beauty talk gives him a good excuse to hold some woman's hand as he admires her French manicure."

Like the big, bad Wolf who dressed in Grandmother's nightie to catch Little Red Riding Hood, men like Mike may act like one of the girls—even if they have to learn more about bikini waxes than they ever wanted to—so they'll seem safe to you. Oddly enough, as such films as *Tootsie* and *Mrs. Doubtfire* show, many men are intrigued by the idea of temporarily masquerading as women so they can penetrate the mysterious world of the opposite sex and find out our secrets. It's their way of gaining a seductive edge over other men, who just don't understand us the way they do.

He's Mastered the Game of Love

Although your lover probably wasn't all that popular with the girls when he was in high school—and may have lost his virginity later than most of his peers—as an adult, he's made an almost obsessive study of the art of seduction. Like a chess grand master, he's explored every imaginable strategy—and has discovered dozens of winning moves. He's gotten very adept at sizing up women quickly, and knows when it's best to make a bold advance, and when to hold back and let them pursue *him*. He's great at all the little games and intrigues that make romance so much fun and can play a woman's heart with all the skill of a virtuoso.

He's a Little Too Smooth

Since he's devoted so much time to polishing his lines, you may feel that your Romeo doesn't ring true as he's romancing you. His compliments are pretty—but practiced—and his style is seductive, but slick. You may also notice he goes overboard in trying to impress you, and other women. Some flirts flaunt their money, power, or important friends with an almost desperate eagerness, or pile up extravagant, sexy toys, such as ultraexpensive sports cars, to bolster their allure. Even if he's utterly impoverished, a Don Juan will devise some way to compensate for it, such as cultivating a hip downtown style, cobbling together a chic look from thrift-shop finds and taking you to funky bistros where the celebrities slum.

Before Flirting, He May Fire Himself Up with a Bit of Liquid Courage

Although these seductive charmers don't necessarily have a problem with alcohol, some feel their lines come out a lot more smoothly after they lubricate themselves with a drink or two. That can inspire the kind of outrageously over-the-top antics Beth complains of. "If my boyfriend is around women, and he has had so much as a whiff of liquor, he turns into Howard Stern and goes into a comedy routine. The other day, we were at a bar, and some women nearby were talking about Tourette's syndrome. Pretty soon he was acting out the tics, twitches, and random bursts of obscenity that are symptoms of this disorder for them. They laughed so hard they almost wet their pants, while I wanted to crawl under the bar and *die* of embarrassment."

If It Weren't So Painful, He'd Probably Carve a Notch in His Penis Every Time He Scored with a Woman

Some Casanovas are content to just win a woman with their eyes, or speak suggestively to her until they feel she would be theirs for the taking, if they wanted her (luckily for you, most of them stop at this point); but others are hard-core philanderers who are not satisfied until they've actually seduced her into bed. Most extreme of all are sex addicts. Regardless of how far a flirt may go or how many women he charms, he never feels that it's enough to convince him he's okay. Just as the phallic-snouted Wolf can gobble up every female in sight and still be as hungry as ever, your man is gnawed by an insatiable craving for fresh conquests, because he constantly needs *more* reassurance about his masculinity.

He Always Has at Least One Woman Waiting in the Wings in Case His Current Relationship Fails

If your lover wasn't involved with anyone when you met him—even tangentially—he's probably not a compulsive flirt, since these restless romantics usually have a long history of *over-lapping* love affairs. Josh, for example, says he nearly always has "an extra girl or two up my sleeve, even if I'm madly in love." For him, flirting is like an insurance policy—he hopes his current love affair will last forever, but just in case it doesn't he makes sure he has *other* romantic options.

He Views You as His "Home Base"

Is your partner a "covert flirt," who hid his wolfish ways until after he had captured your heart? Or does he have a pattern of loving and leaving others—whether it's after a brief flirtation or a full-blown affair—but always coming back to you? Some men need the security of a steady relationship to feel *confident* enough to chase women. That's why you may not realize he's a ladies' man at first: Until he is sure he has you hooked, and knows his bait *works*, he's too insecure to troll for other romantic prey.

He's Fascinated with Other People's Sex Lives

Jody jokes there's a surefire way to get her husband's attention: "You just whisper 'adultery' in a crowded room, and he'll be bounding over two seconds later to savor the juicy details. He loves any sexy gossip, even about people he doesn't know, and focuses in like a laser on the slightest sexual innuendo, especially from a woman. He also has a knack for turning any conversation to his favorite topic—sex—and would happily spend hours speculating about what our friends do in bed and if any of them are having affairs. He thinks everyone has some sexual secret, so if he sees someone he knows at the video store, he'll practically grab the movie she's renting out of her hand to see if it's X-rated."

Despite All His Hot Talk, He's a Bit of a Dud in Bed

Eva says that her last lover's lascivious looks and erotic talk soon ignited a white-hot fever of desire in her—until she slept with him. "What a disappointment! I was expecting something sublime, but instead his performance was just that—a performance. He had an impersonal, one-size-fits-all sexual routine that he stuck to, no matter how I responded. As he was busily inserting tab A into slot B according to some sex manual he had in his head, I felt as if he happened to be doing this with me but would do it just the same way with another woman—probably tomorrow. Because he was the McDonald's of lovers, there should be a sign over his head saying, 'Over 10 million served.' "

This, alas, is not an uncommon complaint about flirts, since their seductive moves are highly choreographed. Most are best at one-night stands because the sex is relatively anonymous, and he knows he can leave afterward. In longer relationships, however, the opening night is often as good as it gets, because as the intimacy of the love affair increases, his erotic performance typically declines—perhaps literally, as some Don Juans have episodes of impotence, ejaculate too quickly, or are afflicted by other sexual problems.

What Makes the Wolf Whistle

The "wild man" movement instructs men who want to unleash their wild side to "listen to the wisdom of the penis," and that's just what your lover thinks he's doing. Before you laugh and say that you've already noticed that he's led around by his loins—since you never believed that it was his *brain* that goes into overdrive whenever he sees a good-looking woman— what you need to realize is that your lover is getting some very *disturbing* messages from the sage inside his pants. Far from being a lusty free spirit who simply happens to have an overactive libido, your partner is actually reacting to a desperate plea from his anxious, insecure penis: "Help! I'm puny and weak—so you'd better do something about it before anyone finds out you're not much of a man at all."

Even if your boyfriend isn't literally undersized, he's still caught up in a childhood stage that every boy goes through when he compares himself with his father, and sees his penis doesn't begin to measure up to the impressive organ that dangles between Daddy's legs. Although most boys get over their anxiety when they mature, and see they've developed to *adult* dimensions, your lover may have undergone some trauma that crystallized this fear in his mind so it remains as sharp and fresh today as it was then. Perhaps he's the baby of the family, and had older brothers who laughed at his comparatively puny organ, or was slow to reach puberty, and was the target of locker-room ridicule at school.

He may have felt physically inadequate in other ways as well. Many future flirts were hopelessly inept at athletics as boys, and are haunted as adults by a lingering insecurity about never having "made the team" of macho men. While this might not seem like much of a wound to you—because if you couldn't catch, hit, or throw as a girl, you probably thought it only *enhanced* your femininity—one survey found that a surprising seventy percent of adult men report their first significant *failure* in life occurred during sports. (Now you know why ads for penile enlargement are often found on the *sports* pages of the newspaper.)

Others, like Steve, were late bloomers, and recall their teen years as pure agony. "Not only did I have terrible buck teeth and a mouthful of metal braces, but I was skinny, prone to pimples, and generally awkward with girls in high school. If I ever got up the nerve to ask someone to dance with me, I'd instantly turn into all elbows and left feet, since I'd invariably bump her in the ribs or step all over her toes. I was friendly with a girl from the chess club, but I was so shy I never even *tried* to go out with her—no less make love to her. In college, however, I got my braces off, my skin finally cleared up, and I stopped looking like a ninety-eight-pound nerd. Suddenly women that I only fantasized about were actually interested in me."

Even after he transformed from ugly duckling to seductive swan, Steve, like many compulsive flirts, never fully outgrew his poor body image. In his heart, he still feels like a ninety-eight-pound nerd with pimples, and believes, like Little Red Riding Hood's Wolf, that the only way to get women in bed is by *tricking* them. "It took awhile for me to get my rap down, but now I know how to chat women up, and charm them out of their panties. Since I have a steady girlfriend, I don't really need to have one-night stands, but what interests me more than the sex is the *game* of seduction."

It's revealing that Steve and other flirtatious males devote themselves to a pursuit of passion they readily admit they don't need or even necessarily want. What's important to them isn't so much getting women into bed with them, as being *recognized* as winners of the erotic sweepstakes. Part of the reason they feel so determined to be seen as players is to impress other men— Steve, for example, doesn't feel so bad about being a ninety-eight-pound weakling as long as the other guys know that ninety-seven pounds is his victorious penis. The problem, of course, is that he only feels as potent as his last conquest, so he soon needs to prove himself all over again at the next party or in the next singles bar.

Another fear that fuels a man's flirting is often triggered by his first sexual experience. Charles was not only slow to lose his virginity—he was shot down by girl after girl until he finally met one who wasn't put off by his awkward overtures—but he sheepishly admits that "when the big moment finally came—so did I, much too quickly. After months of plotting and planning to get her into bed—and fantasizing how great it would be— when Bryna finally agreed to sleep with me, I got so excited that the entire thing was over in about sixty seconds. I'll never forget the look of disappointment on her face as she said, 'Was that it?' I smashed my fist through the headboard of her bed in a fury—at her, myself, and the world—then walked out. Something in me broke that day—besides my wrist."

While such experiences may sound like they'd put a man off sex for good, they only goad a flirt on to greater efforts. That's due to another key component of the compulsive flirt—an over-powering need to rebel against the very *first* woman in his life: his clingy mother, who hugged him to herself when he was growing up, in a futile effort to keep him as her little boy forever. She loathes every woman he's ever dated—including *you*—and acts as if they are her romantic rivals. Her cloying affections ignited a fiery mix of anger and guilt in your lover, which he replays by turning you into "home base," and then flaunting his flirtations with others. It is his revenge against a mom who tried (and to some extent, succeeded) in keeping him from becoming a man.

Shortly after Marissa met her man, she invited him to live with her, since he was new in town. Their relationship was great for the first year, until his wolflike ways caused him to stray. Not content to flirt discreetly, he flaunted each conquest in front of her. And the more she nagged him about his behavior, the more outrageous it became—just like a little boy *daring* his mother to punish him.

The Call of the Wild

Intriguingly, the same force that draws you to a flirt is also the one that compels him to shoot his amorous arrows at every woman in his sights: Both of you are defying a mother who tried to stifle your sexuality as you were growing up. Like Little Red Riding Hood, who conveniently "forgets" her mother's warnings and tells the Wolf exactly how to get to Grandmother's bed, you may also be responding to the lure of the *forbidden* when you fall for a seductive charmer. The more you were raised to be a good little girl, the more you may yearn to feel the hot breath of the big, bad Wolf—who represents everything your mother told you *not* to do—and romp with him in the wild woods of passion.

What makes this rogue an ideal partner in a romantic rebellion is that he is sexual enough to alarm your mother, but not enough of an erotic predator to alarm you. That's because you quickly figure out his *little* secret, which is that he's not really all that big—or bad. Far from being the stud that he claims to be, he's more of a sheep in wolf's clothing, which is very appealing if you're a bit inhibited in bed yourself, as women who are drawn to flirts usually are. What keeps him from being totally tame, however, is that he's still got an edge of danger—his power to wound you with his wanton ways. It's this heady brew of danger and safety that's the essence of a flirt's allure.

A mate who keeps making a *huge* statement about his masculinity may appeal to you because you feel there's some question about your feminine charms. After all, if all these women are after him, it's an ego boost to be the one he goes home with—at least for tonight. Some women willingly endure the agonies of jealousy their partner's seductive style provokes in them because they also gain a vicarious pleasure from his conquests. To them, every notch he carves in his penis is, in some sense, *their* notch as well since it's yet another woman he's given up to be with them. But, as they congratulate themselves for having this luscious man every woman wants, they never question whether they can ever really "have" a man who constantly flirts around.

Other women act as "home base" for their roving lover because this role feels a *lot* like home to them. As children, they always had to compete with their mother or sisters for their dad's fickle affections, and grew up with an unconscious tug toward situations where they'll have to share a man with other women. Or it may be that your father, like Karen's, was a philanderer who finally left her mother for one of his mistresses. "It took me years to notice that there was a strange symmetry between my daddy's love life and mine, because I actually fooled myself into thinking that it was a coincidence that every guy I dated ended up in the arms of another woman. Now I've stopped picking men who are destined to leave and started looking for someone who is stable enough to stay in a love affair for the long term."

Can You Live Happily Ever After?

Soon the Wolf heard a gentle tap at the door. "Open the latch and come in," he said in a quavering old lady's voice. When he saw Little Red Riding Hood enter, he softened his voice and added, "I'm not feeling very well, so why don't you put down that heavy basket, and get into bed with me?"

Eager to comfort her grandmother, she rushed to the bedside to present her bouquet of flowers. "Granny," she exclaimed, "what big eyes you have!"

"All the better to see you with, my dear," replied the wily Wolf, licking his chops hungrily.

"Granny," continued the girl, "what big hands you have!"

"All the better to hug you with, my dear."

By now Little Red Riding Hood was frightened. Her grandmother suddenly seemed very strange. "Granny, what big teeth you have!"

"All the better to eat you with!" the Wolf shouted as he leapt onto Little Red Riding Hood. Just before he pounced, she shouted for help.

A nearby woodsman heard her call and hurried into the house as the little red hood was disappearing down the greedy Wolf's gullet. With a mighty blow of his axe, the woodsman knocked the Wolf to the floor and slit its belly open. Out tumbled the girl and her grandmother. Seeing the Wolf looking small and sadly deflated, Little Red Riding Hood burst into laughter and gave him a contemptuous whack with her picnic basket. Whimpering pathetically, the wicked Wolf limped off into the woods and swore off little girls for good.

Can you curb a wolf's consuming passion for other women before it destroys your relationship? Since flirting can be an addiction, keeping him from straying can be a daunting task indeed. Only when *he's* just as committed as you are to attacking—and overcoming—his obsessive need to make new conquests is there any *realistic* hope of a future of mutual fidelity. If you're willing to take a chance on him, these strategies can help.

Decide What Is Acceptable, and What's Not

How far can your flirt go without inflaming you to jealousy? Is it okay for him to look at the ladies but not to talk suggestively to them? Is some verbal flirtation acceptable, if he keeps his hands to himself; or are you comfortable with *light* physical contact, like his giving a woman a social kiss, or a quick embrace? Wherever you draw the line, sex (or any activity that's usually done in a horizontal position on a bed, a floor, or a deserted beach) should be beyond the limit. You may rationalize, in order to avoid having him end the relationship, that it's okay for him to sleep around. But here's a news flash: If he does, you don't have a relationship! Leave now, while you still have a shred or two of self-esteem left.

Let Him Know What the Limits Are, but Avoid a Power Struggle

The more you tell your lover not to flirt, the more he'll defy you and *intensify* his attentions to other women. That's because giving him rules to follow makes him feel he's being treated like a little boy, which not only arouses his anxieties about being less of a man than his peers, but fuels an overpowering need to rebel against his controlling mother. Instead, focus on *your* feelings as you discuss the issue with him: "Seeing you slow dancing with Suzy made me feel unhappy and jealous. I want to be the only woman in your arms." While you may be reluctant to open up and reveal yourself this way, since you would feel vulnerable in front of a lover who has the power to hurt with his behavior, unless you take a few emotional risks you'll never get the love you want.

Help Him Feel Big—In and Out of Bed

Since the overwhelming anxiety that drives him to other women is his fear that he doesn't measure up as a man, the best way to defuse his desire to woo other women is by assuring him that he is more than manly enough for you. Remember how Little Red Riding Hood thrilled her Wolf by describing how *big* his eyes, hands, and teeth were? During sex, you'll delight your lover by telling him how much he pleases you as graphically as you can, because his greatest sexual thrill is knowing he's turning you on. Even if he asks a thousand times—and he probably will!—don't compare him to your past lovers. Just whisper affectionately that you don't want to talk about them, because he is the one who really excites you.

Even if you can honestly tell him he's the best, he won't fully believe you because of his self-doubts. The more details you provide about your past lovers, the more he'll inflate them out of proportion—and again feel small in comparison. Worse still, he may feel the need to outdo you in his sexual exploits—if he hasn't already—by having wild, *new* erotic adventures with someone else.

Outside of the boudoir, remember that he feels his masculinity is on the line if even the tiniest crisis arises. That's why it is perilous to laugh at him when he is ineptly trying to change a flat tire, or has been cruising around in circles for hours in search of an unfamiliar address. Your smartest move is to hail him as a hero when he finally fixes the tire or finds the right road. Otherwise he'll be extremely tempted to replenish his self-esteem in the only way that he knows—romancing other women.

Expect Some Lapses and Deal with Them Firmly

Since flirting is a compulsion for him, he is not going to break the habit instantly, no matter how supportive you are. If you see that he is acting overly seductive with another woman, hold up a stop sign, as Carolyn did. "What worked for me was taking a stand in public, by walking up to him at a crowded party and saying, 'George, remember how I told you that I don't like you to flirt with other women, and then catch my eye to see if I'm jealous? If you want to marry this woman, deal with her alone, and I'll back off.' An awful pall fell over the room, but he never did it again."

Doesn't sound quite like *your* style? Another way to teach him an unforgettable lesson is through some outrageous flirting of your own. The idea isn't to play games—though this form of revenge can be tempting indeed—but to show him how painful it is to have a partner whose eyes are constantly roaming. When he complains later about your seductive moves toward other men, you might say, "I understand just how you must feel, because it hurt *me* to see you with other women. Why don't we both cool it?" Or you could discover that a touch of judicious flirting on your part heats up the relationship—since an edge of sexual jealousy can fire up renewed passion in the bedroom.

If You Suspect He's in the Throes of a Temporary Sexy Spell, Decide Whether It's Worth Waiting It Out

With a lover who is young (and isn't ready to settle down until he's walked on the wild side a little further), is going through a midlife crisis (and flirts to make sure his allure hasn't faded), or is recovering from a serious illness (and wants to affirm his life force), you have two choices. You can either let him go—he may be back, and ready to make a real commitment sooner than you imagine—or stick with him, at least for now, and set a firm deadline for improvement. Don't fool yourself, however. If he's still chasing every woman he sees six to twelve months from now, it's not a passing phase, it's his life.

Be Ready to Walk Away

Setting limits is meaningless if your flirt knows you'll forgive *any* betrayal. The bottom line has to be that if he has sex with anyone else, he'll lose you. Hopefully, it will never happen, but if he strays, having you leave could be just the jolt he needs to get him to give up his wolfish ways for good—and focus on winning you back as his one and only love.

5

THE GRANDIOSE DREAMER

*U*ntil the great cyclone came, Dorothy lived in a vast gray prairie with her gaunt, gray aunt and uncle. Because she was a lonely orphan, her one joy was playing with her dog, Toto. While Dorothy was wishing to be swept away from her bleak circumstances, the sky suddenly turned even grayer, and a twister roared toward the farm. Dorothy ran to get Toto, and was still in the house when it was sent whirling through the air like a balloon.

After it landed with a jolt, Dorothy peered outside, and was astonished to see she was in a land of marvelous beauty. A crowd of curiously small men and one woman cheered at the sight of Dorothy. "Hail, great sorceress," exclaimed the woman, introducing herself as the Good Witch of the North. "You've destroyed the Wicked Witch of the East, one of the two wicked witches of Oz, and freed the Munchkins from bondage."

Dorothy stepped outside and said, "I'm no sorceress—just an innocent girl from Kansas who never killed anyone." She gasped as the woman pointed out two skinny legs that were sticking out from under Dorothy's front steps. "Oh, no!" cried

Dorothy as the feet vaporized, leaving only the witch's silver shoes.

"These shoes, which have a secret charm, are yours now," the Good Witch said, kissing Dorothy, and leaving a shiny, magical mark on her forehead. When Dorothy sobbed that she just wanted to go home, the Good Witch told her to take the yellow brick road to Emerald City, where a great wizard lived, and ask his help.

Along the road, Dorothy met a Scarecrow who bemoaned his lack of brains; a Tin Woodsman who groaned about having no heart; and a Lion who cried that without courage, he was the most cowardly of all beasts. All three went with her to Emerald City, where the guardian at the gate gave them green spectacles to wear and locked the glasses on their faces, as the Wizard of Oz had ordered.

At first the Wizard would not see them, but when he heard of Dorothy's silver shoes and the shining mark on her forehead, he relented. She was ushered into a vast room sparkling with emeralds. Suspended over the green marble throne was an enormous head, which stared at her and said, "I am Oz, the Great and Terrible. Who are you, and why have you come to me?"

"I am Dorothy the Small and Meek," she answered. "I need your help to send me home."

"If I do, there will be a price," the head insisted. "You say you are small and meek, but you have killed the Wicked Witch of the East. So if you want me to use my magic, you must first kill the Wicked Witch of the West." The head trembled slightly, and for a second Dorothy suspected the entire setup was a scam. As she moved closer to the head, it said, "If you ever want to see your home again, do as I command, or you'll be lost forever."

Sadly disturbed, she returned to her friends, only to learn each had also had an audience with the Wizard. Though he appeared to each in a different form—the Scarecrow saw a lovely lady, the Tin Man a terrifying beast, and the Lion a huge ball of fire—he gave all the same reply: Their wish would only be granted if the Wicked Witch were dead.

Not knowing what else to do, the four travelers and Toto left Emerald City and headed west. . . .

Are you in love with a magical man who makes very extravagant promises but never really delivers on them? At first, Hilary was dazzled by her new boyfriend's delicious wit, fascinating tales of adventure, and wildly inventive and terrifically *intense* lovemaking. Now she wonders, "What's wrong with this picture?" since her dream lover has turned out to have some nightmarish traits.

After sweeping her off her feet with lush, romantic overtures, he took her off for a passion-filled weekend at a cozy country inn. "I thought that everything was wonderful—particularly the sex—but I kept feeling I'd disappointed him and couldn't imagine how. When we were driving home, he abruptly turned to me and announced, in an icy voice, 'I planned to fall in love with you this weekend, but it just didn't happen. I think we should stop seeing each other.' It was such a complete bolt from the blue I couldn't think of anything at all to say."

Days later, just as her broken heart was starting to mend, she found a charming little note under her door from him—asking her to go ice-skating with him, so they could hold hands and talk. When all her friends advised her to say she'd skate with him when hell froze over, she did exactly what most of us do if we fall for a bad boy—hesitated for about two seconds, then dialed his number. Now she's caught up in an on-again, off-again affair that is as compelling as it is frustrating.

His Telltale Traits

Hot and cold passions are just *part* of the problem if your man is a grandiose dreamer, since each quality that attracts you to him has an unfortunate flip side. Just as the Wizard of Oz revealingly describes himself as both "the Great *and* Terrible," you soon notice that your lover is a mix of both: His hilarious anecdotes are often gross exaggerations or out and out lies; while his lavish romantic gestures spring from an almost absurdly impulsive personality. His mood can swing from sunny to stormy and back again as suddenly as a weather vane.

Even his hot-blooded sexuality may have an edge of desperation about it—you sense that he's never truly satisfied, or that he desires more *lurid* turn-ons—while his feelings about you can abruptly turn very frosty, especially if he thinks you're getting too close to him, or are making demands of him without giving him something *first*. Like the Great Oz who made Dorothy kill the witch before he would try to send her home, your boyfriend wants to be paid up front before he'll promise to fulfill your wish, because he is afraid he can't live up to his grandiose claims.

Here are other ways to recognize a would-be wizard.

He Thinks Big—Maybe Too Big

You dream of getting a twenty percent pay raise; he's feverishly figuring out how to amass his first million and has already decided how to decorate his future mansion—and both his yachts. You hope there's a nice promotion waiting for you down the road; he's already printed business cards naming himself the president and CEO of various enterprises. Listening to his gaudy, grandiose ambitions and promises makes *your* daydreams suddenly seem as drab as the dusty plains of Kansas. Even though you may suspect the emeralds on his imaginary throne in Oz are probably just paste, there is still something dazzling—even magical—about a man who dreams so big. After all, even impossible-sounding wishes *sometimes* come true—don't they?

His Life Is Littered with False Starts

Though he's constantly building castles in the sky, his past is full of discarded dreams. Sandy's boyfriend is typical. Not only has he been an advertising salesman, a writer, and a limousine driver; but he's had four different fiancées (three of whom still call him). Even his closet may reveal this tendency: Like the Great Oz, who never appears in the same guise twice, Mona's partner has a wardrobe that spans the fashion spectrum from surfer dude T-shirts to conservative pin-striped suits—and just about any imaginable style in between. "Leroy changes his look so often that you'd think his clothes belonged to ten different people—or someone with an identity crisis," she says.

He Has a Very High Energy Level

Many grandiose dreamers are compulsive about their exercise routine or are drawn to physically challenging activities like mountain climbing or marathon running. Others fling themselves into a new sport with wild enthusiasm—just as they may do with a new career or love relationship—only to lose interest a few months later. Even Wizards who aren't sports buffs, like Ellen's lover, usually seem physically charged up in some way. "It's almost as though a chair can't quite contain Eric, since he's always leaping up to get something. He literally can't sit still, even at a meeting. Instead, his feet start fidgeting, his fingers begin to tap, and pretty soon he's almost jumping out of his skin."

He's in a Hurry for Love—and Everything Else

A home that's crammed with mementoes of his past love affairs, accoutrements from abandoned careers (an architect's drawing board or a chef's hat), or dusty debris of his brief flirtations with photography and surfing may make you suspect your lover is fickle, but actually he's wildly *impatient*. He'll flit from job to job if he feels he is not moving up *fast* enough, or turn sour on a sport if he can't master it right away. That's why it's a mistake to play hard to get with this guy; he's apt to move on to an *easier* conquest. But you shouldn't sleep with him on the first date either—or else he'll have nothing to dream about.

This craving for almost instant gratification can also express itself in other ways too. Paige says her boyfriend hates to wait for anything, especially food. "Burger King is just about the only restaurant with service fast enough for him—and even there he will often complain that he's in the 'slow' line. If we go to a bistro, he practically *inhales* the whole bread basket while he's waiting to get his entree—then bolts his food down as if someone was going to snatch it away any second. He's the same way behind the wheel too: Even a momentary traffic delay drives him crazy because he's always in such a rush to get there."

He's an Incurable Show-Off

Unlike the compulsive flirt, who is starved for female attention, the grandiose dreamer is delighted to dazzle any audience—man, woman or child—with his anecdotes or antics. Over the years, he's perfected some kind of crowd-pleasing act: Perhaps he's adept at magic tricks or juggling, knows hundreds of great jokes, or tells spellbinding stories about his adventures. Although he *usually* stops just short of being obnoxiously arrogant, and is judicious about name-dropping (even the most tenuous link to a celebrity or VIP is sure to surface somewhere in his conversation), it's still extremely important to him that people appreciate his special powers, superior knowledge, or impressive social connections.

He's Bursting with Ideas

Whether or not your man is a marathon runner, he's almost certainly a marathon *talker*, especially if he's egged on by an appreciative audience. While this behavior may not necessarily be a sign of a psychological problem, you should be concerned if your lover takes it to an *extreme*, as talking jags can be a symptom of manic-depression or a milder mood disorder. (During a manic spell, people may start talking more and more quickly as if they are struggling to keep up with their racing thoughts. As words cascade from their lips, the logical connection between one concept and the next may get lost in their torrent of speech, so it's hard for others to follow what they're saying.)

He Has Episodes of Intense Self-Doubt

Although he's usually supremely self-confident, or even boastful, in public, a Wizard may suffer agonies of insecurity in private. During his gloomy phases, while he's wondering if he only has *delusions* of grandeur, he's apt to be very irritable, easily distracted, and difficult to get along with. Or he may grow lethargic and withdrawn—if he hasn't called you for two weeks, this is probably why—and avoid people until his self-esteem again soars into the stratosphere. Don't fool yourself into thinking the improvement is permanent, however—an up-and-down cycle is often a recurring pattern with this man.

He Sometimes Goes on Reckless Spending Sprees

If you marry one of these magicians, don't expect a secure old age, since money slips through his fingers as fast as words tumble from his mouth if he's in a manic mood. It's not just a case of boys and their toys, however, because objects represent *power* to him. Just as a Wizard is nothing without his props, for your partner, acquiring the right possessions is a way of signaling his status, special talents, and overall importance. Unfortunately for his bank balance, the magic of that new windsurfing board, electronic gadget, or trendy jacket soon wears off— meaning that it's time to go shopping again.

He Has a Huge Sexual Appetite

The one time a Wizard *isn't* in a rush is when he's making love. He is, however, every bit as intense in bed as he is everywhere else—and has a vast repertoire of erotic tricks that leave you gasping in exhausted ecstasy. He, on the other hand, believes there's no such thing as *too* much sex. He's always up for erotic action—even if he is *alone*. Some manic magicians are so insatiable that they can make love all night long, and still have enough erotic energy to masturbate the next morning; and for a few, self-gratification is actually a compulsion.

You may also sense there's a wild side to him. Sexual games could appeal to him partly because he'd like to dazzle you and be your most *memorable* lover—after all, how many other guys have ever wanted to picnic naked on the beach at midnight and lick champagne off your nipples?—and partly because he is always seeking the *ultimate* erotic high. That's why he sometimes seems curiously discontent after a wild night of bedroom gymnastics—he's sure there is an even grander way of making love that's eluded him so far.

Inside the Ego of Oz

Dorothy is right to suspect the Great Oz is a sham—since all Wizards secretly believe they're frauds, and live in constant fear of being found out. Their trickery is a way of keeping a guard at the psychological gates to their inner self, who turns away anyone who hasn't bought their magic act. Only true believers who put on the special green spectacles that show these Wizards in their best light are admitted to their throne room—but even there, all their audience is permitted to see is *more* illusions, as the supposed magicians hide their true faces behind yet another screen of secrecy.

It is not surprising that your Wizard considers himself to be an imposter: One psychological study reports that forty percent of men—even ones who are very successful—suffer from feelings of fraudulence, and believe themselves undeserving of whatever they've achieved in life. The reason many of them feel this way is that they've grown up in a household where women had all the power, and men had none, as Sean did. "You know how novelists often describe the father in their story as 'a shadowy figure'? Well mine really was, since my mother dominated the family so thoroughly I hardly even noticed if Dad was home or not. She doted on my two sisters, but always made me feel that I was a huge disappointment to her, just like Dad was. To get any attention at all from her, I felt that I had to pretend to be more than I really was."

Your lover has learned two potent lessons from his childhood, each of which is an important key to understanding why he acts the way he does with you. *First, he believes once a woman realizes he has no power, she'll reject him.* That's why he makes such a show of being a grandiose partner: He hopes all of his overblown promises, dazzling romantic rhetoric, and exhilarating lovemaking will fool you into thinking that he's special and superpowerful. All this sleight of hand is designed to keep you from discovering how hollow he feels inside—that in some sense, there's nothing up his sleeve except a couple of cheap tricks.

The second key to his psychology is his view that *all women are witches with both good and evil powers*. Just like his mother, they have a dual nature—they can bestow their love and attention, and make a man's life enchanting; or they turn mean and rejecting, and use their sorcery to shrivel up all his self-esteem. It's no wonder that the Wizard is attracted to Dorothy when he hears that she has gifts from both the good and wicked witches on her—he hopes that she'll be more benevolent than his mother was—and that his first demand is that she destroy the bad witch for him.

This unconscious wish is the guilty secret that underlies the imposter syndrome: Your lover is furious at his mother for making him put on an act. Just as the Wizard of Oz eventually reveals to Dorothy that he used to be a balloonist who acted as a shill for a circus, and then a ventriloquist who tricked people by throwing his voice around the room, your partner is still replaying a childhood when he believed his mother didn't love him for who he really was. To avoid disappointing her, he felt that he had to resort to flimflam and make-believe.

Along with feeling angry, your man is understandably jealous of the magic he believes his mother—and all women—possess. The good and bad witches are like breasts to him: They can nourish or they can deprive, according to the woman's whim. There's another part of your body he envies and fears even more—your womb—since a woman's ultimate power, in his view, is to create life. If his mother can make him, she can also destroy him, he feels, which is why he still sees her—or any woman that he's involved with—as a terrifying sorceress who must be tricked into staying safely away from his true self.

It's intriguing that the Wizard insists on being seen in a *green* light, since it's a hue that's symbolically associated with jealousy (which is what he feels toward women) as well as being linked to money (the dazzling successes that he aspires to), witches (bad mothers), and nature and fertility (good mothers). What the Wizard of Oz and your man are unconsciously saying is that they're green with envy because you have the power they only pretend to possess.

Why You're with a Wizard

What's the magnetism a magician holds for you? Like Dorothy, you may feel lost and powerless and look to a grandiose dreamer to grant your greatest wish—to be taken to a place where you will be enveloped in love and feel truly at home. Just as her companions yearned for the Wizard of Oz to give them brains, a heart, and courage, you yearn for a lover who will magically supply these missing parts of you and make you feel clever, passionate, and self-confident. That's an impossible task, so you turn to a merchant of dreams who promises you everything—but ultimately does nothing. Yet even after you take off your green-colored glasses and see him for the humbug he is, you still want desperately to believe in his promises.

The reason that you are so willing to let yourself be fooled by a false Wizard is that at heart, you feel like an imposter too. Your secret, however, is the mirror image of his. He pretends to be big and strong because he dreads having somebody discover his *lack* of power; and you pretend to be little and weak because you are afraid of your power. That's because, deep down, you believe you really are the magical being that your wizard wishes he were—and have the power to *destroy*.

This feeling originates in the magical thinking of childhood, when you imagined that your feelings of anger or hate toward your parents could actually injure them. What may have reinforced this fear is losing one or both of your parents as you were growing up, either literally—because of death, illness, divorce, or adoption—or in an emotional sense. Perhaps you felt your parents abandoned you by being cold and neglectful or that they rejected you in some other way. Any of these traumas could have left you with terrible guilt as a child, since you believed the punishment for your "bad" thoughts was losing your parents—or their love.

As a result, you hide your true self for exactly the opposite reason your boyfriend does: He thinks he has to pretend to be *more* than he really is, while you pretend to be *less* so you won't scare people away. Dorothy is a perfect example of this game of denial: Instead of admitting she's furious with her biological parents for deserting her through death—while she's left to live without love, laughter, or friends on a dusty farm in the middle of nowhere—she "accidentally" kills the *two* wicked witches who rule the imaginary kingdom of Oz, an intriguingly symbolic action for an angry orphan. Even when the Wizard realizes immediately that she's mightier than he is—otherwise, why doesn't he kill the Wicked Witch of the West himself?—she still insists that she's "small and meek."

Similarly, Dorothy isn't really taken in by the Great Oz—she suspects he's a hoax from the start. Instead, both pretend to buy the other's act because it fits their psychological needs so well, which is exactly what you and your lover are doing. Like Dorothy, you're unconsciously saying, "I know you're a fake, but I want you to give me the home I never had anyway"; while he's saying, "Sure, I'll pretend you are a helpless little orphan if you want, because it puffs up my ego—but I still expect you to kill off my witch of a mother. That should be easy for you, since you have already got rid of *your* parents."

That you are estranged from your parents or consider yourself a psychological orphan can be a big part of what draws your wizard to you or you to him. Not only does your man gain an irresistible opportunity to pose as the savior that you've been waiting for, he feels secretly relieved not to have to deal with two *new* powerful figures—your mother and father—in your life who would be sure to be a lot more skeptical about him than you are since they wouldn't be wearing the magic lenses of love that make him seem so splendid. You, on the other hand, are eager to view him as he'd prefer to be seen, since flinging yourself into the arms of a man who says he has a magic wand that will make your troubles disappear means that you don't have to depend on your dangerous powers.

While some women want to fly away with an illusionist because they are hiding from disturbingly potent emotions, such as intense anger at their rejecting parents, others disown the female power a Wizard finds most frightening—their fertility. May, for example, says she never wants children. "It's not that I just hate kids or something—actually, I love playing with my sister's baby. It's a perfect relationship for me, since I get to do all the fun stuff—like buying her toys or dressing her up in pretty clothes—without any of the awful responsibilities of parenthood. If she starts to cry or needs a diaper change, I can just hand her to my sister and let her take care of the problem."

Such sentiments, if you have them, could also be an important element of your relationship with your lover, since they hold very significant hidden meanings for both of you. For you, it can be a way of asking your partner for permission to be a carefree child—since you feel your unloving parents robbed you of your *real* childhood. To him, it's a wish he's only too glad to grant, as a woman who doesn't want children surrenders the power of her womb that he fears so in his mother. And, best of all, in his view, not having kids to compete with guarantees him that with you, he'll always be exactly where he want to be—at the center of your attention.

Can You Live Happily Ever After?

As soon as Dorothy and her friends reached the realm of the Wicked Witch of the West, they were attacked by winged monkeys, who took Dorothy to the Witch. Looking into Dorothy's innocent eyes, the old sorceress realized the girl wasn't aware of the power her silver shoes had. She tricked Dorothy and snatched one of the shoes away from her. Furious, Dorothy flung her bucket of water at the Witch, who melted into a puddle of sludge. Shocked and apologetic, the girl held her nose and fished out her shoe.

After she rescued her friends, they returned to Oz to claim their reward. The throne room, however, was empty, and the solemn voice of the Wizard told them to return tomorrow. Angry that the Wizard wasn't keeping his word, the Lion let out a roar. Toto leapt in alarm, crashing into a screen, which had been concealing a bald, little man.

"Who are you?" asked the Tin Woodsman, raising his axe.

"I am Oz, the Great and Terrible—but please, don't hurt me," the little man begged.

"Why you're nothing but a great and terrible humbug,"

Dorothy replied indignantly as the others pressed forward and demanded he produce brains, a heart, and courage. "Don't forget to send me to Kansas," she added, shaking her finger.

"How can I help but be a humbug when people keep asking me to do things that are impossible?" the little man lamented. "I am really a good man—but a bad wizard." Seeing Dorothy's puzzled look, he explained he was once a ventriloquist and used his voice and props to create his illusions. "In Omaha, I was also a balloonist until my balloon drifted away to Oz, where the people took me for a wizard."

He unlocked Dorothy's glasses, so she saw that everything was actually rather drab and ordinary, not emerald green. When the travelers still insisted that he keep his promises, he stuffed the Scarecrow's head with pins and cereal. "You'll be sharp as a pin with your bran-new brains." Next, he put a pink satin heart in the Woodsman's chest, and poured a strong-smelling green potion for the Lion. "Drink this, and you'll always have courage inside you."

Helping Dorothy was harder, but after several days he built a hot-air balloon to carry them both to Kansas. When the balloon was almost full, Dorothy noticed Toto had run off. As she ran to catch him, the Wizard shouted for her to hurry. Just as she had the dog in her arms and was about to climb aboard, a rope broke and the balloon soared into the sky without her. "Don't fly away," she screamed, "I want to go too!"

To keep your Wizard from floating off in a balloon full of hot air and inflated promises while you're left on the ground shouting in frustration, use these guidelines.

Listen to Your Internal Watchdog

There's a powerful message in this story for any woman who loves a Wizard: She should find and embrace Toto, the playful puppy that lives inside her. This lighthearted little dog is the true magician in Dorothy's life, since he helps her escape the gray plains of Kansas and start her journey of self-discovery. Unlike her three needy companions—the Scarecrow who feels stupid, the Woodsman who laments his lack of a heart, and the Lion who considers himself craven—this feisty little pet listens to his shrewd instincts. It's he who unmasks the would-be wizard—and prevents Dorothy from being blown away by his hot air. Let the smart little Toto inside you puncture the illusions that your lover weaves around himself, and lead you to the truth about him.

Give Up Your Need to Be Rescued

Intriguingly, as soon as the Wizard floats away, Dorothy discovers she *always* had the power to go home: All she had to do was click the heels of her silver shoes three times and command them to take her wherever she wanted to go. There's an equally powerful magic in you—the problem is that you're afraid to unleash it, because you fear it's fueled by a terrible, destructive rage. What you need to do is remind yourself that it is okay to be angry—as long as you use the anger as a healthy force for change. Why wait for a Wizard to lift you above the bleak circumstances of your life, or painful memories of the past, when you can attack these problems on your own? Learn to love yourself, and you will always be "home," whether there's a man in your life or not.

Claim Your Power—Slowly

If you show your full strength too quickly, your magician is likely to do a disappearing act, since it evokes alarming images of his controlling mother. Remember that to him, all women are either good witches who accept him for himself—or at least *pretend* to be fooled by his illusions—and wicked ones, who make him feel psychologically impotent. Because his great fear is being exposed as nothing more than a bald-headed little guy with delusions of grandeur, if you want to keep him, it's crucial not to deflate his fantasies by suddenly revealing yourself as Superwoman. Instead, gradually show him that you don't *need* rescuing, but there is still an important way he can help you—by lifting you up to new heights, through the power of his love.

Once You Find Out What's Behind His Screen, Decide If You Can Accept It

Can you get over the disenchantment of discovering that your lover is more of a wanna-be than a great wizard? Is it really okay that he's a bit of a humbug who can't magically solve all your problems—despite his inflated promises? Look into your heart and ask yourself if there is enough that's *genuinely* magical about this man to make you truly happy. It may be that after you abandon *your* illusions, you'll decide you don't need his. Or you may find that for all his flaws and fakery, he'll always be the Great Oz to you.

If He Is What You Want, Let Him Know He Doesn't Need to Put On an Act to Impress You

The secret of having a successful love affair with a would-be Wizard is to make him feel magical for who he really is—not his artful trickery or ingenious disguises. Reassure him that you accept and love every part of him, even that bald little fraud he's got hidden behind the screen. While he'll probably need lots of reassurance from you before he's comfortable enough to let out this secret side of himself, when he does, he'll be just as relieved as the Wizard was to finally be *freed* of the burden of trying to grant other people's impossible wishes and demands.

Show Him You Can Make Magic Together

Another secret of achieving the relationship you want is to renegotiate the balance of power. Right now, both of you are in the wrong roles. You're not the lost little girl you pretend to be, and he's not the all-powerful Oz he poses as—nor is he just the frightened fraud that he fears he is in his darkest moments. Each of you needs to claim what is genuinely strong and weak in yourself, and allow yourself to be completed—not rescued—by the other. Be willing to grow—and the two of you could work real wizardry together!

6

*M*ISUNDERSTOOD— AND MARRIED

eep under the ocean in a castle made of coral lived the King of the Sea. He'd been a widower for many years and devoted himself to his six daughters, while his mother kept house for him. Though he loved all of the beautiful mermaid princesses, the youngest was his favorite. Unlike her sisters, who swam all around the undersea realm befriending everybody they met, she was a quiet, solitary child who spent most of her time dreaming of the marvelous world of the mortals.

Even the little garden she planted outside her father's castle reflected her fantasies of that other world. She designed it to be as round as the sun, and filled it with bright red flowers. When a shipwreck dropped a statue of a handsome boy, carved out of pure, white marble, to the bottom of the sea, she made it the centerpiece of the garden, and planted a weeping willow by its pedestal. As it grew, she fancied the branches and roots were playfully kissing one another.

On her eighteenth birthday, her father finally allowed her to swim up to the sea's surface. As she floated lightly on the waves, she saw a splendid ship decorated with colorful lanterns and banners. It was full of elegantly dressed mortals, but the most handsome by far was the young prince. As she saw the queen fondly embrace him and congratulate him, she learned it was his birthday too—and was fascinated by the face of the beautiful boy who shared this special bond with her.

As hundreds of brilliant rockets began exploding into the sky, the Mermaid felt a sudden turbulence in the sea and knew a terrible storm was coming. The waves leapt higher and higher, and the great ship snapped in two. As lightning flashed, she saw the prince sink into the depths. At first, she was delighted that he would be with her under the sea, until she remembered a mortal could only come to her father's kingdom as a corpse. She searched through the wreckage, at risk of being crushed herself, and found the prince unconscious.

She kissed his pale, handsome mouth, which reminded her of the marble statue in her garden, and carried him through the raging sea to shore. As she put him on the sand, the bells of a nearby tower began ringing loudly. Frightened, the Mermaid dove into the water and hid her face and breasts with sea foam so no one could see her. A young woman came out of the holy temple and rushed to help the prince. He opened his eyes; and believing she'd saved his life, he gave her his gold ring as a reward and a pledge.

"I should be wearing his ring," the Mermaid thought sadly as she swam back down to her father's home. "He doesn't know it, but I'm the one who risked my life to save his."

Every morning and every night, the Little Mermaid returned to the spot where she'd left the prince, but it was empty. Her only comfort was hugging and kissing the marble statue which resembled the prince. But in her sorrow, she stopped taking care of her flowers, and they grew in wild confusion over the paths, so that her garden soon became a wild jungle.

Finally, in desperation, she hurried to the icy black whirlpools that led to the realm of the Sea Witch, whose house was made of the bones of drowned mortals. "I know why you're here," the Witch said as she let a hideous toad eat from her lips. "I will give you the ugly stumps the mortals call legs, but if I do, each step you take will be like walking on a knife as sharp as a *two-edged sword. And I demand a high price. You have the loveliest voice of all . . . and it shall be mine."*

"This is what I want," the Mermaid said, turning deathly pale.

"Your wish shall only bring you misfortune," the Witch warned. "If you don't win the prince, you can never become a mermaid again. The morning after he marries another, your heart will break and you will become foam on the water."

"So be it," the Mermaid answered, parting her rosy lips to reveal her tongue and waiting for the agonizing slash of the witch's knife. . . .

Are you pining for a man who has pledged his heart to another, whether it's his wife, ex-wife, fiancée, or live-in lover? Roberta has been having a torrid affair with her boss, a married real estate broker, for the past three years, but longs, like the Little Mermaid, to be his bride. "He keeps saying that he wants to be with me, but there is always some reason why he can't get a divorce right now. First he was up for a promotion, and was afraid a scandal would spoil his chances; then he was concerned about how his daughter would react, and insisted on delaying until she left for college—which she did, last fall. Now he wants to wait for the real estate market to get better, so he and his wife will get a better price for the property they own jointly. At this rate, the only move he's going to make is to a cemetery."

Charlotte admits there's little evidence that her lover, a top trial lawyer, has any desire for a divorce. He's too sophisticated to tell her his wife doesn't understand him—and besides, his often repeated complaint that she is overly suspicious suggests she does, all too well. Instead, he contends that the problem is "a lack of communication," probably because he lies to her almost daily about where he goes, whom he sees, and what he does.

With Charlotte, he has also been deceitful—after a few dates, he cheerfully admitted that when he previously told her that he was "separated" from his wife, he didn't mean that he's actually broken off with her, just that she wasn't physically with him at that very moment. Despite this less than auspicious opening of their affair, Charlotte recently took heart at his observation that she's "a nice girl—not at all like the bimbos I *usually* date."

Nancy, on the other hand, has the opposite problem. She spent months wishing her boyfriend would leave his wife for her—but once he did, she didn't want him anymore. "That he was so reluctant to leave her only made him *more* attractive to me, but now that there's nothing to *stop* me from sleeping with him, the thrill is gone. The electricity of the affair came from the idea that it was forbidden, illicit, even taboo. I loved to feel that I was *stealing* him: Once I surprised him at the airport when he was flying back from a meeting and drove him to my apartment for a quickie before sending him home to his mousy little wife. In the car, I was running my hand up his legs and being so wildly sexual that he was shocked. I'm sure that his wife never did that in her whole life—let alone recent memory.

"The whole game was about capturing him, but since he had made no promises, I never actually expected to get him. Sometimes I had fantasies about his getting divorced and being with me, but I never actually pushed him to do it. I guess I knew somehow that I didn't really want that, even though I told myself I did. But when it was suddenly a reality—last month he showed up unexpectedly at my door to announce that he'd left his wife and family, and was looking for a house where we could live together—my blood ran cold. I felt so bad about the whole thing that I practically *begged* him to go back to her."

His Telltale Traits

Here's a rundown of the characteristics a runaround husband may have:

He Tries to Run Rings Around You

Spotting a married man who is on the prowl can be trickier than you might think, since there is a continuum between the two types of philanderers—those who try to hide their marital status, and those who actually *flaunt* it. The first type can sometimes be recognized by a suspicious tan line on their ring finger. If they're even sneakier (or smarter), they've learned to avoid such obvious tip-offs—having stopped wearing their wedding bands years ago, when they first started fooling around. These wayward husbands usually get around to mentioning that they're married eventually—but not until *after* they get you in bed with them.

After hours of passionate lovemaking, Selena walked her new lover to the elevator at her apartment building. Making conversation until the elevator came, she murmured breathlessly, "You must have been married once, hmm?" "I *am* married," he said, in a tone that implied, "Isn't everyone?"

The second type, who boldly announce they're married, then act surprised if you view their wife as an obstacle to romance (since they certainly don't), have a different seduction strategy. They've found out that in the eyes of many women—such as Nancy, and maybe even *you*—being unavailable, except for covert trysts, only increases their allure.

He Justifies Having an Affair by Blaming His Wife—or Himself

Though some wayward husbands have an apparently endless litany of complaints about their wife (she's cold, critical, and unappreciative) or vaguely intimate that there is some discord, but leave it to you to fill in the blanks, others get angry or defensive if you imply there's any problem with their partner. Rona's married boyfriend, for example, claims his spouse is practically a candidate for sainthood—which certainly helps explain why he spends so much time in bad girls' bedrooms: A saint isn't too sexy. He, however, says the reason he's had ten affairs is that he is "a terrible person"—not nearly good enough for such an angelic wife.

Some men say that their wife doesn't mind their extramarital flings—or is having an affair herself. Your lover may even tell you he has "an open marriage," as Jennifer's former boyfriend did. "I figured that this would be news to his wife, since claiming to have an open marriage has to be the oldest line in the book. But after I slept with him a few times, he decided to reveal his *real* agenda—it seemed that his wife had sent him out to find somebody who would be willing to go to bed with *both* of them! That is way too 'open' for me, so I broke up with him on the spot."

He's Tired of Taking Out the Trash

Whether or not he tells you about it, most men who look outside their marriages for love—or sex—have a much less exotic motivation than arranging a ménage à trois: They feel that they're taken for granted at home. In his heart, your lover may think of himself as a romantic swashbuckler, or a Lone Ranger who is always up for another adventure, while his wife treats him like a paycheck with legs. He's resentful that no one in the family appreciates that he's out there every day grinding down his spirit at a dull job to make money to pay for his wife's clothes or the kids' college.

Rather than being praised and treated like a prince when he gets home after a hard day at the office—as he feels is his due—he's nagged about leaving dirty socks on the floor, and ordered to empty the garbage. It's more often a buildup of such prosaic slights than a lust to find a lover who knows seventeen ways of performing fellatio that makes most married men stray (a good point to keep in mind should you ever succeed in wooing him away from his wife, though knowing lots of techniques to give him oral pleasure couldn't *hurt*.)

He Longs to Live Out His Fantasies

Tedious responsibilities are only part of the problem, however. He also feels misunderstood by his wife, who treats him like an ordinary mortal—not the sexy stud he fancies himself in his dreams—so he conjures up a lover who will give him more. Very often, a husband may spend years having romantic and sexual fantasies about other women before he acts them out with an actual affair. What he wants is the magic of falling in love, the joy of being with someone who makes him the center of her life, the thrill of making love with somebody new for the very first time. In other words, he longs to recapture the fun of being single, younger, and carefree—at least temporarily.

It's also possible that there's some erotic variation his wife won't do with him—or that he lacks the nerve to tell the mother of his children he wants her to wear crotchless panties and talk dirty to him. Or he may have slipped into a sexual rut with his wife and views an affair as an exciting opportunity to do all the deliciously naughty things that he's only dreamed of, as Dara's boyfriend does. "He's never actually told me that his wife refuses to have sex with him in black leather and heels, but he was thrilled when I said I'd try it. And you know what, it was fun!"

He's Looking for a Trophy

Particularly if your man married young—when he had less power, success, cash, and self-confidence—he may secretly believe that he's entitled to a reward for what he has achieved: a woman who is more suitable for his new status than the wife who accepted him when he had less to offer. That doesn't necessarily mean that he's going to do a Donald Trump and dump his aging wife—even if you are as hot as Marla Maples. He might just enjoy having you on his arm to pump his self-esteem even further, and show the world that he's still a virile stud, even if he's not so young anymore.

No Matter What He Claims in the Heat of Passion, He Probably Doesn't Want a Divorce

Statistics show that the odds are against getting him away from his wife—the majority of men who have affairs end up staying with their current spouse. Along with the obvious reasons like children, money, religious beliefs, and disapproving relatives, there are a number of psychological inhibitions that keep most married men married. One of the most important is the fear of losing control: As long as he has his wife, your lover always has a safety net to land in should your love affair collapse.

Running away with you, however, forces him to leave everything that's familiar, surrender to passions that secretly alarm him, and risk getting hurt. It's scary for him to even think about it since he can never be one hundred percent sure that you'd stay with him if he did agree to sacrifice his security and take a chance on life with you. What especially terrifies him about the idea is that he might end up all alone—without a wife or a mistress to console him.

He Gives You Just Enough Hope to Keep You Hanging On

Because he doesn't want to lose you either, your lover may drop hints that he might someday make you his bride, or whisper in your ear that your love makes his life worth living. He probably throws real energy, far more than any single guy would, into wooing you, even after he has gotten you into bed. Perhaps he calls you three times a day—from the office or car phone, of course, or when he's out walking the family dog— or surprises you with a gold locket on your birthday (or two days later, after he gets back from taking his sons to Cub Scout camp). Or maybe he takes you to romantic restaurants and holds your hand under the table, takes you to hotels for torrid nights of passion, or spends a small fortune giving you anything your heart desires—except for a wedding ring.

He Has a Self-Indulgent Streak

Not only does your partner treat you well—at least, until the affair is over—but he treats himself even better. Secretly he believes that by having you and his wife he's getting the best of both worlds—a playmate for his nights out, and a companion at home he can always count on. He's not as burdened by guilt as you may think—he tells himself he is entirely justified in having both of you, since neither of you is meeting *all* of his needs. It's gratifying to him to have two women competing over him—even if one of them doesn't realize it.

Why He Cheats on His Wife

Millions of married men are tired of taking out the garbage, feel unappreciated at home, or fantasize about having wild sexual adventures, but studies show that most of them *don't* fool around. What makes your man different? Is it just that his wife is worse than most—as he may imply—or is there a *deeper* reason why he is having an illicit affair?

To understand why your boyfriend is drawn to a love triangle, you need to examine the *first* three-way relationship in his
life—the primal threesome of mother, father, and child, which is
always the model for our later romantic relationships, and represents the roots of any later love triangle we might get involved
in. In the case of your lover, the key figure in this primal triangle
was his rather seductive mother, who gave him mixed messages.
On the one hand, she was constantly hugging him and telling
him how special he was, as the queen does with the Little Mermaid's prince (which is where your partner's self-indulgent
streak comes from—he was spoiled by his mother); but on the
other hand, she ultimately rejected him in favor of his father.

The result is that your prince is still petulant and irritated
about being hurt by his mother when he was a boy. Because he
never got to reign supreme in her heart, as she seemed to promise
him, he feels he deserves *two* women to make up for this injury:
an improved mother who always puts him first, and a lover who
lets him into her bed (which was his secret childhood desire as his
mother kissed him and told him he was her favorite).

When he first met his wife, she seemed to satisfy both
desires: In the initial throes of fresh love, she probably lavished
him with all the attention that he craved, yet was unfamiliar and
mysterious enough to be erotically intriguing to him. After they
were married and had a baby (making them three), however,
being part of a family triangle started to stir up disturbing emotions from his childhood. Now that his wife has given birth, she
starts seeming *too* much like Mommy, which makes sleeping
with her taboo.

These feelings don't necessarily *stop* him from having sex
with his wife completely—no matter what he tells you. They just
inhibit him so he does it less often, or in less exciting ways,
which makes it feel enough like "proper" married sex to quell
these unconscious concerns about incest. (To him it's okay to
sleep with this Mommy, as long as he doesn't enjoy it *too* much,
which would be threatening and induce guilt.) What this situation often does, however, is rekindle your partner's need for a
lover to fulfill the seductive fantasies his mother evoked in him

as a child. That, of course, is where you fit in, since you are mysterious, unfamiliar, and sexy as his wife once was to him.

Unfortunately, it's also a potent reason why he may eventually cheat on *you*, as Vivian discovered. "Back when I was single, I ran around with lots of married men and never felt the least bit guilty about it, since I figured if their fat, nagging wives couldn't keep them at home it was hardly *my* fault. Then I got married to one of them, and realized one day—after he made some flimsy excuse why he would be staying out late for the third night in a row—that he was having an affair. I looked down at myself—six months pregnant and absolutely *huge*—and saw, with a shock, that I'd turned into a fat, nagging wife who couldn't keep her man at home."

What if your lover doesn't have children? There are a variety of other ways his childhood triangle could be spurring him on to an affair. One of the most common is that he's entering midlife, and sees he's not the cute little boy his mother used to dote on anymore. One man recalls looking in the mirror one day and noticing that his butt was losing muscle. First he bought a red sports car, but that didn't quite do it for him, so he turned to a much younger redhead, who gives him the illusion that he could be immortal. It's his way of starting his life all over—or at least temporarily escaping the scary reality his wife and mirror represent. His butt isn't lifted any higher, but his spirits certainly are, at least for now.

Another possibility is that your man has a claustrophic sense that the adult world is rapidly closing in on him, and wants to run after his boyhood fantasies before it's too late for him to be like James Bond or the dashing captain of the ski patrol. Like a little boy, he wants to sneak past Mommy and steal a treat from the cookie jar, with an affair that gives him some naughty fun—plus an inside joke on the wife who dismisses his dreams and tells him to grow up and act like a man. He may see you as the key he needs to unlock the trap that holds him in the "husband" role.

Though some married men want a private indulgence, others leave a trail of clues to their adultery that even the most obtuse wife is sure to stumble upon eventually, such as daily calls to an out-of-town number she'll see on their phone bill month after month, or extravagant charges for flowers and hotel rooms on their American Express card. That could be good news for you, since this behavior suggests your lover *wants* to be caught. It's a covert way of telling her and hurting her at the same time, because deep down, he is very angry with his wife for disappointing him, as his mother did, which is why he picked this cruel method of announcing that he'd like a divorce.

Last, but by no means least, your lover may be using an affair as a way of avoiding deeper intimacy with his wife, as was the case with Jim, who was faithful to his wife for twenty years—until she told him she wanted a closer relationship now that their three sons had left home. "That remark was a turning point in our marriage—but not in the way that I'd hoped for," she recalls. "Not long after that, he started sleeping with a female young law associate at his firm. As soon as I discovered he was having an affair and confronted him, he packed his bags and moved in with *her*. What I wonder, now they're married, is if any of this would have happened if I'd kept quiet and never told him that I wanted more."

What Entices You into a Love Triangle

As you might suspect, your motives for getting involved with a married man are much like his: a fascination with the forbidden, erotic desires of your original love triangle. Actually, you are acting out a slightly different drama from childhood. It's the competition with another *woman* that's a secret seduction to you, almost a sibling rivalry—except that the sibling is Mom.

Unlike your lover, whose doting, but ultimately disappointing, mother made him feel that he was entitled to two women as an adult, your family triangle left you with the sense that all you actually deserve is *half* of a man—or even less. By accepting the obviously subordinate role of "the other woman" in your lover's life—as does the Little Mermaid when she hides her face and allows another woman to wear the prince's ring—you re-create a childhood situation where you were locked in a conflict with "the wife" (your mother) for the "husband" (your father).

(Since the Mermaid's mother died when she was very young, she could never resolve the conflicts of her first romantic triangle. Instead, she acted out her rivalries with her grandmother, the Witch . . . and the woman her prince married.)

The main problem that you had with your primal power struggle was that you couldn't decide what would be better, winning or losing. That's a dilemma that you're still trying to resolve since you secretly believe that actually getting your father—or your lover—would be gratifying but alarming. Each time you steal your partner away from his wife for another torrid night in your arms, it's your secret revenge against a mother who kept you away from your father. That's why Monique takes such pleasure in the time she actually met her paramour's wife at a party. "I felt triumph as I looked at her and thought, 'Ha-ha, you don't know it, but I am sleeping with your husband!'

"It gave me an incredible feeling of power to finally see her face—especially since she had a smudge of lipstick on her tooth—and know exactly who I was giving pain to, even if she didn't know it. It's kind of a painful pleasure though, since it combined the thrill of conquest with the shock of realizing, 'Oh my God, there really is a wife.' "

The flip side of these victories, however, is that the closer you come to actually getting your guy away from his wife, the less desirable he may seem to you. That's because you've unconsciously equated winning your lover with winning Daddy, which is erotically off-putting because of the guilt it induces. It's this taboo that makes the Little Mermaid go for unavailable men—it's her tactic to deal with a father who is much too available, since he's a widower who possessively envelops her as his favorite. It is no wonder that she prefers the marble statue she so lovingly puts up on a pedestal—and the prince who has given his ring to another woman!

To avoid confronting uncomfortable anxieties about winning or losing your lover, you, like the Mermaid, may feel the best choice is a compromise. By letting his wife get the bigger share—but not all of him—you can win and lose at the same time, which could be what makes an illicit affair seem just right for you. Women who are attracted to married men are repeating their childhood pattern: sneaking around to become Daddy's secret lover. But because the incest taboo makes this scenario too threatening, you unconsciously set up your future relationships as no-win situations.

Can You Live Happily Ever After?

Through a haze of pain, the Little Mermaid, now mute forever, watched the witch brew a magic potion. Into the kettle dripped crocodile tears and black blood from the Sea Witch's breast. The Mermaid drank it in one gulp and fainted dead away. When she awoke, she was on the beach looking up at the handsome prince. As he stared at her, she looked down, and saw her fish tail was gone. Instead, she had two lovely legs—but was totally naked.

Blushing, she wrapped her long hair around herself. When the prince asked who she was, she looked at him sadly, since she could not speak. "If only he knew I gave up my voice for all eternity—just to be with him," she thought as the prince led her to his castle. As the Witch had warned, each step she took was like walking on razor blades, but she willingly endured this just to be at his side.

The prince called her his little foundling, and said that she would stay with him forever. Every day he grew fonder of her, and soon gave her a velvet cushion so she could sleep outside his room; but the idea of making her his bride never occurred to him.

"Don't you love me best of all?" her eyes asked him when he took her into his arms and kissed her.

"Of course I do," he replied, "because you are so devoted to me. You look like a woman who once saved my life. Though she is the only one I could ever really love, and has my ring, your face has almost replaced hers in my heart."

"If only I could tell him that I was the one who saved him," the Mermaid thought. "But since he doesn't know where that

woman is, and I'm with him now, I'll take such good care of him—sacrifice myself for him—and love him so well that he'll choose me over her."

Soon the Mermaid heard servants gossiping that the king had found a bride for his son. "I am so happy," the prince told her. "Since you love me so well, you will be overjoyed to hear that my parents have found the woman I have dreamed of, the one who saved me from the raging sea. She and I will be married tonight." The Mermaid felt her heart begin to break, and knew she would be dead by morning.

The wedding was held aboard a splendid ship whose cannons and colorful lanterns reminded her of the one where the prince celebrated his birthday the night the Mermaid first saw him. Because she knew it would please the prince, she stood holding his bride's train throughout the festivities. This time the Little Mermaid didn't feel the sharp knives under her delicate feet, because the pain in her heart cut more deeply. Blissfully unaware of the Mermaid's agony, the prince kissed his bride and glided toward their marital bed, while the Mermaid stayed on the deck awaiting dawn.

Her sisters suddenly surfaced with a magical knife obtained from the witch in exchange for their treasured tresses. They told her if she plunged it into the prince's heart before sunrise and let his warm blood splash on her feet, she would grow a tail, and be a mermaid again.

She took it to the marriage chamber and drew back the curtain, revealing the happily married couple sleeping entwined in each other's arms. As the Mermaid stole one last kiss, the prince murmured his wife's name. She alone was in his dreams now. Since in a sense the Mermaid had already sacrificed her life for his, she knew she couldn't kill him.

Instead, she threw the knife far out into the waves, which turned red, as though drops of blood were boiling up from the sea. With one last sad glance at the prince, she dove from the ship and felt her body melting into foam.

Are you also suffering all sorts of agony as you try to win your prince away from his wife? These ideas could help you move beyond being part of an unhappy triangle and gain the one-on-one love you yearn for.

Ask Yourself If You'd Really Want Him If He Were Available

In the midst of an exciting illicit affair, it's hard for you to be objective, but it's important for you to explore your feelings as fully as you can, and find out if it's simply the *challenge* of taking him away from his wife that's the real attraction. Try to step outside of your fairy-tale fantasies of romance, and imagine what life with him would be like if there were no sneaking around for torrid encounters in hotel rooms. Is this the man you'd like to have children with? Can you see yourself sharing the bathroom with him every day? Would he still seem irresistible to you when he trudges home after an annoying day at the office, grabs a beer, and collapses in front of the TV?

If So, Is There Any Concrete Evidence That He's Preparing to Leave His Wife?

Even if he hasn't consulted his lawyer yet, there are several subtle psychological signs that a married man might be getting ready to make the big move. Very often, the first one you may notice is that he's started experimenting with new lifestyles—by finding new friends who don't see him as half of a couple or by taking up activities or interests his spouse doesn't share. He might also alter his attitudes, habits, or personal appearance, so it could be cause for celebration if your married lover suddenly grew a goatee, and abandoned his archconservative beliefs in favor of a left-wing cause *you* favor.

What would be better yet is if he began taking *practical* steps to pave the way for his life with you, as Linda's married boyfriend recently did. First he went to his doctor to see if his vasectomy could be reversed so they could have children together, and then he saw his attorney to discuss how a divorce would impact him financially.

If having an affair with you is the *only* change your lover has made in his life—as is typically the case with these men—the prognosis for a happy future together is poor, since he is showing no sign of wanting to alter the status quo. Abbey felt she was making progress with her married lover of several years, until he suddenly told her that he and his wife were buying a new house—together. Then he couldn't understand why she was less than thrilled about spending hours helping him pick it out!

Find Your Voice and Tell Him Exactly What You Want

Don't be like the Little Mermaid, who sacrificed her lovely voice (her power) in a futile effort to get her guy—only to have her bubble burst when he failed to read her mind. Instead, decide whether you'd be content to stay with your lover if he never got divorced. This means losing your voice forever and sacrificing having children with a full-time father, steady companionship, and the emotional and financial security of being a wife.

If not, how long are you willing to put your life on hold: six months, a year, two years? Then let him know what your timetable is—without giving a hostile ultimatum like "Marry me, or else!" Once he realizes you will only wait that long—and no longer—he might discover, after he's forced to examine his heart, that he truly does want to make his fantasies with you into reality.

While it is terrifying to confront the possibility of losing him, unless you are prepared to leave him if he doesn't take action, your deadline is meaningless. If you don't speak up for what should rightfully be yours, the whole of him, not just the crumbs his wife leaves on the table, you may never get it. One woman spent five years having an affair with a man who made no significant move toward marrying her; she sacrificed financial and emotional security, and spent all her holidays alone, until she finally told him there was one sacrifice she wouldn't make—giving up her chance to have children. "I said if he hadn't filed for a divorce by my thirty-seventh birthday—which was coming up later that year—that was it. I wasn't feeling all that optimistic, but he did it, and now we're married, with a baby on the way."

Until He Actually Leaves His Wife, Even the Playing Field by Dating Other Men

This isn't a manipulative ploy to drive him mad with jealousy—though it may be just the spur he needs to goad him into action—but simple fairness. Why should your man be the only one with another romantic option, while you sit home and wait for his call? Even if you feel no one else could ever take his place, you'll have company on those lonely nights when he's busy with his family. It's a mistake to shut yourself off to other possibilities before he has committed himself to you—and only you—since he may never give you one hundred percent of his love. And who knows, there just may be someone out there who is as special as he is, but doesn't have the excess baggage of a wife!

Create a Healing Triangle

Instead of walking on knives to please him as you suffer in silence, why not add another presence to the relationship—by seeking out a therapist, support group, or trusted friends to add new perspectives and balance to your life? By reaching outside the unhappy triangle you're caught up in, you could gain a positive, self-affirming outlook that builds you up—which could ultimately free you to let go of damaging old patterns and find a man who will make you his one and only love, whether it is this partner, or the next one you meet.

7

MR. POWER MAD

*O*nce upon a time, there was a country gentleman whose second wife was the meanest and haughtiest woman in the world. She brought along two daughters, who, like her, wore ostentatious finery but were black of heart. Neither this new wife nor her girls could stand the lord's daughter from his first marriage, since she was as beautiful as she was virtuous. Seeing that she was gentle and easily taken advantage of, they stole her pretty clothes and turned her into a household drudge who had to wait on them hand and foot. The poor child patiently endured these insults, realizing that if she protested to her father he would scold her, as he was completely dominated by his wife. She took to hiding by the fireplace near the ashes, a habit her stepmother mocked by calling her "Cinderella."

One day, the king's son invited every eligible damsel in the land to a ball so he could choose a most suitable wife. The stepsisters ordered Cinderella to clean their most costly gowns and style their hair. As she ironed their fine petticoats, she begged her stepmother to take her as well. "What a ridiculous idea," the *stepmother replied. "What would a dirty little cinder girl like you do at a ball?"*

As they rode off to the ball, leaving Cinderella to scrub the floors and outhouses, she wept. Suddenly her fairy godmother was standing next to her. "Bring me a pumpkin from the garden, and I'll grant your wish to go to the ball." As soon as Cinderella picked the best one, the fairy touched it with her magic wand and turned it into a gold coach. Then she went to the mousetrap and released the six mice, tapping them with the wand and turning them into a set of fine horses. From the rattrap, her godmother picked the rat with the largest beard, and transformed it into a coachman with luxuriant whiskers. Six lizards from the garden became six footmen in full livery.

Touching Cinderella with her magic wand, the fairy godmother turned her rags into a ball gown covered with jewels, and then handed her a pair of glass slippers. "Now you're ready," she said. As Cinderella stepped into the coach, her godmother warned her to leave the ball before midnight, when everything would change back to what had been before.

When the prince heard that a great princess had arrived whom no one knew, he rushed to receive her. He never left her side or took his eyes off her the whole evening, giving her many compliments and fine speeches. If someone else wanted to dance with her, the prince told him firmly, "This is my partner," and sent him away.

All too soon, Cinderella heard a clock start to strike twelve, and fled from the ball so fast that she lost one of her glass slippers. The prince ran after her, but tripped over it on the palace walk. As she sped home to her familiar spot by the fireplace, he proclaimed, "No other maiden shall be my wife but the one whose foot fits this slipper!"

Does the man in your life demand that you "fit" yourself into his way of doing things? Deirdre jokes that her boyfriend has his house so meticulously organized that it looks like a museum. "All that is missing are velvet ropes around the furniture. I'm almost afraid to touch anything—even to get a pickle out of the fridge—because everything he owns, including the food, is arranged with a military precision, and he hates it when I move anything out of its place. Even his *garbage* is unusually neat—before he throws out a cereal box, he folds it exactly in half. I'm surprised he doesn't mark it with the date and time as well."

Lauren's lover isn't quite so obsessive about *his* belongings, but he's begun taking over hers. "First it was my remote control, which he practically grabs out of my hand every time he comes over so he can watch fifteen seconds of every show that's on the air. Next, it was moving around my stereo speakers until the sound was to his liking; and now it's my car—whenever I pick him up at the office, his usual greeting is, 'Slide over, I'll drive.' He seems to feel that, as a man, he should be the master of all things mechanical—and I guess that on some level I must agree with him, since I have yet to figure out how to program my VCR, while he's always talking about surfing the Internet and other high-tech stuff."

Stephanie's boyfriend is so controlling that she's seriously considering breaking up with him. "I used to be flattered by all the attention Teddy paid to my looks, since my previous boy-friend probably wouldn't have noticed if I dyed my hair green and showed up in toe shoes. After a while, however, I started feeling as if I were entering a beauty contest every time we went out—with *him* as the judge—because he'll make little comments like, 'Don't you think that blouse is a bit tight?' or 'I wonder if a red lipstick would be prettier on you.' What's worse is that he's now decided I should lose weight and watches every morsel I put into my mouth as if he were the diet police."

Why would anyone put up with such an absolute control freak? Almost paradoxically, many women who would never tolerate gender-based inequality at work gladly—even ecstatically—agree to give men the upper hand in love. More surprising still, in this postfeminist age, is how many women think their lover isn't masterful *enough*, a complaint I've often heard in my psychiatric practice.

His Telltale Traits

Is your boyfriend more dominating than most men? Here's how to detect a would-be "master of the universe" who is just waiting for an opportunity to take over:

He's Ruled by Rituals

Because there's an obsessive thrust to his personality, a controlling man is preoccupied by schedules, lists, rules, or petty details. It's his way of imposing order on his life—or yours. He may insist, like Deirdre's boyfriend, that every object in his apartment be precisely positioned in a certain place; or he may keep a very elaborate appointment diary, as Stanley does, using four different pens to color-code his various activities into the proper categories. "Next, he'll probably get a red pen to mark down when he plans to have sex each month," says his girlfriend, Nina. While he probably doesn't take it to a compulsive extreme, your man may also have fixed rituals he likes to follow. At bedtime, for example, his routine could include making sure certain lights are left on, double-checking that every door and window is securely locked, and having the exact same bedtime snack.

He's a Neat Freak—Most of the Time

This trait may express itself as a horror of germs, or elaborate precautions to avoid them. Hector, for example, spends at least ten minutes washing up before eating, but seldom can he finish a meal without leaving the dining table at least once to scrub his already spotless hands again. His fixation with cleanliness doesn't stop with food either—at work, he checks his secretary's fingernails for dirt each morning before he allows her to open his mail; and at home, he expects his girlfriend to shower and shave her legs before he'll even *think* about sex.

This doesn't necessarily mean that every inch of his home is as immaculate as a hospital operating room. Some dominating men are fastidious in some ways and slobs in others. Brian is typical: He's so particular about how his laundry is done that at age thirty-two, he still sends it home to his mother every week, while the rest of his apartment looks like a biology experiment gone amok. Mary's lover, she says, "has a home that looks like Felix Unger and Oscar Madison were taking turns living there, since he sometimes goes on cleaning binges, and sometimes lets things slowly fall into chaos."

He May Be Overly Sensitive to Smells and Tastes

For some of these men, the best foreplay would be for each of you to take long, steamy showers—separately—followed by plenty of toothbrushing and flossing, as they find the faintest whiff of garlic on your breath or a lingering odor of cigarettes on your clothes a total turnoff. One man actually broke up with his fiancée because he insisted that her body had a strange scent—a vague, unpleasant aroma no previous lovers of hers had ever detected. Your lover may also feel anxious about how *he* smells, and douse himself with cologne, or be addicted to breath mints.

Part of his excessive concern with bodily odor and bodily functions—his or yours—stems from his dread of dirt. This may make him quite sensitive to supposedly "off" flavors in his food that could signal spoilage and germs. Refusing to kiss you because you're wearing a perfume that offends his delicate nostrils or have eaten spicy foods can also be a way of distancing himself from you—literally—when he fears that his feelings for you are getting out of control, since imposing finicky rules about what you eat or what scent you use makes him feel he is in command again.

He's Stingy and Withholding

Along with keeping a tight rein on his feelings, your man is probably equally tight with his money, or even a bit miserly. No matter how well his job pays or how much he has in the bank, it's not nearly enough to make him feel secure, since he's worried that some sudden catastrophe will wipe him out—unless he keeps on hoarding. As a creature of habit, he might also develop thrifty rituals, and become fanatical about turning off the lights, bringing his own popcorn to the movies, or driving an extra ten miles every day to avoid a fifty-cent toll. Don't let yourself be too flattered if he tells you how he loves your cooking—after all, it's a free meal.

Not only does your partner still have the first dollar he ever made, but he may have the first pair of shoes he ever bought with his own money. And if you dare try to toss out that old moth-eaten sweater he sometimes wears on the weekends he may howl with all the hurt of a child whose security blanket has been yanked out of his hand. In fact, your prince is unable to discard *any* worn-out or worthless objects—except when he considers *you* to be one.

He Has a High-Powered Job or Aspires to Have One

Since the last thing your man wants is to take orders from someone else, it's extremely important to him to be a boss at work, even if he only is in charge of a few people, or has to start his own business. He is just as stubborn and inflexible at the office as he is at home: His basic attitude toward his coworkers is, "It's my way or the highway." He is attracted to a high-status career—he'd love to be a surgeon, a movie director, or a corporate CEO.

Though he may profess a distaste for office politics, secretly he relishes power games, and is likely to be masterful at playing—and winning—them. His relentless determination to get the edge on the competition at work, so he can advance to a position that puts him in charge of *more* people, could turn your partner into a bit of a workaholic. It's not just his ambition that has him working long hours, however. He's also very concerned about getting every minor detail just right—and may meticulously review everything he or his staff does over and over until he's sure it measures up to his high standards.

He Wants a Perfect Princess

Initially, a dominating man may worship you as a goddess and tell you he's never met anyone who is so beautiful, intelligent, or utterly delightful to be with. During this idyllic phase, you may not even realize how controlling he is, since he's showering you with compliments and seems enchanted with everything you say and do. All too soon, however, your lover makes the same disconcerting discovery Cinderella's prince does: that his beloved isn't the idealized princess he had hoped for, but a flesh-and-blood woman with *flaws*—and what flaw could be worse to a man with a dread of dirt than finding out that the elegant lady he has fallen for is actually a soiled little cinder girl who sleeps in a pile of ashes?

At first, these imperfections, though a bit troubling to him, are tolerable—even intriguing—since deep down he has a love-hate relationship with dirt (which is what your flaws represent to him) and finds it both repellent and fascinating. It's okay for you to be imperfect, he feels at first, since that means he's superior to you. Soon, however, the blemishes that he's detected in you begin to grate on him, and he looks for ways to correct them. He may get overly invested in your appearance, as Stephanie's boyfriend does, and demand that you change everything from your hairstyle to your hemline; or he may try to take over your finances, reorganize your life, or get you to change jobs.

He Feels Justified in Taking Over Your Life

For him, the world is made up of opposites—everything is either black or white, right or wrong, clean or dirty. Because he believes clean is best, though dirt has a secret allure for him, he feels that it's his duty to lead you to the right path—by fixing your flaws and helping you be the perfect princess he fantasizes about. He may even frame the shape-up program he plans for you in moral terms, and tell you that the reason he's so intent on having you lose weight or quit smoking is that it is wrong to abuse your body with unhealthy habits.

If you fail to embrace the sometimes fanatical standards he lays out for you, you risk rebuff because your man doesn't want to be contaminated by your imperfections. He sets strict standards for himself as well and despises himself if he doesn't live up to them. So he'd never want your flaws to reflect badly on him, for fear his own shortcomings will be illuminated.

He's also very alert for possible clues that you're rebelling against his authority. If you aren't prompt about meeting him for a date, for example, he will take every minute you are late as a personal affront, because that was a minute when you apparently didn't want to be with him, and a minute when his power over you ebbed. Don't be surprised if he's quick to retaliate for this fancied injury: Melanie says her lover once sold two hard-to-come-by tickets to a Broadway show when she was ten minutes late—then spent the rest of the evening complaining that *she'd* cost him his only chance to see this hit show.

He Measures His Potency by How Much Control He Has over You

The more effectively he dominates you—by dictating where you eat, what movies you see, and what activities you do together—the more virile and masculine he feels. That makes him quick to pick up on new ways to control you, such as sneering at what you've selected from the restaurant menu— "Oysters in *August*? Are you *sure* that's what you want?"—until you break down and ask *him* to order for you. Your power-mad prince prefers to do things himself, or have you do them his way. Since he lost his early power struggle with his parents, he's reenacting it with you. Now he's even more determined to win—and winning means not letting his romantic feelings for you get out of control. He insists on regulating the pace of your relationship by finding excuses to slow it down, or even ending it, at least for a while, if he doesn't feel *firmly* in command.

Leah's heart surged with delight every time her lover told her, "I can't stop thinking about you. I can't work. I can't sleep. I'm so in love with you it makes me crazy!" The more he repeated this, the more she felt the relationship was heading toward the altar. One day, however, she realized that for Winston, feeling crazy about her *wasn't* a positive sign. Instead, his terror at being out of control sent him packing.

In Bed—and Everywhere Else—
He Wants to Be on Top

Nowhere do his controlling qualities show themselves more strongly than when you're having sex with him. He's likely to have a favorite erotic routine that he is convinced is the one and only *right* way to make love—and make you feel like a dirty slut should you suggest something different. He's also averse to sexual activities that make him feel out of control, such as letting you be on top, or putting his penis in your mouth (which may make him very anxious).

Letting go—even for an orgasm—may be difficult for him. Or you may notice that he can only climax in places where he feels he can be in control, such as *his* bed. When it comes to making *you* come, he can be almost obsessive about giving you an orgasm, since driving you wild with passion only makes him feel more masculine. Sally says her lover can't rest until he's sure he has given her the ultimate pleasure, whether she wants it or not. "Sometimes I'm tempted just to fake it, because otherwise I know that he'll spend all night exhausting his erotic repertoire to get those little quivers out of me, as he did the first time we made love. The next morning, I was so sore that I could hardly walk—while he was happy, since I finally did have a climax."

Almost paradoxically, since your mate is so intent on having the upper hand in bed, he may fantasize about sadomasochistic sex (with him in the *submissive* role), or engage in it secretly, with anonymous partners. (Or he may even have a kinkier interest, as Cinderella's prince does with his shoe fetish.) Don't expect the man in your life to explore his fascination with erotic surrender with you, or even admit he has one. Since it would give you much too much power over him, he'd consider it more scary than sexy to submit to you in bed—or anywhere. Being with a strange woman he doesn't love—or necessarily even like—permits your boyfriend to feel superior enough to her to let go in bed, at last.

His Dominance Dilemma

Why does your lover have such a lust for power and control, especially over women? Hiding inside your power-mad partner is a penis-mad little boy, since his relentless drive to be on top—in and out of bed—springs from anxieties about his masculinity that he developed early in life. His apparent rage to rule is his way of reassuring himself that his penis is strong and powerful. The reason he's compelled to prove this over and over—by keeping you firmly in line—is that he secretly lives in terror of *losing* his manhood.

All men share this fear to some degree—that's why males all over the world felt such a horrified fascination with the case of John Wayne Bobbit, whose wife, Lorena, sliced off his penis with a knife as he was sleeping. (Many women, on the other hand, were oddly amused by—or even approved of—this ultimate act of vengeance by his horribly abused wife.) Being unmanned by a woman isn't what your man is *most* afraid of. (He may, however, like to look at pornographic images of naked women to remind himself that we *don't* have a penis, and he does, which makes him feel superior.)

What your mate is actually worried about is having evoked the wrath of the man with the most powerful penis of all—his father—as he was growing up. Like all little boys, he tried to charm and seduce his mother—maybe by pretending to be sick so he could stay home with her while Dad was at work, or sneaking into his parents' bed so he could snuggle in Mommy's arms—until he noticed that his innocent desire to have her all to himself seemed to be angering his father. Suddenly your partner realized that he was putting himself at risk for terrible retaliation from Dad—and what could be worse, for a male, than having his precious penis taken away?

What made this terrifying prospect seem more real to your man than it was for men who don't share his compulsive need to control is that his father is an unusually powerful person. For example, Evan's father was an extraordinarily successful businessman. "On Wall Street, the top currency traders are called the 'big swinging dicks,' and my dad let everyone know he was the biggest swinging dick of them all, a real master of the universe who made over five million dollars a year outsmarting the other big dicks. At home, he practically expected us to grovel on the floor when he graced us with his presence, and to treat him like a god."

Even if your partner's father was not particularly successful or rich, he may have been punitive or physically intimidating like Mark's father, a forklift operator. "Even at age fifty-five, my dad has a body most weight lifters would envy. Not only is he huge, but he's got a mean streak. When he came to visit me at college, I told my friends not to shake hands with him, because he'll get you in this grip that makes it feel as if he'll break every bone in your hand. I wouldn't exactly call him abusive, but he's definitely one scary guy to be around, especially when I was small."

Having a frightening father like Mark's or Evan's may be what convinced your man that the best way to protect his penis is to be such a big swinging dick that no one *dares* to try to take it away. Even a high-powered career or a woman he can dominate doesn't make him feel completely secure, which is why he may develop rituals to make sure everything—including his penis—is in its proper place. It's also why he hates to be out of control in bed: To him, giving up his power, even to obtain pleasure, is like losing his manhood. (Now you know why getting oral sex is so threatening to him—guess what anxieties putting his penis in your mouth, next to your sharp teeth, would arouse.)

When Cinderella's prince wanders around the kingdom with his cherished glass slipper, testing it on every woman's foot, he's symbolically acting out his boyhood desire to "repair" his mother, by giving her the penis she appeared to lack. When the shoe fits Cinderella's foot, the prince is reassured that everything is "perfect" again—and his castration anxieties subside. (This is also part of the reason your prince is so eager to correct your supposed "flaws," and make *you* perfect.)

In extreme cases, these same childhood concerns about loss of masculinity cause some controlling men to develop sexual fetishes, a perversion that's virtually unknown in women. Using women's shoes, bras, panties, or other garments to gain sexual gratification, or fantasizing about doing so, has an additional appeal to dominating males, one man says, because a fetish is "a portable arousal mechanism that gives guys *control* over sex—an area where a man feels chronically out of control, since he has to approach women and hope they will want to have sex with him. Women have always had power over him, from his mother telling him to stop eating candy, to his teacher telling him to do his homework, to his girlfriend telling him to shape up. Finally, when he's told, 'You didn't call when you said you would, so no sex for you,' he rolls his eyes and thinks, 'Bring on the shoes!' "

What about your man's cleanliness compulsion? This originated in his very *first* power struggle with his parents: toilet training. The more they shamed and humiliated him over soiling his pants or his bed, the more he resisted their commands by withholding his feces—an attitude he now expresses by being stingy with his money and emotions, since he's still angry with them for trying to control his body and force him to measure up to *their* standards of hygiene. He's developed an ambivalence about mess: Part of him is still a little boy who finds a secret pleasure in being "good and dirty"—and defying his uptight parents—while another part of him relishes being tidy, since that makes him feel in control of his body and his environment. (So if you think your lover sometimes acts like a real tight ass, this is why!)

A Controlling Passion

What's the magnetism that a forceful man has for you? Sex may be a more important aspect of this attraction than you think, since power is the ultimate aphrodisiac, as Henry Kissinger has remarked. Many of us are secretly intrigued—or aroused—by the idea of being erotically overpowered by a male: One survey reported that it's the favorite sex fantasy of half the women polled. What's appealing about being swept off our feet—and into bed—by a masterful man is that we can avoid feeling as dirty as Cinderella for having dirty thoughts, and wanting sex.

Instead, we can pretend that it's not our fault if we happen to have fun in bed, since we were *forced* to have pleasure by our dominating lover.

Many women enjoy giving up power in bed, just as many men like the feeling of being on top—both literally and figuratively. They relish the opportunity to control and conquer, while many of us are delighted to surrender to our man's strength, his power, and most of all, his penis. A take-charge man doesn't just seduce us sexually; for some of us, he also offers a potent emotional come-on—a chance to lose our inhibitions, our adult responsibilities, even ourselves in his arms. He makes us feel he's strong enough to shelter us and protect us from a dangerous world.

One reason you may be drawn to a man who seems like a powerful daddy is that your real one *didn't* make you feel safe or well cared for as you were growing up. Like Cinderella's hopelessly henpecked father, yours may have also been completely under the thumb of your domineering mother, had pitifully low self-esteem, or simply been an ineffectual wimp. That's left you hungry for a powerful prince you can confidently turn to in a crisis—a man whose penis is as strong as your father's was weak. What you're hoping is that this partner will finally give you the childhood you never had: a paradise where a powerful person will take care of all your needs and solve all of your problems for you.

You may also feel that wearing his glass slipper will give you some of your prince's power. Perhaps you envy what his penis seems to have brought him: freedom from the glass ceiling and sexism that still can keep a woman from rising to the top in the workplace. Or you may find it hard to shake off those cultural messages that tell you it's feminine to be submissive—and masculine to be in charge—so vicariously live out your own dreams of world domination through him. Inside you may be a potential mistress of the universe who is waiting for the right moment to take over—if your lover would only let you!

Can You Live Happily Ever After?

The prince scoured the land, trying the glass slipper on each and every damsel, from royalty to commoners. Eventually, he came to Cinderella's house and asked the first stepsister to try it on. She took it aside and soon saw that her big toe was too large. Giving her a knife, the stepmother whispered, "Cut off the toe. Once you're queen you won't need to walk anymore." The daughter sliced off her toe and jammed her foot into the shoe. She swallowed the pain so well that the prince rode off with her to make her his bride, but noticed along the way the trail of blood she was leaving.

He brought her back home at once, saying that she unquestionably was not the right woman for him. When the second stepsister next tried on the shoe and her heel wouldn't fit, the stepmother urged her to cut off a piece of it. "Once you're queen, you won't need to walk anymore." The daughter did as she was told and the prince took her off to be his bride. But along the way, he saw red stains on her stockings, and turned his horse around.

"This is not the right woman either," he told the stepmother. "Have you no other daughter?"

"The only other girl here is a mousy little drudge who couldn't possibly be the one you're looking for." The prince insisted that she get Cinderella anyway, refusing to budge until he overcame the stepmother's protests that the girl was far too dirty for him to see.

Cinderella excitedly washed her face and hands as best she could, then came into the room and curtsied gracefully to the prince. He was taken aback to see her in such a filthy gray gown, but he knelt down and, with a flourish, proffered the glass slipper. It fit her foot perfectly, and as she took the matching shoe from her pocket, he looked closely at her, and recognized that he'd finally found the right princess.

You may be right for him, but is your power-mad prince really right for *you?* And if you think he is, wouldn't you rather have a more balanced relationship with him? These tactics could help you and your bossy boyfriend share power in ways that fit comfortably for both of you:

Don't Let Him Love You Too Much Too Fast

As tempting as it is to encourage your prince to fall madly in love with you, keep reminding yourself to take it slow. When men who need to be in control fall in love, it feels as though their world is "falling" apart.

"Too much. Too strong. Too fast," was Winston's distraught explanation to Leah as he raced off. "I need time," he added under his breath. Give your power-mad man all the time he needs to feel safe and allow his romantic feeling for you to grow at a pace *he's* comfortable with. It's difficult for a man who has carefully guarded his emotions all his life to avoid being overwhelmed and vulnerable.

It's hard not to be as irresistibly gorgeous, warm, and seductive as you can—especially when you feel he's *the* one—but be alert for warning signs that he's becoming scared of the heady rush of falling in love. These signs can include his vacillating between wanting to make mad, passionate love and not wanting to have sex at all, his backing out of plans the two of you made to spend the weekend together, and his getting that deer-caught-in-the-headlights look when he sees you.

Set Limits Right Away

If you stand by meekly the first time he pulls a power play— perhaps because the issue doesn't strike you as *worth* fighting over—you may become imprisoned by his rules over time and find it impossible to speak up when he goes over the top, since you already gave in on everything else. Mary Kay Blakely, an essayist for the *New York Times*, remembers that she and her husband started their marriage as equals—until the day when he objected to a $1.95 carton of ice cream she wanted to buy, claiming that it was too expensive. Instead of telling him not to be such a cheapskate, she obediently put it back, even though it was her favorite brand.

Later she realized that by saying, "I defer all ice-cream judgments to you," she'd relinquished any right to views on vacuuming, entertainment, sex, children, or any other topic. By the time she got the courage to rebel—by buying the forbidden brand of ice cream—it was too late. That purchase, as her husband had warned, proved to be costly indeed, since she later decided that this tiny act of rebellion marked the end of their marriage.

Be Cautious About Compromise

It's important to realize you and your man have different ideas of what's a fair split of power, so as soon as you give an inch, he'll take a *foot* (as Cinderella's prince does). That's why you have to be very clear about what you will and won't accept. If, for example, your boyfriend asks if he can drive your car one night, you have to make sure he understands this isn't a *permanent* arrangement (unless you've always wanted to have a chauffeur). As you hand over the keys, you might say, "I'm happy to have you drive tonight, but generally I like to do my own driving."

What if he's a terrible driver, or you just don't want him at the wheel of your car? Instead of attacking him or forbidding him to touch your keys—either of which could set off a power struggle he'll go all out to win—focus on your own feelings or needs. You might tell him that your insurance doesn't cover other drivers (if true), or that you find driving helps you relax from the stress of work, so you can enjoy his company even more. Make him feel that he's not giving up a lot of territory by respecting your feelings about this topic, as he gains more than he loses by going along with you.

Hang On to Your Realm by Maintaining Your Friendships, Your Job, and Your Money

What you need in this relationship is a sphere of independence where you can rule as queen—even if it's a small one—as a counterweight to all the spheres where he rules as king. Not only is it crucial to show him that you have a power base of your own, so he'll see you are not completely dependent on him for everything, but it's even more essential that you convince *your-self* that you have some resources of your own to fall back on—or some support, should you decide he isn't for you after all.

Recognize That He'll Respond to Problems in His Life by Being More Controlling

If he feels his power is being threatened by the outside world—maybe because his company is downsizing, and his job could be in jeopardy—his first reaction is to grab more tightly to everything he has (which includes *you*). That doesn't mean you have to tiptoe around on eggshells whenever he's under stress, just that you should realize that what he's really doing is trying to protect himself from *loss* (which makes him feel his masculinity is snatched away). Let him know that he's still important—and virile—in your eyes, and subtly assure him he's not about to lose you. That should encourage him to loosen the reins.

Don't Humbly Ask His Permission to Be Independent

Avoiding mixed messages like this can be more difficult than it sounds, since some of us find the idea of taking responsibility for our own life scary—that's why we're drawn to a dominating man—and may unconsciously sabotage our attempts to break free of his control. Consider Katy, who has told her boyfriend that she finds him too bossy, but keeps making comments that provoke him to jump in and take over, such as: "It may be a mistake, but I'm thinking of applying for a job in the sales division." Quite predictably, he finds such remarks to be an irresistible invitation to interject *his* opinions about what career moves she should make.

A better tactic, if you are sure you really want your freedom, is to announce your decisions in a casual manner, as if you weren't anticipating any disagreement from him. Rather than asking for her lover's approval *before* she applies for that sales job, which gives him veto power over her decision—or forces her to challenge him if he says no to it—Katy might instead mention over dinner that she's applied for this job, and hopes he'll keep his fingers crossed that she'll get it.

Prove Yourself Worthy of His Trust and He'll Gradually Loosen Up

Since a controlling man can be rigid in his ways, he's not going to agree to play by your rules—which include having a more equal partnership—right away. What's working in your favor, over the long term, is that he may secretly find his need to be in control all the time just as burdensome as you do. After all, it's lonely and frightening on top, where your man feels he is under constant pressure to maintain his powerful image of perfection, and avoid any little mistake that could shatter it. Imagine how exhausting it is for him to have to vigilantly monitor everything to make sure it's in its place, and everybody, in case they're trying to steal his power.

Although he probably won't admit it to you, he'd secretly love to let go of some of his awful responsibility. Convince him you're committed to being a trustworthy, competent *partner* for him and you could be surprised how willing he is to step down from his pedestal and relax in a *mutually* gratifying love affair with you.

If His Shoe Fits You, Wear It

Since it is unlikely that you will ever achieve total equality with your power-mad prince, decide if you're really comfortable with being the way he wants you to be. Is his fantasy of you a good fit for your true personality, or does it chafe on you like a shoe that's too tight? If you feel you have to chop off precious parts of yourself to please your boyfriend, as Cinderella's stepsisters do in their vain efforts to get the prince, then it's time for you to stand up on your own two (intact) feet, and look for a lover who lets your spirit—and his—run *free*.

8

*T*HE COMMITMENT
PHOBE

*O*nce upon a time, there was a handsome prince who
wanted to be certain that the woman he married was a
"real" princess. He traveled all over the world in search of
one, but the more that he looked, the more frustrated he got. There
were plenty of pretty women who claimed to be princesses, but
whether they were real ones or not, he couldn't find out, because
something about each woman he met always seemed to be not
quite right, so he never got too close. At last, he returned home and
was very sad, since he wished so hard for such a princess.

His mother suggested he hold a contest to find the right wife,
and told him of a secret test that could distinguish between a
true princess and a fake one. As soon as the competition was
announced, women started lining up outside his door—all of
them purporting to be genuine princesses.

The first woman in line looked exactly like a princess, so the
prince invited her to spend the night at the castle. While she was
having dinner, he crept into her bedroom and put a dried pea on
the bedstead. Then he ordered the maids to cover it with twenty
mattresses and twenty down quilts. When the alleged princess

went in the bedroom, she found the bed piled so high she needed a ladder to get into it.

Though she found this bed oddly uncomfortable, when the prince asked the next morning how she'd slept, she was reluctant to offend him, so she smiled, and purred in an ingratiating tone, "I slept like a baby in the lovely bed you prepared for me."

The prince sent her on her way, and invited the next applicant in. After she took her jeweled tiara off and climbed into the bed, she fell into such a sound sleep that she was only vaguely aware of an irritating lump in the bed. By morning, she'd convinced herself it was only a dream, and assured the prince she'd slept like a baby in the bed.

Each day the prince was increasingly weary and disheartened as yet another supposed princess failed the test. Some of them sensed the pea, but tried to please the prince by pretending not to notice it, while others were too insensitive to detect it.

After all the women had left, a raging thunderstorm broke over the palace. Suddenly there was a knock on the door. "Who would be out in such a frightful gale?" the prince and his parents asked each other as he went to open the door.

Outside stood a soaking wet woman. Her clothes were muddy and her hair was a mess from the wind and rain. Water was running down her body and pouring out of her shoes, yet when the prince inquired who she was, she said through her chattering teeth, "I am a real p-p-p-princess."

"We'll see about that," thought the prince, who had never in his life seen a woman who looked less like a princess. Still, there was a spark of hope in his heart as he escorted her into his palace....

Is your lover leery of making even the smallest commitment to a future with you? After she'd been seeing her boyfriend for six months, Elly suggested she leave some lingerie at his apartment so she'd have a pair of fresh panties to change into the next time she slept over. "He said that would be okay, but after I left, he apparently decided that having even one of my intimate garments in his home was way too intimate for him, and sent my panties back by messenger later that day," she ruefully recalls.

Wendy's beau, on the other hand, decided that after a year of dating he was ready for what he considers a long-term commitment—he bought them tickets for a concert that would be held the following month. She, on the other hand, longs for more permanent plans, and explains, "The trouble is that even the most casual mention of marriage, babies, or even moving in together someday makes him get the terrified stare of a rabbit caught in a trap. Though he's told me he loves me—usually when we're in bed together—I am seriously questioning whether it's worth investing any more time in this relationship."

Victoria feels precisely the opposite way about her intimacy-averse boyfriend. "I was only mildly interested in him at first, but after he announced, on our second date, that he'd been married twice and had no intention of ever tying the knot again, I took it as a challenge—'Catch me if you can'—and began pursuing him with all the steely intensity of a mating salmon swimming upstream. So far he's still playing hard to get, but I've made some headway and feel that it's just a matter of time before he is ready to produce a ring."

His Telltale Traits

Is your partner picky, but receptive to a deeper relationship once his heart tells him you're right for him, or does he actively *avoid* intimacy by setting up an impossible test that even the truest of princesses might fail? To find out, give him a test of your own—by measuring him against these commitment-phobe characteristics.

He's Idealistic to a Fault

While some men have a wish list of qualities that they'd like to find in a lover and let it gently guide them toward appropriate partners, these princes have a checklist that defines their dream girl down to the last detail. Often the characteristics that they are looking for are so specific—and eclectic—that they seem to be on a never-ending scavenger hunt as they wander the world in search of the one woman who has them all. Compounding the dilemma is their paralyzing fear of mistakenly missing out on true love with Ms. Right by being too quick to settle for Ms. Not Quite Right.

He's Left a Long Line of Women in His Wake

Your man's real problem is not just that he hasn't found the right woman yet—he's probably dated plenty of promising prospects over the years, along with some losers—but that he doesn't stay with any of his girlfriends long enough to be able to tell if she is a real princess or just a good-looking imposter. Even if the romance is as delectable as sinking into a sensuously soft pile of down quilts, the annoying little lump that keeps him tossing and turning uncomfortably is his secret conviction that there's someone even better out there.

His past romances may follow a predictable pattern, as was the case with Carlton, who began each one by proclaiming that the woman he was with was the best thing to ever happen to him. A few months later, however, he'd suddenly start complaining to his friends that he'd noticed something off-putting about his new lady: She wore too much makeup, mispronounced a certain word, or disliked his favorite sport. Rather than tell his lover what's bothering him about her—and find out if she is willing to change—he considers it "kinder" to drop her with the same chilly words he's used to dismiss all her predecessors: "It's my fault. I just don't feel anything for you."

He Has Sneaky Ways to Avoid Confrontation

Carlton's passive-aggressive style is very typical of a true commitment phobe. Under the guise of not wanting to hurt the woman in his life by revealing the truth, he actually causes even more pain, since she's left with an impression that her faults are too awful and all-encompassing to even mention. Similarly, your prince may use covert—and sometimes hurtful—tactics to slither out of unwanted intimacies. Should you invite him to have dinner with your parents, he probably won't tell you the idea alarms him; instead, he may let you go ahead and make the plans, then call with a last-minute excuse to cancel, or simply "forget" to show up.

That's because, to him, confrontation, which would require him to reveal what he's feeling, is actually a form of intimacy, which is precisely what he's trying to *avoid*. If his extremely sensitive antenna tells him that you're moving in on him—either figuratively or literally—his emotional alarms go off, and he puts up a passive-aggressive defense to push you away from his inner zones. Like Elly's panty-phobic partner, he won't say that he doesn't want you to leave your lingerie—or your heart—with him; he'll just wait until you're not around to confront him, and then send it back by messenger. Though he pretends he's just being nice, deep down he know his ploys hurt you, and he doesn't care, since he knows you'll back off—at least for the moment.

He Avoids or Delays Any Move Toward Deeper Intimacy

Along with devising excuses and ploys to escape commitments you suggest, he'll also try to steer safely clear of actions that could advance the relationship. For your birthday, he's much more likely to give you a cute teddy bear or a cappuccino maker than a pair of gold earrings. (Even a friendship bracelet strikes him as far too reminiscent of an engagement ring.) Don't expect him to introduce you to his pals right off—they probably don't have a clue that he even knows you—or bring you home to Mom, in *this* decade anyway.

At Work, or with His Friends, He's No Team Player

It's not just you that he keeps at arm's length, it's the world, since he's averse to *any* commitment, whether it's doing a favor for a friend or taking on a long-term project at the office. He's not a joiner, and panics or performs poorly if he's forced to be part of a group. Although he keeps a wall around himself to ward off the world, he's often oddly reluctant to say no to anything—but doesn't definitely say yes either. Instead, he may either devise a passive-aggressive ploy to wriggle out of an unwanted obligation, or just leave people hanging until they give up and call someone else.

His Penis Chills If He Feels That the Relationship Is Getting Too Hot

As much as he likes having you sleep over, he gets scared if he feels it's getting to be a habit, or you take it for granted that you'll be back next weekend—or ever. As soon as you propose leaving so much as an old toothbrush at his place, he may suddenly feel he's being lured onto a slippery slope that leads inexorably to living together, marriage, and a baby. Since such thoughts are about as appealing to your prince as having a bucket of cold water poured over his penis would be, don't be surprised if he turns off to you sexually if he feels you're getting too close for comfort.

Not all commitment phobes object to having you keep undies or your toothbrush at their home, since some are open to more intimacy than others, and may even go as far as to live with you or agree to get engaged—some time far in the future. What all of them have in common, however, is that they draw the line somewhere—and it stops short of marriage. Even though your lover won't tell you where his limit is, you'll know if you are getting close to it because that's when his penis ices over and you feel an abrupt sexual chill in the air. It's another of his covert tactics to evade confrontation and avoid intimacy.

Even Though He's No Sex Hound, He Prefers to Keep His Erotic Options Open

While your partner's sexual appetite may not be all that big, he likes to be free to sample any tasty dish that tempts his finicky palate. He hates the thought of having any woman tell him that he cannot have sex whenever—and with whomever—he wants. Not only does he consider reserving his right to erotic freedom an escape route from a real commitment to you, but he's afraid that a permanent menu of monogamy may be monotonous and dreary—even if he finds making love to you delicious indeed. After all, who's to say that sex with some other princess might not be more sublime still?

Or he might be agreeable to having all his X-rated adventures with you, but insists he's entitled to get some R-rated excitement elsewhere, as Ramon does. When his girlfriend complained that his once-a-month habit of going to striptease clubs with the boys made her feel he didn't cherish her, he replied, "When you have a Pinto, you want to see what a Ferrari looks like." That's the irreverent, bad-boy attitude many commitment phobes display when they feel you are trying to corner them—or curtail their sexual freedom.

He's a Fanatic About Birth Control

Unlike some of the guys Cheryl has slept with, who don't bother to ask about birth control until *after* they've climaxed, her current partner is so determined not to be trapped into marriage by an accidental pregnancy that he armors himself for their amorous encounters with *two* condoms—then insists she use a spermicide as well. "I'm sure if he could, he'd wear a full-body condom, or safer still, find a way to have sex by E-mail, so his sperm wouldn't even be in the same *room* with me," she jokes.

Michele's lover is equally paranoid about pregnancy—or is he? Recently, she feels that she's spotted an intriguing ambiguity that makes her question whether he's as much of a commitment phobe as he appears. "He's always been conscientious about reminding me to put my diaphragm in, but last week he showed me an article in the paper about a woman who secretly cut a heart-shaped hole in her diaphragm so she could conceive her boyfriend's baby without his knowing what she was up to. '*You* wouldn't do anything like that, would you?' he asked with a teasing tone that made me wonder whether he was giving me a warning—or a dare!"

Why Intimacy Intimidates Him

Michele's right to suspect that her lover has mixed feelings—but fatherhood isn't all that he's afraid of. A man who constantly flees from commitment, and finds fault with every woman he's with, is really running from something that he finds even scarier: having anyone get close enough to see *his* flaws. By going on the offense and finding your faults first, he hopes to shield himself from hurt, shame, and rejection.

This explains why your boyfriend may act cruelly jubilant when he spots even a very small imperfection in you, as Gloria's partner did. "One day when I was taking a shower, I saw that a beauty mark on my abdomen was swollen and bleeding. I completely freaked out—I was sure it was cancer—and demanded that my dermatologist remove it immediately. Fortunately, it wasn't, but instead of being happy I didn't have melanoma, my boyfriend was upset about the scar I had from the biopsy—which was all of a quarter of an inch long. Every time that I got undressed in front of him, his eyes would *gravitate* to the scar, until I felt like the ugliest woman on earth."

As long as her lover can keep Gloria focused on her tiny scar, he feels safe, since her attention is distracted away from the huge psychological blemishes he believes he has. Though he's making her miserable about her looks, the scar isn't really an issue with him: Secretly, he thinks he doesn't deserve a woman this good, and plays on her insecurities to keep her from discovering just how unlovable *he* really is.

Similarly, if you're a divorcée, a commitment phobe may fixate on the failure of your marriage, and subtly imply that he views you as tarnished by it. The more he suggests that being divorced makes you less desirable, the more he's letting you know how *dangerous* he feels you are. No matter why you actually split with your ex, your lover's fantasy is that the real reason why you've broken your marriage vows is because you've discovered your ex-husband's fatal flaw—and will dump him as well after you find his. That seems like a bigger risk with you than with the other women he's dated—since he thinks you've already proved you're perceptive enough to look into a man's secret soul and read exactly what his failings are.

Whether you're divorced or not, your partner may have another reason why he is reluctant to wed: His parents' marriage makes him shudder. Perhaps it ended in an acrimonious divorce that left him scarred—and scared of intimacy—or was bitterly unhappy behind a white picket fence. Either way, the institution of marriage might seem like a prison to him, where any woman he takes as a wife will inevitably become the warden who controls him in the same way that his mother did his father. Being hurt in his previous romances by lovers who gained power over him, and then used it to hurt him, may have reinforced these feelings—and convinced him that saying "I do" really means "I surrender."

Although his childhood left him terrified of being controlled by a woman, in some ways, your lover is still ruled by his mother. He's picky because he wants someone who is flawless enough to pass his critical mother's secret test: a task *he's* been failing at all his life. No matter how hard he tried to be a perfect little boy, she always found some unforgivable failing he'd tried to hide, and pointed it out. That's left him ambivalent about intimacy: On the one hand, he's afraid if he lets you share his mattress, you'll discover his defects, and dump him; but on the other, he wants a woman just as fastidious as his mother is—a princess who can detect one tiny dried pea of a defect even when it's hidden under twenty feather beds.

There is also a less common reason why some commitment phobes seem so wary of intimate relationships: They are not one hundred percent committed to *heterosexuality*. It's possible the real reason why every woman seems wrong for your partner is that she's not a *man*. Consciously or unconsciously, he may be keeping himself from getting too close to you because making a commitment to any woman would force him to make a lifelong decision about his sexual orientation. That could be an issue your boyfriend isn't ready to address right now, since his disturbingly *ambiguous* erotic feelings may seem like a flaw he has to hide from everyone—especially you.

Why You Lust After an Elusive Lover

What makes a hard-to-get guy so curiously captivating? Is it the thrill of the hunt that has you hooked, or the sheer challenge of capturing him after so many other women have failed? Actually, the true attraction is probably the very quality that you complain of: that he flees from a deeper relationship with you. That could be more *reassuring* to you than you realize, since you may secretly be just as intent on avoiding intimacy as he is.

Chasing a man you suspect you'll never catch gives you a good excuse not to confront your own fear of closeness, because you can blame your elusive boyfriend if the two of you never commit to one another. What could actually be holding you back is an anxiety much like your partner's—you don't want anybody to spot the flaws that make you feel damaged and unlovable. A lover who never gets near enough to be able to tell a true princess from an imposter is ideal for you, since he'll never notice how imperfect *you* are.

Not quite sure if this is the dynamic that keeps your romance stalled at the starting gate? One test that can reveal your inner feelings about intimacy is to examine what happens when your lover suddenly seems *attainable*. Mandy, for example, spent years trying to talk her boyfriend into getting married, but just when it appeared her heart's desire might be at hand, things mysteriously went awry. "After an incredible week in the Caribbean that was like a honeymoon, we never felt closer and more in love. When we got back, Louis began talking seriously about marriage, and gave me a necklace as a pre-engagement gift. He also began wanting to be with me every night, which he'd carefully avoided in the past.

"Just when he was at his most vulnerable, putty in my hands, I began finding reasons *not* to be with him, even though I was the one who was pushing before. It was as if he had called my bluff, since I backed off and tried to drop the relationship down to a lower level of intensity. In my mind, it was just temporary, until I could catch my breath, but pretty soon he had the walls back up, and was pretending that it was no big deal. Now that he's cooled off, I want him to get hot and heavy again, but I don't think he'll ever risk being rejected *twice*."

What Mandy has discovered is the intriguing paradox of these often futile attractions: The pretense that one partner is avidly pursuing the other is what keeps the relationship alive. Without the exciting illusion of *movement* this endless chase creates, the romance loses all its drama and tension. That is because you and your partner recognize that, by definition, a courtship needs the climax of a commitment. As long as you can convince yourself the relationship is building to a peak—no matter how imperceptible—you'll never feel empty and alone.

By simultaneously running after intimacy you're not sure you really want and running away from it by picking a lover who will always be elusive, you could also be re-creating a childhood situation that you hope to reverse. You may be attracted to an aloof, hard-to-please man because he poses the same challenge your father did: to discover how to get past all the barriers he's put up, and find a way into his heart. If you could manipulate your marriage-shy boyfriend into committing to you, it would be like winning your unattainable father's love, at last.

This scenario could seem very scary to you, however, since it puts you in the same position as the storybook woman who showed up at the prince's door trembling with cold and emotion to take his secret test and see if he'd accept her as a true princess. That's an awfully vulnerable situation to find yourself in if your childhood—or past love relationships—have taught you that opening the door to a deeper relationship can be dangerously risky.

Can You Live Happily Ever After?

When the young woman came down to breakfast the next morning, both the prince and his mother eagerly asked how she'd slept.

"Miserably, I'm sorry to say," she told them both. "I scarcely closed my eyes because there was a hard little lump in my bed that had me tossing and turning and made me black and blue."

The prince and his parents rejoiced at her complaints, knowing that only a true princess would be sensitive enough to feel a dried pea through twenty mattresses and twenty down quilts . . . and tell the truth about it.

The prince immediately asked for her hand in marriage, and had the pea put on display in the town museum, where it remains to this day.

Will *your* picky prince ever propose? And even if he does get around to it eventually, will you still want him? These guidelines could help you get him if you decide he's really worth waiting for:

Catch Him by Not Seeming to Pursue Him

Since your skittery sweetheart may be scared off by any sign that you're closing in on him, why not try *reverse* psychology—and make him chase *you*? Hide your eagerness for intimacy, and allow the love affair to progress at a pace that is comfortable for him. True, it might seem almost imperceptibly slow to you, but if the impetus toward deeper intimacy is coming from him, he won't be constantly backing off in alarm when he feels you intruding into his danger zones. Instead, if you maintain a friendly distance, he may discover that he wants to open the door to his psychological palace—and invite you in.

Avoid Pressing Him for More—Even in Jest

When Erica joked to her lover that thanks to his recent promotion, he could now support her in the style to which she would like to become accustomed, she thought he'd realize she was just teasing him. He, however, heard her remark as the sound of a bear trap snapping shut on his foot—and panicked. For a true commitment phobe, there is nothing funny about even the most lighthearted reference to kids, wedding rings, or a future together. You may think you're just being cute if you make an innocent jest about one of these taboo topics, but to him, humor of this kind is a sugarcoated guise for letting your secret feelings emerge.

Before you protest too much that you mean nothing of the sort, recognize that in a way, he's right. After all, if the idea of having kids with him, or being his wife, had never even crossed your mind, would you be joking about it? What you need to realize is that you are bringing these things up for a reason—to trick him into agreeing to greater intimacy. If he nervously laughs along with you, or at least doesn't vehemently *reject* the possibilities you've raised through your little joke, you can interpret (or misinterpret) it as evidence he's more open to marriage than he pretends to be. Though this tactic may give you temporary solace, in the long run it works against you, since he'll resent being put in this awkward position.

Prove You Are Trustworthy by Acknowledging That He Has Flaws, but They Are Only the Size of a Pea

Since your lover's great fear is that you'll discover his hidden deficiencies—then reject him—show him you are the right princess for him by letting him know you have noticed that his emotional mattress is a bit lumpy, but accept him anyway. You shouldn't besiege him with criticisms, which would seem too threatening; instead, just gently draw his attention to mistakes you see him making, or offer constructive suggestions that could empower him to do better. While you may be tempted just to keep quiet about flaws you see in him to avoid alienating him, it is a major mistake with this guy. He'll simply conclude that he's found *your* imperfection: that you are either dishonest or lacking in discernment.

Will This Man Still Do for You If He Never Says, "I Do"?

Ask yourself what your ultimate goal is—being with this guy, or having *somebody's* ring on your finger, even if it's not his. If *he's* more important to you, forget about marriage, at least for now, and just focus on enjoying the love you've found with this special man. But even if he's unwilling to commit to matrimony, insist that he agree to *monogamy*. It's fine for him to say he wants to keep his options open—which also leaves *you* free to move on to the next studmuffin who might catch your fancy—as long as you refuse to share him sexually with other women, which could be hazardous to your self-respect and your health, in this age of AIDS.

If, on the other hand, a wedding is what you truly want, there are two choices to consider. You can either leave now and look for a more marriage-minded mate, or set a limit on how long you'll wait to see if your current lover comes to share your feelings. Wondering what a realistic time frame would be? *Bride's* magazine reports the average man dates his future bride for almost three and a half years before he pops the question— and marries her one year later.

Don't Try to Snare Him with a "Surprise" Pregnancy

If you, like Michele, are thinking about secretly snipping a heart-shaped hole in your diaphragm, here's a word of advice: *Don't.* It can be a seductive fantasy to imagine that your commitment-phobic partner will suddenly realize he longs to spend his life with you after he learns you are carrying his child, but the reality is that he will always resent you for having trapped him this way—even if he does agree to marry you. And you will always wonder if he does truly love you—or if he only married you because you were pregnant.

Don't let romantic novels brainwash you into believing a baby is a solution for relationship problems: Pregnancy should never be a deceptive ploy to trick a man into staying with you, but a joint decision by two people who are firmly committed to each other—and their future family. If children are important to you, but not to your boyfriend, be truthful, and let him know that without a baby, you'd have a hole in your life (although not in your diaphragm).

Avoid an Ultimatum Unless You're Absolutely Certain That You Mean It

Setting a limit on how long you'll wait for a commitment or a child is not the same as giving your boyfriend a "Marry me or else" ultimatum, since you don't necessarily have to *tell* him what your timetable is—or even that you have one. Instead, you might prefer to use it as a *private* goalpost to measure the progress of your relationship, or to give him a *gentle* nudge forward, as Kathy did when she told her shy sweetheart that she loved him very much and hoped they might get married in the next couple of years. "He trembled a little—and didn't commit himself one way or the other, but since then, I can see that he's at least *considering* it."

Before you threaten to leave if your lover doesn't come across with an engagement ring by a certain date, be *very* certain that you can live with the results, no matter what they may be. Brenda, for example, decided to play her final card—by telling the man she had been dating for five years not to call again unless he was ready to commit—and *lost*. "I thought he'd realize he couldn't live without me, but he decided he could—and started dating somebody else. I'm very sad about it, because I'd love to be with him, and now I never will."

Watch Out for Ways You May Be Sabotaging His Attempts to Get Closer to You

Is it just your boyfriend who is so cautious about commitment—or are you unconsciously keeping him away? Sarah says she was surprised by her reaction when her intimacy-avoiding lover unexpectedly indicated he did want to have a future with her. "All of a sudden, there was a total role reversal in our relationship—because I started telling him that I wasn't sure and needed space, which are the lines that he used on me back when I was giving him the impression that all he had to do was whistle and I'd marry him two seconds later. I guess I'm still hurt from all those years of painful breakups after watching him always measuring me, or hearing him say he didn't feel enough for me. Or maybe I just want to get even—by pushing *him* away."

If You Ever Win Him, You May Discover You Don't Want Him

As Sarah's case illustrates, the good news about a commitment phobe is that he may have a change of heart eventually—if you hang in there until he realizes that you're the best thing that's ever happened to him; but the bad news is that by the time he does, he's not the intriguingly elusive charmer you fell in love with. That could provoke you to spurn him—until your partner is ready to resume the dance of avoidance that the two of you find so much more compelling than doing a duet of *true* intimacy with each other.

To move beyond this stalemate, you need to explain to your partner that your fears of commitment may cause you to do or say things that push him away. Try to get him to see how he may be doing this too. Then, each of you should make a promise to help the other person better understand the ways your anxieties about being rejected or swallowed up are leading you to sabotage the relationship. By working hand in hand to solve the problems—and giving each other breathing room at crucial times along the path to deeper intimacy—you could ultimately become closer, and more in love, than you ever imagined was possible!

9

*T*HE WOUNDED
POET

*T*here was once a merchant who suddenly was plagued by
misfortune. His ships were lost at sea, and then his fine
house in the city burned down. He and his three daughters had to move to a woodcutter's hut at the edge of the forest.
His youngest daughter, who was so lovely that everyone called
her Beauty, worked alongside her sad father as he planted crops.
She devoted herself to encouraging him, measuring her success
by his hard-won smiles. Her two older sisters, however, did
nothing but grumble all day long.

One day joyous news arrived. A ship had returned to port with
a rich cargo aboard that would restore his fortune. Before setting
off to claim his riches, the merchant asked each daughter what gift
she'd like from the city. "A diamond tiara!" demanded the oldest.
"Ball gowns!" said the second. "What about you, Beauty?" her
father asked. "All I want is your safe return," she replied. Her sisters snickered at this, and her father urged her to name a wish. "A
rose," she finally said. "Just one beautiful red rose."

In the city, the merchant learned his partners had stolen all
the money, leaving him as poor as before. On the way back he

got lost in a raging snowstorm, and happened upon a castle. Inside, he found a fire, and food on the table. The somber castle seemed deserted, so he ate his fill and fell asleep. In the morning, he saw a hedge of roses outside, and plucked one. "At least Beauty will be pleased," he thought.

Just then a terrifying Beast leapt out. "Is this how you repay me?" he roared. "You eat my food, sleep in my bed, and now you dare to steal from me. You will die for this!" The merchant begged for mercy, for the sake of his children. "I'll spare you on one condition," the Beast replied. "One of your daughters must agree to come and die in your stead. Otherwise I'll find you and kill you!"

When he reached the hut, the merchant handed Beauty the rose, telling her of its terrible price. Her sisters grabbed the flower and ripped off its petals. "Your ridiculous request has killed our father!" the oldest said. "Who would have guessed that asking for a rose would cause such misery?" Beauty said sadly. She insisted on riding off to the dark, foreboding castle of the Beast to keep her father's promise.

To her astonishment, magnificent fireworks burst into the sky when she reached the castle. "The Beast must be very hungry," she thought, "to rejoice so at the arrival of his prey." The Beast appeared, and asked in a terrifying voice if she came of her own free will. Trembling at the sight of him, she assured him she had, and he left her to marvel at the rich treasures in the palace.

She soon fell asleep, and dreamed about a handsome prince, who promised her every wish would come true. "Try to find me, no matter how I may be disguised. By making me happy, you will find your own happiness." Tenderly, she replied, "What can I do, Prince, to give you joy?" His enchanting voice pierced her heart when he implored, "Above all, do not desert me, because I need you to save me from my cruel misery."

Have you fallen in love with a man of hidden talents—or even genius—who would be your perfect prince if it weren't for the dark moods which sometimes make him act like a real beast? Sheila would love to transform her charming but petulant boyfriend. She's tired of hearing all about his allegedly traumatic childhood (among his insensitive daddy's "crimes" were demanding that his six-foot-tall, fourteen-year-old son mow the yard once a week and clean his own room); his imaginary ailments (he sometimes wakes her up at night to take his pulse or listen to him breathe); and his artistic frustrations (he's a government bureaucrat, but feels he'd be great at making *noir* films—if only somebody would take a chance on him). What keeps her hooked, however, is a hope he's *right*, since through the cloud of gloom that often surrounds him, she detects marvelous flashes of true brilliance.

Terry was thrilled when her new lover, a struggling novelist, called her his muse—until she discovered the dark side of her new role. "He told me that being with me was so inspiring that he was modeling a new character in the story after me. Almost every day, he'd hand me the pages he'd just written as if they were a gift to me. Everything was great, until I made a tiny criticism. He fell into this almost suicidal funk, and walked out. Three weeks later I finally heard from him—he said he'd had terrible writer's block and it was all my fault. We finally made up, but now I shudder if he shows me a chapter, for fear I'll say the wrong thing."

Wendy's boyfriend is sensitive to the point of being paranoid, she feels. "It's almost as if he's bent on destroying his career—which is finally taking off now that he's sold some of his songs to a Broadway producer—because he sees rejection where there is none, and lashes out. The other day, he was invited to a party with some important people from the music business, and somebody asked him to play the piano. The first song he played was so arresting that the guests stopped in their tracks and gathered to listen. Anyone else would have been delighted, but he suddenly crashed his hands down—and began shouting at his hostess because he thought she'd insulted his talent by letting him play on a piano that was ever so slightly out of tune."

What's the magnetic attraction that a misunderstood genius who acts out his "cruel misery" through black moods, emotional fireworks, or downright *beastly* public behavior has for so many of us? Here's an intimate look at these brooding Beasts and the enchantments they may weave for us.

His Telltale Traits

Do you feel there's something tragic—but supremely *romantic*—about your lover? If he's a wounded poet (who, of course, could be a bass player, a screenwriter, an artist, or just a bureaucrat with a movie camera and a dream), he's sure to show some or all of these characteristics:

He Lives Under a Perpetual Thundercloud

Because this is the poetic personality's most potent trait, if your lover doesn't brood at all, he's definitely *not* a misunderstood minstrel. Typically, he is all too willing to talk about his woes as soon as you meet. It's part of his *seduction* technique, since he knows that women are often eager to hop into bed with a sensitive man who shares his inner pain, so they can console him with sex.

It's also possible, as with Terry's literary lover, that he might mask his misery under a jovial veneer at first, either because he wants to get you firmly hooked before showing his true self, or because the wild excitement of a new love affair has temporarily lifted his fog of gloom. This facade of cheer won't last long, though, since these creative souls yearn for your sympathy.

He's Easily Offended or Annoyed

Like the Beast, who roared with anguished rage and hurt after Beauty's father picked one rose from a hedge of hundreds because he considered this trivial theft to be a personal affront, Andrea's oversensitive boyfriend howls with pain at even the tiniest slight. "Sometimes we'll spend a night out with friends, and I'll think we had a great time, but when we get home, he turns to me and says, 'Did you hear what Bruce said?' Then he'll make a huge deal about how insulted he was by some comment that I thought was harmless enough, and go on about it until I begin to wonder if there's something wrong with *my* perceptions, or I'm just too naive to *notice* somebody's being insulting."

He Blames Other People, Especially His Father, for His Woes

Often, this type of man has a long list of lovers, therapists, and family or friends who have let him down over the years by failing to recognize or appreciate his artistic talent and depth of soul. Since he is likely to latch on to each new person in his life as a potential savior, he's cruelly disappointed when they *don't* have a magical elixir to instantly cure his ills. Although he uses these people as an emotional Band-Aid to temporarily soothe his wound, he's furious that they haven't healed him. If they're not the solution, he reasons, they must be the problem, so he holds them responsible for whatever is wrong in his life.

One therapist says he once had a patient who showed him a box of burned matches, explaining that each stood for a psychiatrist who had cruelly disappointed him. This doctor, well aware that he was being set up as the latest scapegoat to account for the man's own failures, tried to give him a reality check by lighting one of the matches, blowing it out, then handing it to him, saying, "That will be a hundred fifty dollars." Similarly, the man in your life may be carrying around a box of extinguished hopes in a vain search for someone who will rekindle them for him.

He's Overly Concerned with His Health

While some melancholy bards fixate on their hurt feelings, others fret unduly about minor physical ailments, or imagine that they suffer from some mysterious malady that no doctor can detect. Renee's boyfriend, Frederick, is typical of these hypochondriacs. "He's like a disease-of-the-week movie, because if he gets a cut, he'll start to obsess about flesh-eating bacteria, while he's sure a twinge in the neck is the first sign of meningitis setting in," she says. Pat's live-in lover has a much more off-putting habit: If he feels the least bit sick, he takes his temperature *rectally*, in case his fever is too slight to register on an ordinary oral thermometer.

He May Have Unusual Eating or Sleeping Habits

Along with being overly concerned with their health in general, some wounded poets, like Jeannie's ex-lover, are fantastically picky eaters. "He had this phobia about onions and claimed some dire thing would happen if one even *touched* his lips. At restaurants, he used to make an enormous production of grilling the waiters about the ingredients for each dish on the menu. Since practically everything contains onions, it took forever for him to order. Then, after the entree came, he'd sit there and *pick* through it to see if he could find any trace of onion—and if he spotted so much as a sliver of this offending vegetable, he'd send his food back. After we broke up, he got married and now makes his wife *taste* his food before he'll eat it."

While some men get very picky if they're in a down mood and eat much less than usual, others drown their sorrows in food and pig out on anything in sight. Some melancholy men seek solace in sleep, not snacks, and lie languidly in bed until the clouds part and they feel ready to face another day. Or your lover may rest uneasily if he's unhappy, and complain of insomnia, or waking too early in the morning.

He's Exquisitely Attuned to Himself but Not to You

Whether it's his physical or emotional health that he expects you to be so solicitous of, your brooding beast probably assigns a very low priority to any need of yours—or acts annoyed that you have problems at all. Pat, for example, says her hypochondriacal lover behaves like a helpless baby if he gets sick. "All day long, he has me running up and down the stairs to get him books and pillows and soup and cups of hot milk, but if I get ill, I'm lucky if he looks in the room once a day to make sure I'm not dead in there or something. He seems to find it irritating when I get sick right after he does—probably because I caught *his* cold—and acts like I'm faking just to get even with him. He's like a little boy who gets mad at Mom for daring to get sick when she's supposed to be taking care of *him*."

He's a Master of Self-Sabotage

Fearful of both failure and success, he unconsciously shoots himself in the foot when presented with an opportunity to let his talent shine. At these moments, he panics—realizing that catching his dream means having to let go of his wounds. Mimi's boyfriend Dave, a would-be TV personality, kept "forgetting" to record any of the television appearances that he was fortunate enough to land. Each time he had another excuse: First his VCR wasn't working; then, just as the show was starting, he'd discover he was out of tapes. Even when he called his mother for help, she recorded the wrong program.

Soon Mimi devoted herself to recording his every appearance. If she missed one, she drove across town to a recording studio, where they sold it to her for a small fortune. But Dave rewarded her efforts with only lukewarm appreciation, because Mimi was *interfering* with his self-sabotage. Now he'd be able to make those demo tapes after all, and his career might actually take off—which is precisely what he was trying to avoid.

He's a Hopeless Romantic

Even though he isn't very helpful in practical ways—like taking care of your flat tire—he can be very charming when he feels up to it. He's the kind of man who might send you a handmade valentine, a beautiful love letter, or a poem he wrote especially for you. These sweet gestures remind you why you fell for him in the first place—his vulnerable, artistic, and achingly soulful nature—and help move you past his dark side: those moody moments when he overwhelms you with his needy, greedy, and sometimes clingy behavior. He also has another saving grace—he's probably *very* good in bed, since his creative imagination can spark true erotic originality!

Portrait of an Artist

Why is your lover so maddeningly moody? Both a raging Beast and a sad-eyed, dreamy prince live inside him, which isn't nearly so contradictory as it sounds, because depression is anger that's turned inward. What's infuriating and frustrating your prince is a cruel twist of fate he believes has hidden his magnificence and unique talents from the world. In his heart, he's the prince of poets, or a Rembrandt in the rough, but feels some cruel sorcerer has cast a dark spell over him that keeps people from seeing past his plain, unlovable exterior and appreciating just how special he is.

The source of his sorrow and anger is a childhood that left him so wounded that he is *still* brooding about it. That's why he fusses over his food and acts like a baby if he gets sick. He's asking for the love and nurture he lacked while he was growing up. What the prince inside your lover wants is an ever devoted woman—in other words, a *mommy*—to undo his childhood hurts and be his life preserver. The Beast in him is acting out a child's rage toward the bad daddy—Beauty's father—who deprived him. He wails at the slightest pain, refuses to share his flowers, and makes absurd threats against the father: "You will die for this!" the baby Beast roars, then lets Daddy off when he is promised his heart's desire: a woman to love him.

The reason your wounded poet hates his dad so much is that he sees his father as the sorcerer who put an evil spell on him—with constant criticism that eroded his self-esteem. At age three, Joe realized he'd never be macho enough to satisfy his father, an avid motorcycle racer. The first time his dad lifted him onto a custom-built baby motorbike, he was terrified by the roar of the engine, but had to hide his fears and tears. Over the next ten years, his father devoted endless hours to trying to train his son to excel at a sport he detested. Finally, at thirteen, Joe rebelled—by taking up the saxophone. "Even when I got in the school band, my father kept on belittling the sax as an instrument for 'sissies' who were presumably too scared to have nine hundred fifty cc's of hot, throbbing power between their legs."

Wilson had the opposite problem: His father, a truck driver who loathed his work, was determined to turn his son into everything he *wasn't*. To fulfill his father's fantasy, all he had to do was give up his own dream, he says. "My father was after me all the time to take practical courses, like math or science, so I could get ahead and be the successful businessman he wanted me to be. When I told him one day that I loved to draw and wanted to be an architect, he jeered. 'What kind of stupid idea is that? You don't have the talent, and if you don't shape up and learn something useful, you'll end up hauling lettuce up and down I-95, as you suck up *my* exhaust—because you'll be driving the truck right behind mine.' "

A father like this creates a double bind, because Wilson has two choices—both of which are wrong. If he chases his dream, he's faced with the terrifying threat of losing his father's love; but if he sacrifices his creative desires on the altar of his father's ego, he loses what he most prizes in himself, his creativity.

This creates a terrible conflict, which explains why a wounded poet often is reluctant to put his talent to the test. Wilson, for example, waited until he was thirty-five to study architecture, and now, two years after getting his degree, has yet to apply for a job in his field. Procrastinating is the ideal way for him to rebel and *not* rebel at the same time, since he isn't really defying his dad unless he starts designing buildings. That's a truly frightening prospect for him because he's now internalized the critical voice of his father that whispers, "You're not good enough, and you never will be." This is your poet's wound, because his greatest fear is that Daddy is *right* and he's destined to fail as an artist.

A Poetic Passion

Why is a poet who oozes angst from every pore so appealing to you? Like Beauty, you may have such a tender heart that you can't resist a man in distress. Her whole life is a never ending rescue mission, as she unhesitatingly volunteers to sacrifice her life to save her unfortunate father; instantly accepts the job of bringing joy to the sorrowful prince of her dreams; and even shows sympathy for the monster she believes is gleefully plotting her destruction: "The Beast must be very hungry, if he rejoices so at the arrival of his prey."

Although *you'd* probably think it was a very small consolation indeed to feel that you were helping out a hungry beast by letting him gobble you up, you might be more like Beauty than you realize. Think of all the times you've let men you love hurt you, then made excuses for their wicked ways. Or do you still blame yourself for your last breakup, thinking that if only you were prettier, better in bed, or more supportive, your previous boyfriend would still be with you? If you feel it's up to you to make the men in your life happy—or feel guilty if you fail to fix their problems—ask yourself why you're so willing to take responsibility for curing *their* pain.

One explanation is that you're a bit of a wounded poet yourself, and take on the job of being your partner's support and sunshine as a way of escaping your *own* sorrows. For years, Merry believed that she was just as upbeat and bubbly as her name suggests, even though her smile masked a lot of sadness, even depression. "I was so busy rushing to the rescue every time Larry was rejected for a part in a movie, or couldn't get out of bed to go to another audition, that I had no time to take a hard look at myself, and admit that I felt empty and unhappy with my life."

Being a melancholy bard's muse can also be secretly gratifying because it makes us feel powerful. Ginger, for example, is glad to take charge of her lover's chaotic life—he's a talented but hopelessly impractical musician—because she loves to feel needed. "If it weren't for me, he'd probably wear the same outfit until it fell apart, sleep over a warm subway grating, and strum his guitar as he slowly starved to death," she says, with a smug note of superiority sneaking into her voice, as she reminds everybody of how strong and competent *she* is.

Women like Ginger, who needs to be the "superwoman" who solves every problem for her helpless lover, are often overcompensating for problems they were unable to repair as children, such as not curing their father's sadness, or being unable to give him the fortune and success he yearned for. It could be that you find a melancholy poet irresistible because you secretly feel guilty about causing—or not healing—your father's hurt, and are trying to make up for it as an adult, through love affairs with wounded men. Like Ginger, you may brag about what good care you take of your boyfriend so you can say to the world, "I know how to make a man happy, so I'm not really a bad daughter at all."

An *extreme* need to please—and appease—troubled men suggests a darker scenario, a childhood in which you were abused, or had to act as the caretaker of an alcoholic or emotionally disturbed father or mother. What you may be acting out by rescuing your lovers is your own urgent need to be rescued from a painful past.

For some women, it's not pain but *pleasure* that draws them to creative partners. As a girl, Nona was attracted to the arts, and loved to sketch and sculpt. "As I got older, I felt frustrated as I'd conjure up beautiful images in my mind, but never quite caught them on paper or in clay. Eventually I realized I didn't have enough talent to be an artist, so I decided to use my eye for artistry to discover someone who really *could* create a masterpiece." She took a job at a small art magazine, and prowled the galleries until she spotted a man of hidden talents. Now she's his lover, his model, and his muse, and vicariously lives out her dream of being a great artist by helping him achieve success.

Women who have a fear of success for themselves may abandon their own pursuit of it by becoming entirely devoted to cultivating success in their man instead. Since it takes an unending supply of devotion to transform a wounded poet into a victorious achiever, a woman can easily become so consumed by this task that she is oblivious to losing her own chances of catching the brass ring.

There's also a mysterious affinity between moody, talented men and upbeat, supportive women. What's often appealing is the sheer *challenge* these men pose—both the task of figuring out how to turn all that raw talent and creative energy into the success he yearns for, and the equally intriguing problem of how to make him happy. Since his smiles are so hard to get, if you do win one, it's more of a reward than with a partner who is sunny and easy to please. Another reason why these opposites attract is that some lighthearted women *lack* a dark side, and may feel that men who are beset with sorrows have more depth of soul than they do.

Expressive, artistic men also have a distinctly *erotic* allure to many women. Almost paradoxically, they seduce us by *not* trying to seduce us. Unlike sexually aggressive men—who may threaten us with their overpowering, out-of-control eroticism— these delicate, soulful poets seem enticingly approachable. It's up to us to make the first move, as we tenderly fold him into our embrace and start making love to *him*.

Can You Live Happily Ever After?

When Beauty woke from her dream, she found that her supper was ready. As she began her lonely meal, she heard the Beast approach, and feared he'd come to eat her up. Instead, he sat down, and they talked for an hour. She found he wasn't so fierce as she'd thought. Then he rose, and asked gruffly, "Do you love me, Beauty? Will you marry me?" Her voice shook as she said no. To her relief, he just bid her a gruff good-night, but then looked crestfallen and sad.

In her room, she saw a gold locket dangling from a chandelier, and was amazed to find it held a portrait of the prince. She fell asleep with the locket next to her heart, and thought she heard him say, "Why do you treat me so unkindly? I fear I am doomed to long months of unhappiness." Each day after that she amused herself by exploring the palace, and often discovered enchanting objects and new pictures of the prince. The Beast visited her every night, and always repeated his two questions. With each "no" he became more despondent, then left her to dream of her beloved prince.

One evening, the Beast failed to appear for dinner. That night, she had a nightmare. As she walked down a lonely path in the Beast's garden, she heard heartrending groans from a nearby cave. Inside, the Beast lay dying. Terrified, she leapt from bed and raced through the palace, screaming the Beast's name over and over. No one answered. Exhausted, she stopped to catch her breath, and saw she was on the lonely path from her dream. She ran to the cave, and found the Beast inside, still as death.

"He's dead, and it's all my fault," she sobbed, but then saw him take a faint breath. She brought water to revive him. Finally, he asked weakly, "Could you ever love such an ugly beast as me?" This time, she said, "Yes, I never knew how much I loved you until I feared it was too late to save your life. I will marry you." Just then, words blazed across the sky, each letter made from millions of fireflies: "Long live the Prince and his Bride." She turned to the Beast in bewilderment, and found he'd changed into the prince she'd so often dreamed of.

Will your love work a similar wizardry on your wounded poet? Try these tactics to tame the Beast in your boyfriend, and entice the handsome Prince to emerge.

Never Underestimate How Sensitive Your Lover Is

While he may be irritable or a bit gruff (like the Beast), he's easily hurt, because even an unintentionally tactless remark you make reminds him of all the *past* wounds he feels have scarred him for life.

Be Supersupportive of His Work, but Avoid False Flattery

Since he's so prickly, it's tempting to placate him by telling him anything he creates is one hundred percent perfect. That's a mistake, however, since there's no higher superlative to offer if he *improves*. As his muse, your role should be to inspire him to greater heights, not to feed his ego with insincere praise.

Give Constructive Criticism, in Minute Doses

Since your partner reacts so strongly to the faintest whiff of criticism—because it sets off blaring alarms from his childhood, when his parents put down his artistic dreams—it may seem safest not to tell him if you spot a glaring flaw in his work.

Actually, you jeopardize the romance by *not* telling him, since his friends or professional associates will undoubtedly detect it too, and will point it out a lot more bluntly than you would.

Understandably, since he hears even a whisper of criticism amplified through the loudspeaker of his insecurities, he'll be furious at *you* for throwing him to the wolves. Be brave enough to tactfully tell him as much truth as he can handle—even if it makes him mad. One screenwriter says that if his wife or agent suggests his latest plot is less than perfect, "I fly into a rage and denounce them as fools and knaves who wouldn't know a good story if it jumped up and bit them on the butt, but the next morning, after I cool off, I often decide the fools and knaves are *right* and make the changes."

Help Him Remove Obstacles and Find Solutions

One woman, whose boyfriend was an aspiring singer with a nine-to-five job, suggested he could carve out more time to practice by waking up an hour earlier. To show her support, she got up with him and made him a cup of coffee, then read the paper as he went through the scales. Another woman, whose partner yearned to break into broadcasting, kept an eye out for people he could network with, and eventually learned of a promising job opening for him.

You might also consider taking a course in his craft with him. He'll have an extra reason to make the commitment, while you could gain an interesting insight into his art.

Don't Let His Creative Career Become Your Sole Obsession

Fran says that breaking up with her boyfriend, a fledgling newspaper reporter, "was painful, but incredibly *liberating*, because I was so focused on advancing his journalistic career in any way I could that it was like a black hole that sucked away my energy for myself. It got to the point where I got up at dawn to read all four city newspapers from cover to cover so I could clip out anything remotely related to his beat—politics—and went to all sorts of incredibly boring meetings in search of story ideas for him. Finally, I realized that even if he won a Pulitzer Prize, it wasn't worth it, because I was sacrificing my own life."

If He's Very Depressed, Urge Him to Get Therapy

Although many creative people think, sometimes correctly, that an *edge* of angst inspires artistry, *severe* depression can keep your lover's talent from flowering to its fullest. Such symptoms as inertia, hopelessness or suicidal urges, poor concentration, and a cloudy memory (all of which are characteristics of clinical depression); eating or sleeping too much or too little; and headaches, backaches, and other physical complaints with no medical basis can get in the way of artistic success, and make your lover more miserable than he has to be.

New treatments for depression, which include increasingly effective medication as well as psychotherapy, could have your hopeless poet feeling much less wounded—and ready to believe that there is a light at the end of the cave he's languishing in.

Encourage His Dream, but Don't Push Him Too Fast

Remember that he has underlying fears about both failure *and* success. The more you encourage him to expose his hidden talents to the world, the more vulnerable he feels. That's because it triggers a whole new set of anxieties. Instead of fearing his parents were right, and he's a talentless dreamer who will never amount to much, he's now worried that doing too well, too fast, would be like swinging a bigger penis than his father—which no son wants to do, as he'd risk terrible *retaliation*. (You can just imagine what that might be!)

Instead, ease him forward gently, in baby steps if necessary, until he is ready to *run* on his own, and grab the success he so richly deserves. As you tenderly help him to discover his happiness, you could win the reward the Prince promised Beauty, and discover your own joy—in his arms!

10

THE SELF-ABSORBED
SEDUCER

*O*nce *upon a time a poor wood-carver named Geppetto
found a piece of wood that laughed and cried like a boy.
"I'll make a puppet that can do tricks," he thought,
"and make my fortune." The puppet, which he named Pinocchio, was troublesome from the start. As he carved the nose, it
had the impertinence to defy him by growing and growing until
Geppetto was exhausted from trying to cut it down to size.
Then, just as the feet were done, the puppet dashed out the door
and got into all sorts of mischief.*

*When Pinocchio was unbearably hungry, he returned to
Geppetto's house. Inside, a Talking Cricket told him bad boys
who rebel against their father grow up to be stupid donkeys.
"Chirp all you like," Pinocchio retorted angrily, throwing a
hammer at the Cricket. "I am not like other boys, and don't
intend to be sent to school, and made to learn by love or force. I
want to eat, drink, and play all day."*

*When Geppetto got home, he found Pinocchio had fallen
asleep by the fire and had burned his feet off. As soon as he saw
his father, he wailed so piteously that Geppetto forgot his fury*

and kissed him. "It's all the Cricket's fault," the puppet wept. "Get me a spelling book and fix my feet, and I promise to go to school and be good from now on." His father tried to look stern, but traded his only coat for a spelling book, and made two new feet. When Pinocchio saw his reflection in the water basin, he was very pleased with himself.

"You won't regret it," the puppet told his shivering father, and set off for school. As he passed a puppet theater, however, he forgot his promises and sold the book so he could go to the show. Afterward, his sad story convinced the puppet master to give him gold pieces for Geppetto. Then Pinocchio lost them by boasting of his fortune to a pair of con artists. Fox and Cat cheated him, chased him, and left him for dead.

He woke up in an unfamiliar bed, where a beautiful Fairy with Blue Hair was spooning bitter medicine in his mouth. "How did you get hurt?" she asked.

"I was running to school when I was attacked by robbers," he fibbed, and felt his nose, which was already long, grow two inches. "Actually, I did stop—but only to get a gift for my father." His nose kept growing, and he said, "I was getting him a ticket to the puppet show." At this lie, his nose got so long he couldn't move.

The Blue Fairy laughed. "Why do you tell such silly lies?"

Pinocchio was so ashamed he wanted to run, but his nose held him captive in the room. He implored the Blue Fairy to forgive him. "I don't know why I do all these naughty things. I'd like to be a real boy—not just my papa's puppet."

When she felt he had learned his lesson, the Fairy called in woodpeckers to whittle his nose down to its usual size. "How good you are, dear fairy," Pinocchio said. "I love you."

But, despite Pinocchio's good intentions, he kept getting into mischief and begging for the Blue Fairy and his father to forgive him. One day, searching for the Fairy, he found only a tombstone engraved with, "Here lies the Blue Fairy who died of sorrow on being deserted by Pinocchio." As he was weeping for her, he learned his father had taken off to sea to look for him.

Alone and bereft, Pinocchio continued his misadventures

until he miraculously found the Fairy again. "If you only knew how my heart ached when I thought you were dead," he sobbed.

"That's why I forgive you. Since you were truly sorry, I know you have a good heart," she said. "I'll give you one more chance."

Pinocchio kept his word and became the best student in his school. Finally the Fairy said the words he was longing to hear. "Tomorrow I'll grant your wish and you'll become a real boy!"

With delight, they planned a feast, and Pinocchio went off to invite all his friends. When he invited his best friend, Lampwick, to celebrate the important event, his friend said, "Come with me to Pleasure Island instead, where there are no schools or books, just fun and games for boys." Pinocchio's tiny ears heard the Cricket chirp a faint, urgent warning, but his eyes looked longingly down the road, where the coach to Pleasure Island was waiting. . . .

Lindy's boyfriend has an outrageously in-your-face attitude—he'll cheerfully hold up a line of people at a supermarket to argue about a sixty-cent discount the cashier insists he is not entitled to; often breaks petty regulations, or even laws he is sure don't apply to *him*; and can be unbelievably insulting if a waitress dares serve him a dinner that he deems less than perfect. What saves him from being utterly obnoxious is that along with a narcissistic sense of entitlement, he also has a cocky self-confidence that is curiously captivating.

"Basically, Don is the kind of guy you'd like to slap across the face—then hug and kiss afterward," Lindy notes. "Getting in trouble is his hobby—but luckily he is very good at getting out of it again. He has the heart of a rogue—egotistical, kind of nasty, definitely not burdened with any surplus of scruples—but he's also full of fun and has a boyish love of mischief."

His Telltale Traits

Is your partner like an impertinent little puppet with a real nose for trouble—and sweet-talking lips that he uses to charm his way back into your good graces? If he wears a defiant, hedonistic attitude painted across his face—and *dares* the world to do something about it—he's probably a provocative Pinocchio at heart. Here's how to tell for sure:

He Expects VIP Treatment

Don't hold your breath waiting for him to thank people who bend the rules on his behalf or go out of their way to help him: He sees himself as a very special person who is *entitled* to every favor he gets—and more. His exaggerated sense of self-importance makes him feel he should be recognized as superior without having to earn it through studies, hard work, or impressive achievements. Just being there is his achievement—and he expects everybody to acknowledge it by handing him the best of everything as a tribute.

Like Lindy's lover, he can be haughty and demanding about the service he gets when he goes out. He'll demand a special discount at a store or hotel, expect the bartender to invent a new cocktail just for him—and name it after him—or order a dinner that is *not* on the restaurant menu. To get his way, he may pour on the charm, but if he is thwarted by a clerk or waitress he considers to be an underling, he can turn downright nasty or insolent.

He's in Love with His Own Reflection

Not only may your man be vain about his looks and admire himself in every mirror he sees, but his favorite topic of conversation is himself. He's likely to be intently interested in what you—or other people—think of him, as it's another way of gazing at his endlessly fascinating reflection. He won't necessarily mind if you think he's arrogant or conceited—in fact, he'd probably love to discuss it with you in detail. Like Pinocchio, your boyfriend may fly into a fury, however, if he feels somebody is criticizing him, and smack the offender right back with a scathing insult or two of his own.

Self-absorbed and filled with fantasies of unlimited success, good looks, power, brilliance, and the ideal love, your guy shirks responsibility in the real world. He'd rather fantasize than be confronted by the challenges of work, school, or love in his real life.

He Pretends to Be a Puppet, Then Pulls Your Strings

Another major trait your lover may show is being subtly manipulative. He'd never overtly boss you around—it's just not his style; instead, he lets you feel you're in charge, but has all kinds of cute tricks to charm you into doing what *he* wants. Like the spoiled child that he is, he may pout, flatter, flirt, cajole, or even throw a tantrum if that's what it takes to get his way. Never is he more charming and seductive, however, than when he's trying to woo you back after some especially outrageous escapade: He'll show up with a single rose in his hand—and a sheepish grin—to tell you what an angel you are to put up with a naughty boy like him.

Zina was adamant about not taking her bad-boy lover back after he'd spent a weekend with another woman in what he described as "my *last* fling before we get married." After he called her seven times in the same evening, begging her to let him come over, however, she relented. "I said he could stop by to *talk*, but not to expect sex. Usually when he came over, I wore a lacy teddy from Victoria's Secret, but this time, to show that I was serious, I greeted him in a full-length flannel nightie, and bunny slippers. But I might as well have opened the door nude—with my diaphragm already *in*—since it wasn't more than fifteen minutes before his entreaties had me melting into bed with him!"

He Isn't Above Lying to Achieve His Ends

Toni was attracted to her ex-lover because "he lived on the edge," but didn't discover where that edge actually was until she started working at his firm. "He was careful to stop just short of breaking the law, but he'd do unsavory things to make a deal, including lying to his clients—and the salespeople who worked for him. I'd sit there listening to him lie in such an incredibly convincing manner, and wonder how I could trust anything he'd told *me*. I kept waiting for him to get caught, but he always got away with it since he had that roguish charm that made every-one *want* to believe him, even though they knew he was out for himself, and wouldn't hesitate to rip them off if he could."

Part of his appeal, Toni admits, was how he made her feel like an *accomplice*. "As he was talking someone into risking their money on some pie-in-the-sky deal that he'd dreamed up, he'd kind of wink at me, as if to say that it was just a boyish prank that the two of us were playing on someone who wasn't as smart as us. The message was that since I was supposedly his partner in crime, he'd never try to pull this same stuff on *me*. He was so brilliant at manipulating everyone—including me—that I admired him in a strange kind of way and overlooked how totally self-centered and unscrupulous he really was."

The reason that a Pinocchio can take people in so easily with his lies is that very often he believes them himself—at least for the moment. His fantasies of how he'd like things to be may be so compelling that they start to seem like reality to him. As soon as you confront him with evidence to the contrary, however, he will usually crumble immediately and *admit* that he wasn't telling the truth.

Emotionally, He's Wooden and Unyielding

Just as Pinocchio's little ears don't listen to reason or con-science, your man may only hear what he wants to hear. He's apt to be obstinate, and mulishly ignores any warnings that might interfere with his fun. As well as being headstrong, he can come off as heartless, since he's unempathic. He doesn't like to hear about other people's needs and feelings—including yours—and finds it hard to identify with them. Even if he's madly in love with you, he secretly feels your role is to serve *him* and satisfy his wants.

Some of these seducers are so self-absorbed that it's hard for them to grasp that you could possibly have any wishes or desires of your own, as Hope recently learned. "Every time I go out to a club or restaurant with my boyfriend, he insists we get a corner booth—and then grabs the seat against the wall, so I have to sit with my back to the other people. When I finally told him this was annoying me, he patiently explained that he *needed* the wall seat so he could see if anyone he knew came in. Besides, he added, he could also see if someone came in to rob the restaurant and escape. 'What about me?' I said. '*I* wouldn't be able to escape.' He was bewildered: 'Yeah, so?' He was number one, so as long as he got out, everything was fine with him—even if a restaurant robber shot *me*."

He Acts on His Impulses—Instantly If Possible

The quality Toni remembers most fondly about her lying, live-on-the-edge boss, and boyfriend, is how "he wanted what he wanted *when* he wanted it, not an hour later. Whether it was money or food or sex he craved, he had to have it immediately, no matter how inappropriate the time or place was. We were both single and had our own apartments, but we were always making love on his desk, or in the office bathroom, or in his car after we'd been out on a date, because he didn't want to put off his pleasure until we got home. A few times, we almost got *caught*, but that didn't deter him from doing it again—maybe even later that day!"

Paradoxically, your partner's impulsive personality can make him susceptible to the very danger he's most intent on avoiding: being manipulated by other people. When a whim seizes him, he will pursue it so impetuously that he leaves himself wide open to people who might want to cheat him or take advantage of him. Compounding the problem is his belief that he's smarter than other people—an assumption that any con men he encounters are quick to capitalize on.

He Has Keenly Honed Sexual and Animal Instincts

Since your man is so focused on what will give him pleasure, he's exquisitely in tune with his body and its appetites. Since he wouldn't dream of letting any silly inhibition get in the way of his erotic enjoyment, your partner is likely to be impetuous and passionate in bed, as he strives to satisfy himself to the fullest. Don't think that he'll leave you behind as he takes off to Pleasure Island, however. He adores praise, so he'll try to pull all of the right strings for you, so you'll *applaud* your puppet's impertinent tricks!

What Pulls Pinocchio's Strings

What makes your man so saucy and self-absorbed? If he reminds you of a spoiled boy who constantly defies his doting parents, it's because he was one when he was growing up. From birth, his parents considered him extraordinarily special, even a miracle. Perhaps he was the only son (or the first or lastborn son) of a mother who thought she'd never be able to have a real live boy; was born after a previous baby had died; or had a narrow escape from death himself, due to a childhood illness or near fatal accident. Like Pinocchio, your mate may have been raised by a single parent, or adopted by a couple who couldn't have kids on their own. Whatever the exact circumstances were, *his parents were overly grateful for having him—and let him know it at an early age.*

Having parents who did too much for him—possibly because they were emotionally deprived or poor when they were children, and made up for it by showering their son with all the things they lacked as they were growing up—is what gives your lover an exaggerated sense of self-importance. He expects to get the best table, the tastiest tidbits, and lavish praise that he's done nothing to deserve because that's what he got as a child. Boys being boys, he soon learned to take advantage of his overly indulgent parents—and manipulate them into giving him even *more*, just as he now charms, cajoles, sulks, or shouts until you—and everyone else—give him the special treatment his narcissistic nature tells him he's *entitled* to.

As a child, he also started the cycle of getting into trouble, feeling guilt and shame, and giving lies and abject apologies until he's forgiven (until *next* time) that he now replays with you. It's part of his boyhood need to rebel—and prove he's not his papa's or mama's little puppet, and won't be *yours* either. Defying you, then lying or manipulating his way back into your heart through his charming wiles, makes him feel it's not his nose, but his *penis* that is getting longer, as your Pinocchio never feels like more of a man than when he's showing you his strings can't be pulled by a woman.

It's not that he doesn't hear the chirps of his conscience—he does, and disregards them—but that the sheer delight of getting away with some boyish mischief overpowers this internal voice of reason. Don't make the mistake of thinking his unempathic outer shell means your lover is unaware of your feelings and needs either—after all, he can find your hot buttons easily enough when he senses that he's gone over the line, and is at risk of losing you. Instead, he just *chooses* to disregard them if they might interfere with his fun—he's used to having his parents sacrifice their desires in favor of his, and expects you'll also put him first.

Paradoxically, what he's really acting out with his rebellious bad-boy behavior is unresolved *anger* toward the parents who spoiled him. As a child, he sensed that he wasn't really getting something for nothing when they lavished him with love, praise, and presents—there were definite *strings* attached. Underneath all their giving, his parents were actually very needy, and made your lover fear he'd never be devoted enough or sympathetic enough to repay them for all they had done for him. This is why your lover can seem as heartless or unempathic as a block of wood—it is his defense against others who may also try to devour him with their emotional demands.

Not only does your man still resent this debt of gratitude his parents burdened him with, but it's left him with a need to prove—over and over again—that he will defy anyone who tries to turn him into a puppet that does their bidding. The problem, however, is that as soon as he pulls some outrageous antic, he gets anxious and worries he may have gone too far in testing his parents'—or your—love and is at risk of losing it. That's when he comes scampering back with his most adorable apologies for any pain his mischievous ways might have caused you, and swears a thousand times that he'll never, ever do it again—at least not *today*!

The Seduction of a Self-Absorbed Man

What is the peculiar charm that these manipulative mario-nettes hold for us? Rachel marvels about what she lets her lover get away with. "Yesterday, we were having a game of golf when he complained I was playing too slowly. Though we had nothing else to do all day long, he felt it was unfair for me to delay him, and demanded I stop playing and just drive the cart. I never thought that I'd agree to be a golf caddy for any man, but I spent the entire morning finding his stupid balls every time he hit them in the rough, and wondering why I was letting myself be manipulated this way."

Actually, there are several common reasons why such a mad-deningly self-centered man may be seductive to you.

Your parents may have given you such a strict upbringing that you never had the chance to be mischievous as a child. Their threats and punishments may have stifled your impulses—especially your sexual ones—making you too afraid to hop aboard the coach to Pleasure Island, where the naughty little boys indulge their every whim and eat candy all day long. That could have left you hungry for these forbidden delights—and for a bad boy who puts no limits on his carnal appetites.

Your childhood or past relationships with men have left you with a secret belief that the only way you can get love is by being a long-suffering martyr. What attracts you to the relationship with your lying, live-for-the-moment lover is his pattern of per-petually hurting and disappointing you with his wicked tricks, which gives you an opportunity to gain his gratitude and devo-tion by forgiving him, *again*.

Secretly, you're as mad at your parents as he is at his, and long to rebel. Trouble is, you were raised to be a good girl, who minded her manners, got her homework in on time, and never got mud on her pretty white dress. As an adult, you're tired of being such a responsible, hardworking citizen, who always fol-lows rules and obeys her parents and the boss, and hope that with him at your side, you'll finally find the nerve to tell the world to go to hell—as you roar off into the night on the back of his motorcycle.

Unlike your lover, you were *not* the pampered darling of your parents, and you grew up with a sibling or friend who always got all the attention. Unconsciously, you are so used to the pain of being perpetually on the sidelines watching somebody else get the applause and admiration of the world that without meaning to, you re-create this role with your lover. It's not that you think *he's* necessarily entitled to what he demands, but that you don't think *you* deserve any special treatment.

His cocky self-confidence is just what you lack. Since you're secretly rather shy or insecure, his dramatically *opposite* demeanor has you convinced that he's just as special as he claims to be—and if you hang around him long enough, perhaps some of it might rub off on you!

Despite his uninhibited sexuality that unleashes a wild side you never imagined existed in you, you'd still pull the plug on the relationship, except for one thing—he always repents just in time. You just can't resist him as he's standing outside your door with a heart-shaped box of chocolates in his hands, pleading for one more chance to show you what a good boy he can be. Since you're so softhearted, you can't help but be moved by his lies and manipulative ploys, and start to *pity* him for the misfortunes and pain that have caused him to go astray. Before you know it, you have taken him back into your arms—and a few minutes later, your *bed*.

Can You Live Happily Ever After?

With a pang of regret at disappointing the Blue Fairy again, Pinocchio impulsively hurried to catch the coach to Pleasure Island. As he was about to climb aboard, the donkey that was pulling it wept like a boy, and whispered, "Turn your back on school, and you will cry as I cry now—but it will be too late, you little fool!" Pinocchio obstinately ignored the donkey's advice, and climbed on.

Pleasure Island was even more wonderful than the puppet had imagined, and weeks sped by in a nonstop whirl of play and tasty treats. One morning, Pinocchio had a nasty surprise—

when he saw his reflection in his washbasin, he found he had long donkey ears!

Horrified, he shrieked until a neighbor came over and told him, "You have donkey fever, which is the fate of all self-indulgent boys," she said.

"I am a heartless puppet, with no sense," Pinocchio sobbed. But the more he cried, the longer his ears grew. As the puppet ran about in despair, his hands and feet became hooves, and gray hair sprouted on his body.

And just as he began braying his lament, the coachman who had taken him to Pleasure Island came into the room laughing. Pinocchio put his tail between his legs in shame as the man led him off and sold him to the circus. There he was whipped and made to learn tricks until he fell through a hoop and became lame. His next owner threw him into the sea to drown. The Blue Fairy saved him again, this time by sending fish to eat up all his donkey outsides, freeing the puppet inside.

As he swam toward her, a huge whale swallowed him whole. He sobbed, "Oh poor me! Now I'll never find my papa." But Pinocchio, drawn to flickering candlelight deep within the belly of the beast, was utterly amazed to find his father there. Flinging his arms around Geppetto in joy, he said, "I'll save you, Papa. Climb onto my back, and I'll swim you to shore as soon as the whale opens his mouth again and we can escape."

Once they reached land, they met Cricket, who told Pinocchio the Blue Fairy had been overcome by grief and misfortune and was now in a hospital, too poor even to buy a morsel of bread. Desperate to save the Fairy, the puppet took the first job he could get, pumping buckets of well water for the garden—work so backbreaking that it killed the donkey who previously did it. Working from dawn until well after dark, Pinocchio was able to support his father and the Fairy, and then study until midnight.

One night, the Blue Fairy appeared, fully recovered and more beautiful than ever. She kissed him and said, "Most of the time, a puppet has no heart, and thinks only of his own pleasure, but you have taken care of me and your father so tenderly that I will forgive you all your past misdeeds. I now grant your

*greatest wish, and make you a real boy!" As she spoke, Pinoc-
chio stepped out of his wooden puppet shell, and moved forward to embrace her with his warm arms of flesh and blood.*

What are the odds that your infuriatingly impetuous and
self-absorbed partner will ever develop any real concern for your
needs and feelings? While there are no magic tricks to change a
wooden-hearted puppet into a real boy who will always love you
as you are entitled to be loved—remember that your mate will
resist attempts to pull his strings—these strategies can help:

Be Willing to Accept That He'll Always Be
His Own First Love or Walk Away

Mr. Altruistic he isn't, so about the most that you might
realistically hope for is that your self-involved lover will come to
care about you and your feelings *almost* as much as he does
about himself. Even that might take a while, since he has to tear
himself away from that endlessly intriguing mirror of his for
long enough to see *you* before he can truly start to love and
appreciate you. Should the prospect of patiently waiting for
what might well be slow improvement hold no allure for you,
move on to a man whose heart is easier to carve your name on
than this obstinate block of wood. Otherwise, smooth the way
to gaining more of his empathy by praising him lavishly whenever he does show some insight into your feelings.

Let Him Know There Are No Strings
Attached to Loving You

To your boyfriend, it can be a big deal to show even a small
amount of sympathy or concern for your needs, since it makes
him feel just as vulnerable as if he were swimming near the big,
greedy, *needy* mouth of a whale. Actually, he may see into your
heart more clearly than you imagine, but he hides it from you,
just as he did from his hungry, impoverished parents, out of fear
that he might then be expected to do something about it. That
would put you in control of him, which is exactly what he most

dreads. What you need to help your partner recognize is that *understanding* is enough—you do not expect him to make up for your poor childhood, or take responsibility for you the way his needy parents expected.

Reassure him your needs won't swallow him up, by being precise and positive about what you want from him. As a boy, he got vague, poorly formulated demands from his parents and felt that he'd never satisfy them, since he didn't understand what they were asking for. Use clear, positive statements to say you'd love him to call you up more often or ask you about your job, and you're likely to get your wish granted, while vague hints or little ploys could make him feel you're trying to make him be your marionette, and close his ears to your message.

Don't Flaunt All Your Sacrifices on His Behalf—or Make Ones That Leave You Exhausted or Ill-Nourished

It's also a mistake to use guilt to keep your lover in line— he'll just see it as another tactic to control him. Notice how Geppetto and the Blue Fairy are always *discreetly* rescuing Pinocchio from his self-inflicted woes, when they repeatedly sacrifice, forgive, and patiently try to teach him right from wrong? What they do is offer help and support in a way that lets the naughty puppet accept it—without losing face as they pull him from mischief.

That's what you want to do as well, except that you shouldn't leave yourself shivering with cold, as Geppetto does when he sells his coat to buy the puppet a schoolbook, or bankrupt and starving, as the Blue Fairy does. Calmly, simply, and briefly let him know how it makes you feel when he pulls his various stunts; but don't look for an immediate response. It's enough that your message gets through his little ears and into his wooden head. The lesson you need to learn is that your partner, like Pinocchio, may not come through for you until you're on the brink of abandoning him. Until then, he'll keep on getting into trouble, as you make ever greater sacrifices and put yourself into danger—by giving until you're psychologically exhausted, materially impoverished, and too ill-nourished to rescue *yourself* from the consequences of excessive self-sacrifice.

Let Him Miss You When He's Pursuing Mischievous Impulses

As Pinocchio's story illustrates, there's no need to hover around your partner all the time to make sure that his impetuous impulses don't impel him headfirst into the mouth of misfortune. Always being there to extricate him from his misadventures only encourages him to go even *further* next time, since his provocative naughtiness is intended to test the outer limits of your love. Even if he's deep in the belly of the beast, reveling in some unsavory escapade of his, he's very capable of rescuing himself. As soon as he suspects you are on the verge of giving up on him altogether, he'll swim out of the whale's mouth all by himself—anxious to make amends so you won't leave him alone and hungry.

Allow Him to Make a Total Ass of Himself Through His Mistakes

Your boyfriend's obstinate nature means that it might take lots and lots of time before he learns from his mistakes. He may need to go to the ultimate extremes of pleasure or lazy self-indulgence before he'll admit that his refusal to accept responsibility and earn your respect—or the world's—through actual work is making him act like a real donkey. He has to see for himself that gratifying his every whim is making your feelings for him wither up and die, and keeping him on a merry-go-round that has a lot of entertaining motion, but goes nowhere.

The good news about your partner is that he'll eventually grow up and settle down, because he has a clever cricket of a conscience to guide him—he just doesn't like to listen to it. The younger or more emotionally immature your Pinocchio is now, the more likely he is to believe, as babies do, that he is the center of the universe. It may take many, *many* mistakes or misfortunes to convince him that the world can be a very mean place—unless he has a Blue Fairy like you at his side to lead him to what's beautiful and good.

Show Him There Are Other Ways to Make His Penis Long Besides Lying, Which Must Be Unacceptable

Let him be insolent or defiant if you like—he is never going to be a polite, obedient puppet for anybody, even a woman he *adores*—but draw the line at lying, which makes a relationship impossible. Without trust, love can't thrive, since you'll never be able to open up fully and allow yourself to give your heart to a man who constantly lies to you. Even when you only suspect he may be deceiving you, give him the bitter medicine of the truth: You don't believe what he is telling you or have evidence to contradict it. Be resolutely honest *yourself*, as a model of what you expect from him—or anybody who is an intimate part of your life.

Watch out if he lies frequently or pointlessly—he could be a pathological liar! One recent study found that there are more of these seriously disturbed—and compulsively dishonest—individuals than ever before, so don't dismiss uneasy feelings you may have as mere paranoia. If you have any reason to think that your lover is repeatedly untruthful, end the relationship. Painful as it may be, you could be sparing yourself even worse hurt in the future—and a life with a lover you always have to be wary and suspicious of. (A psychotherapist may be able to straighten him out, but for some of these men, dishonesty is so ingrained they even lie to their therapist—which is the most futile false-hood of all, since telling the truth is the key to psychological recovery.)

Help Him Learn How to Pull His Own Strings

What if it's not your lover's lying, but his ridiculously elon-gated sense of entitlement that frustrates or infuriates you? Don't be a little bird that pecks away at his penis with petty threats, wounded silences, or tearful complaints, which are the sort of games he's so good at. Just remind him, in a firm but gentle way, where your boundaries are. For all of his bravado, he is apt to be as relieved as a spoiled child who feels he's gotten out of control, to have you rein him in.

Just as a naughty boy tests his mother's love, your partner may act up so he can be reassured you care enough to stop him. He may pretend he's having a ball as he strays into trouble—again—but his underlying motive is to test your love and determine where he stands with you. He never feels on solid footing, since he knows that by putting his needs first, yours are left unfulfilled. By insisting he accept limits that are good for him—and you—you'll show him how to pull his own strings, instead of letting his very worst impulses do it for him. That could make your lover's heart of wood beat with flesh-and-blood feelings of real love for *you*—not just for himself!

11

*T*HE MAN OF
MYSTERY

*O*nce upon a time, there was a man who had several magnificent castles, gold and silver plates, and gilded coaches driven by snow-white horses, but who believed he was so ugly that no woman would have him. Actually, he was quite handsome—except for the strange blue beard that hid part of his face. He'd had several love affairs, all of which ended rather mysteriously.

His neighbor, a fine lady, had two beautiful daughters, and he began wooing them both. Neither wanted to marry a man with a blue beard—until he invited them, their mother, and several of their friends to his castle in the country. After a week of hunting parties, balls, and other amusements, the younger daughter began to think that his beard was not so very blue after all, and she agreed to marry him.

Soon after the honeymoon was over, her new husband told her he was going away on business, and urged her to invite some friends to visit. "Here's a key for the bedroom safe, where you'll find money and jewels; and here's a key to the storeroom where the gold and silver plates are kept," he said. "This master key *will unlock every room in the house, and this final key is for the closet at the end of the gallery on the ground floor. Go anywhere you like, and open anything—except the closet, which I strictly forbid you to enter, at the risk of my terrible wrath."*

She promised to observe his instructions, and as soon as he left, she called her friends. Soon they were running through the house, exclaiming over the new gowns he had bought her, the exquisite antiques and rich tapestries, and most of all, a series of jewel-encrusted mirrors—each more costly than the last—in which they could admire themselves. Yet she was unable to enjoy their envy of her good fortune—or the yearning looks her ex-fiancé kept giving her—because she was consumed with the most forbidden desire of all.

At last she could resist it no more, and slipped away from her guests, down the back staircase to the closet at the end of the gallery. With the little key in her trembling hand, she hesitated for some time—thinking about her husband's warning and what unhappiness might befall her—then turned it in the lock.

Are you, like Bluebeard's wife, wondering what skeletons might be in *your* lover's closet? Charlene says that what drives her crazy about the men she has dated is, "They absolutely hate to tell you anything. If I ask the man I'm seeing a question he considers remotely personal, he'll look at me strangely and say, 'Why would you want to know *that?*' as if I was trying to ferret out his deepest, darkest secret—which of course I am, except that I haven't worked up to the really intimate stuff, like why he broke up with his last girlfriend."

Louise says she's so frustrated by her partner's closemouthed ways that she's taken to rifling his pockets and searching his belongings for clues as to what her lover does when she's not with him. Though she has yet to learn anything of interest, she's recently sunk to a new low in her snooping—she's learned his answering machine code so she'll be able to listen to his messages remotely. He, on the other hand, shows so little curiosity about her, she reports, that she could stamp her diary TOP SECRET and leave it out on the kitchen table, confident that he'd never even sneak a single peek.

"Sometimes I'm convinced he goes into suspended animation in the morning, and thaws at five p.m., because according to him, nothing has *ever* happened where he works," she complains. "Then we'll get together with his friends from the office and I'll learn that half the department was laid off last month, or that the office is a hotbed of intrigue because one of them is about to be selected for promotion. It's embarrassing to be the only one in the room who isn't in the know, but when I confront him about it he just shrugs and says, 'Didn't I mention that?' "

Rebecca isn't concerned about details—with her boyfriend it's the big picture that's missing. "He reminds me of that David Bowie character in the movie *The Man Who Fell to Earth.* You'd think he just landed on the planet the day we met because he doesn't seem to have a past—not that he's willing to reveal anyway. He's a lot of fun to be with—and great in bed—but I am starting to wonder if he has something *serious* to hide. Sometimes I'm very tempted to snoop through his stuff and see if I can find some clues as to what this guy is all about."

Do you suspect you might have fallen under the spell of a man of mystery? And exactly what is your silent partner concealing—a wife and six kids, a cupboard full of corpses, or just a private life that he deems too *dull* to dwell on? Here's a look at men who tantalize us with what they *don't* tell, and what their real secret might be.

His Telltale Traits

Is your boyfriend genuinely mysterious? And, if so, is he intentionally hiding something, or unintentionally blocking your way to his innermost thoughts? Or could your lover be a "pseudo" man of mystery, whose enigmatic smile only masks a bland personality with *no* hidden depths at all? Use these clues to decide if your man is as elusive as he seems:

He May Be the Strong, Silent Type
or Have Plenty to Say on
Every Imaginable Topic but One: Himself

Marta says that her lover is bursting with passionate opinions, witty observations, and insightful anecdotes about other people, but has yet to reveal anything about his inner world. "At first, I didn't notice that he wasn't at all forthcoming about himself, because he is so incredibly articulate about everything else. Finally I realized that I know everything he ever thought about the *New York Times*, his favorite music, and national politics, and not a damn thing about himself."

There's an Area of His Life Marked "Hands Off"

Whether it's his mother, his ex-wife or former girlfriends, or what he does for a living that he's loath to discuss, there's sure to be something extremely significant about this aspect of his life. Amy had qualms from the beginning about a man who observed darkly from time to time that he was "unlucky" in love, but refused to reveal any of the specifics about his past romances—and soon found out he had so many strange phobias that she left him too.

He Almost Never Expresses
Anything About His Feelings

Tina, for example, says her boyfriend claims that he only gets depressed about two things—traffic delays and foul weather—while Sherry's husband never feels angry, upset, or gloomy: According to him, he's simply "tired." During his episodes of alleged fatigue, he sometimes spends the entire evening in total silence, compulsively rearranging objects in the living room.

He's Evasive About Where
He Goes or to Whom He Talks

Barbara complains that the man she lives with, a book editor, often murmurs something vague like, "I've got to see some people," and then stays out until the wee hours of the morning. Ann's lover is even worse: He sometimes vanishes for weeks on end, and refuses to give her one word of explanation of where he was or why he didn't call. And Sue says her boyfriend is driving her up the wall with his odd habit of bringing his cordless phone into the bathroom, locking the door, and making long calls that he claims are "business."

He's Artful at Dodging Questions

One of his favorite ploys is to put the spotlight back on you as quickly as possible—either by doling out a tiny nugget of information or just a vague answer, then quickly changing the subject to one very close to your heart: *your* personal life. He probably is so adroit at drawing you out—and flattering you by his apparent fascination with your secrets—that you get too swept up in talking about yourself to probe deeper into his forbidden zones.

Another way a man of mystery stops you from getting too close to his secret self is by telling jokes. Instead of answering your question—or anticipated question—he'll quickly say, "That reminds me of a funny story," or "Did you hear the one about. . . ."

He Has a Seductive Strategy to Lure You Away
from the Door to His Secret—Showering You with
Compliments, Presents, or Romantic Declarations

After all, if he's being so loving, are you going to spoil the mood by giving him the third degree? Or he may resort to the ultimate distraction—sex, which gives him many more interesting things to do with his lips than answer your questions, as he skillfully substitutes intimate acts for the intimate revelations you desire.

If He Senses You're Getting Dangerously Close, He May Create a Sudden Crisis as a Smokescreen to Distract You

Perhaps he decides to reveal something he considers less damaging—and regales you with the details of an annoying problem at the office, or a minor illness he's developed. He may also pick a fight with you, or express doubts about whether the relationship is working out, so you'll be too nervous to pry.

If He Feels You Have Him Truly Cornered, He May Lie, Play Innocent, or Act Hurt That You Suspect Him of Something

One tip-off that he's being evasive is a sudden shift in conversational style: suddenly Mr. Strong and Silent seems positively loquacious, as he unleashes a torrent of words to rush you away from the hiding place; or Mr. Talkative falls into a wounded sulk and hopes you'll feel too guilty to pursue the topic further. His body language may also change, as he fidgets in his chair, bites his lip, touches his mouth often as if to keep the secret in, or refuses to look you in the eye.

Almost Paradoxically, If One of These Tactics Works, a Man of Mystery Will Often Deliberately Make the Secret an Issue Again

As Bluebeard did, he may act provocatively and almost *dare* you to try to find out what he's hiding. Ashley once dated a man who liked to conspicuously lock his briefcase in her presence. "A few times, he even took it in the bathroom with him, as if he thought I would try to pick the lock while he was peeing." Understandably, she became all but obsessed by curiosity about the case's contents. Another woman got her first inkling that her husband might be unfaithful when she noticed he'd left a matchbook from a local motel on their dresser.

In Bed, He Keeps You in the Dark—Perhaps Literally

Don't expect a lot of amorous pillow talk from this guy—he's likely to be such an erotic enigma that you don't have a clue as to what he may think or feel while he's making love to you. Or you may find that he is a bit more communicative in bed than out of it, because when he has his mouth on yours, he knows he doesn't need *words* to express his emotions. Either way, you may wonder afterward, when he rolls over and falls asleep, if you've truly pleased him, or if there's something else he'd like you to do. Another way that your lover may keep you guessing in bed is by surprising you with a new sexual trick from time to time—but never revealing where or how he picked it up!

The Great Pretender

Not sure if any of these traits quite capture your boyfriend's strangely inscrutable qualities? It could be that you've hooked up with a *pseudo* mystery man—a Bluebeard whose cupboard is bare. His only secret is that he has *no* secret because the neutral, impassive exterior that intrigues you so much is all there is. That's why he has no telltale traits—there is nothing to tell, as Betsy finally discovered. "Greg was by far the most beautiful man I ever dated—and an incredible lover. That he was also so shy only attracted me more: Usually really gorgeous guys are horribly conceited and never *stop* talking about themselves. I figured he'd open up when he felt comfortable with me, but when he did, what a disappointment! In his case, still waters ran *very* shallow."

The *real* puzzle however, is why Betsy (or any woman) would be drawn to a lover so devoid of depth. Many of us have unconsciously been programmed by movies or our culture to view the strong, silent type as sexy, while others see such men as a blank screen to project our fantasies on. Just as Pygmalion carved a magnificent ivory statue of a woman, then breathed life into her so she could be his perfect love, we pick a bland, beautiful partner and turn him into whatever we crave the most—a daddy, an appreciative audience, or a soulmate who accepts us unconditionally. As we bask in the attention of our gorgeous creation, it's easy to ignore the little voice that tells us that "there's no *there* there," as Gertrude Stein once said about a city she found singularly dull.

Who Is That Masked Man?

What's the solution to the puzzle *your* boyfriend poses? There are several motives that might underlie a man's elusiveness, but at the heart of all of them is "the Bluebeard syndrome," his conscious or unconscious belief that if you knew what he's hiding it would be fatal to the relationship. That's because he secretly thinks there is something so terrible or flawed about him that you'd abandon him if he ever allowed you to see it. To avoid revealing the skeletons in his psychological closet and risking rejection, your lover feels it's safer to wrap himself in a shroud of mystery—or a tapestry of lies.

To uncover what your man might be concealing behind this self-protective mask, focus on what he's *most* secretive about: Is it his *feelings*, or the *facts*? Then use this brief guide to probe further into what either of these common tendencies may mean.

Five Reasons Why He Hates to Reveal His Feelings

Masculinity Concerns

Imagine how a man would feel if he had a funny-looking blue penis that any woman he ever wanted to have an intimate relationship with would take one look at, and either laugh, or run away, shrieking in terror? That, in essence, is what Bluebeard's problem was, since a beard is as much the emblem of his masculinity as his penis is. Similarly, your lover might feel that he's not as manly as he'd like to be, and uses a strong, silent act to cover up his real or imagined deficiencies. That's a reassuring role for him, since it is both the very stereotype of *male* behavior and a good way to avoid exposing insecurities, fears, or doubts about himself that might diminish him as a man in your eyes.

A Fear of Being Criticized or Controlled

Because men often think of women as being the experts on emotions—and themselves as the amateurs—your lover may worry that you'd find something *wrong* with his feelings, and tell him that his most private emotions are stupid, weird, or inappropriate. He may also feel that telling you too much about himself would make him vulnerable, possibly because he's been hurt in the past by a parent, friend, or lover who found out something about him and used it as a weapon against him. Like those primitive peoples who believe that their soul will be stolen if somebody takes their photograph, he could fear that if you knew his secret, you'd control his innermost self.

Power Plays

Conversely, your man may feel that the less you know about him—and the more he knows about you—the more dominant he'll be in the relationship, since knowledge is a form of power. By refusing to share his troubles with you (which typically is the style of communication favored by women), he's saying, "I'm superior to you, because you have problems, and I have solutions." This tactic appeals both to men who are extremely competitive (and worry that you'll somehow outdo them if they give you even a small psychological edge) and those who feel very insecure (and hope you won't notice that there are some chinks in their armor—emotions that trouble them just as much as the ones you've revealed).

Sexual Secrets

The most intimate secret of all is an erotic inclination that's unusual, even alarming. Ashley, for example, still shudders when she talks about the lover who kept his briefcase locked. "After a while, that black leather case almost seemed alive—it cast a shadow over any room it was in, and pulled my eyes toward it. One day he went out for bagels, and I spotted a small key in a pile of coins on his night table. It was as if I had the key to understanding him, and I opened the case. My first reaction was disappointment, since it was full of files, but then I noticed that each was labeled with a woman's name.

"I opened the first one, and found pages and pages of notes—in this weird little writing—that described, in the most intimate detail imaginable, every time he'd had sex with this woman and how he rated it. Then I saw a folder with *my* name on it, and learned he thought my butt was too big and graded me C+ in oral sex. I was dizzy, disgusted—and very, very frightened—and ran out of his house as fast as I could. I'm sure he figured out what happened because he never called again, thank God!"

Sometimes a man's sexual secret is so disturbing to him that he even hides it from himself, and spends years denying his covert attraction to other men—or a yearning that's even more taboo. One woman was devastated when her husband of six years, who was the father of their three-year-old, announced he wanted a divorce—so he could have a sex-change operation, and experience life as a woman.

Anxieties About Love

Finally, what he may be hiding from is a richer relationship with you. He may be guarding his emotions to *avoid* intimacy—either out of fear, or because he doesn't love you. His secret could be that he's hanging on to you for sex, nurture, or money; or that what he really wants isn't necessarily you, but just the status of having a girlfriend to impress his friends or family, or get even with a woman who rejected him. It's also possible he's holding off for now because he's not emotionally ready to commit to a future with you, and wants to limit his involvement.

Four Reasons He's Reluctant to State the Facts

Childhood Traumas

A key reason why he might be reluctant to dwell on the past is that it's too painful, as Nan finally realized when her ultracontrolled lover got very drunk one night. "Bob had never said a word about his childhood to me, but at this party, he suddenly started sobbing hysterically and told everyone in the room how horribly his father had abused him when he was growing up. His mother was dying of cancer, and his father began going out drinking every night, leaving Bob—who was only eight years old—to care for his mother. One night she abruptly got worse, and while he pounded on a neighbor's door, shouting for help, she died. When his father finally staggered home, drunk as usual, he beat Bob half to death—telling him he'd killed his mother.

"I was crying as hard as he was when he finished talking about years of beatings and accusations that followed his mother's death, but also felt overwhelmed by pity, horror, and even an odd sense of betrayal, because I felt that I'd spent four years dating a man who I never really knew," she says.

A Shady Past—or Present

Whether his crime is as trivial as stealing candy as a boy (and being *caught*!), or as serious as arrests for armed robbery, it's easy to see why your boyfriend keeps his lips firmly sealed. Wanda, for example, only discovered by a total accident that her lover of six months, a very talented artist, also had a prison record—for a series of bank holdups. Your lover's crimes may not be entirely in the past either. When police burst into her boyfriend's home at dawn—catching Sue and her sweetheart naked, in bed—she realized he hadn't entirely misled her when he claimed the mysterious phone calls he made in the bathroom were for "business"; he'd just neglected to explain that he was in the *cocaine* business.

Secret Infidelities

It could also be crimes of passion that your bad boy is covering up—especially if he's suddenly discovered a need for late nights "at the office," spruced up his wardrobe, or taken up new hobbies that don't include you. And don't necessarily assume it's *girls* he's out with: One woman felt reassured to learn that her lover spent his nights out with a male friend, until the day that he confessed that his alleged "buddy" was actually his gay lover, and left her.

Another woman was married for years, and had two children with her husband, before she discovered he was all *too* heterosexual. He had been conducting not one, but two long-standing love affairs with other women, and had children with each of them.

Hidden Addictions

Perhaps your man isn't going out drinking with good-looking girls—or boys—he's just drinking. Many addicts are masters of denial, and may be so convincing that you also overlook how compulsive their drinking, drug use, or gambling really is. Or they may fool you by limiting their habit to occasional binges. Lucille, for example, was under the illusion that her boyfriend was accident-prone, since he'd sometimes vanish for a week or two, then return with mysterious injuries. He couldn't explain to her how he'd gotten hurt, but he vaguely remembered that the evening began with him walking into a cocktail bar.

Seductive Secrets

What is the hidden attraction that an enigmatic male holds for you? The answer lies not in *his* secrets, but in *yours*. Before you protest that you are the most open person imaginable, and have told absolutely everyone you know about your abortion, that kinky ménage à trois you had in college, the time you got caught shoplifting, or some other shameful episode in your past, think back to your childhood, and what secrets your family guarded from the world—or maybe even from you. Did you used to stealthily search your dad's pockets when no one was around? Undoubtedly you were looking for more than loose change. . . .

Perhaps an atmosphere of mystery feels familiar to you because you grew up in a home where you suspected something significant was being hidden from you. Marianne, for example, says she always "knew" in her heart that the parents who raised her weren't her biological parents, but ran up against a brick wall of denial whenever she asked about it. It was not until she was twenty-six, and both her parents had died, that she found the answer she'd been searching for—adoption papers with the names of her *real* mother and father. "Later I tracked them down, and now when I look in a mirror, I finally know who's looking back at me."

As a child, Julia remembers feeling like "a junior Nancy Drew, because I was constantly trying to find a clue as to what was going on with my parents. When I was about ten, they started closing the door to their bedroom, and arguing a lot, but I couldn't quite make out the words. A few years later, they split up, and never told me why. I still don't know what happened, but I think my mother might have had an affair my father found out about."

While some parents conceal secrets from their children, others enlist them in a conspiracy against their spouse. Whenever Lizabet thinks about her father, she can hear him whispering seductively to her, "Don't tell Mommy," after he took her to a racetrack with him, or bought her an expensive dinner. "I always felt that he liked me better than Mommy," she says. "It was almost like being his secret mistress, except that he never touched me sexually." For many young girls, such behavior fuels their most forbidden fantasy: our childhood desire to displace our mother and marry our father.

The most toxic family secret of all is abuse—either physical, sexual, or psychological—by a parent who forced you to keep quiet about it. Because you were made to feel like an accomplice in your own mistreatment, you may unconsciously repeat this pattern in your adult relationships by helping your partners avoid exposing secrets that may be painful or threatening to you. Instead, you feel it is safer *not* to know what a man you love may be hiding.

Even if they were not abused as children, almost all women who get involved with a secretive man *collude* with him to some degree—because on some level they don't want to know the truth, especially if they suspect he's covering up infidelities, an addiction, bisexuality, or a shady past. As long as their man of mystery keeps those disturbing revelations to himself, they're satisfied. Or you might not want to admit your lover is imperfect in some other way, so you make a covert bargain with him: "I'll accept your flaws, as long as you don't tell me what they are."

Some women are so determined to remain in the dark that they adamantly "overlook" even the most obvious clues that their lover is deceiving them. When Marie-Chantal emigrated to the United States from her native France last year, she exuded Parisian sophistication in every way but one. When it came to amour with a charming stranger she met on a California beach, she developed a sudden blind spot, and never questioned his improbable excuse for not telling her his number: He lived with his sister, who didn't let him use the phone. Nor did she find it odd that he never introduced her to his family or *anybody* he knew—she assumed he preferred to be with her.

When friends suggested a more likely scenario—that he had a wife—she was indignant. How could they say such a thing when he had promised to marry *her*? True, he'd said that three weeks ago, after learning she was pregnant with his child, and hadn't done a thing about arranging a wedding since, but he would, she doggedly insisted—as soon as he took care of various business matters and located an affordable apartment for them. Eight weeks later, she was still parroting his flimsy excuses for delaying their trip to the altar—right up to the minute that Federal Express delivered an envelope from him. Inside was a one-way ticket back to Paris, and a two-word note: "I'm sorry."

Other times, ironically enough, you and your lover may be attracted to one another because you share the *same* secret. You both prefer having a veil of mystery between you because each of you has a potent reason to hide from intimacy, such as being hurt in your previous love affairs, or childhood insecurities that make you terrified to expose your inner soul and risk rejection. That's why he keeps his mysteries locked up—and why you're so hesitant to use the key he left so temptingly in view. By protecting his secret, what you're actually protecting is your own: You don't feel lovable. So you prefer mystery to the pain of discovering that he doesn't love you.

Can You Live Happily Ever After?

Still trembling, Bluebeard's wife swung the closet door open. The windowless room was as black as night, and bitterly cold. As she stepped through the doorway, the dank air swirled around her, and she felt bony fingers pulling and pushing her deeper inside. Her eyes adjusted to the darkness and she could now see that she was surrounded by the ghosts of Bluebeard's previous lovers, who had mysteriously disappeared. Their blood-curdling groans terrified her as each phantom wailed of the horrors that Bluebeard had subjected her to. Deafened by the ghastly screams, the wife lifted her hands to cover her ears—and dropped the key. She picked it up and ran from the room, bolting the door behind.

As she stood gasping in the hall, she saw that the key now had a bloodred spot on it. She scrubbed at the stain frantically, but as she rubbed, Bluebeard burst into the room and snatched the keys. "How did blood get on this key?" he asked in a terrible voice. "I don't know," she said, turning pale with fear. "Since you dared to spy on me," he yelled, seizing her by the shoulders, "you must join the other ladies in my closet who betrayed my trust!" Tearfully, his wife threw herself at Bluebeard's feet and begged his forgiveness, promising never to open his closet again. But hard-heartedly, he refused. At this, she wrenched free from his grasp, and fled.

Will your fairy tale end as tragically? Not if your lover is willing to perform a heroic task to win his fair princess—you—by summoning up the courage to confront the psychological ghosts that hover around his secret, and *voluntarily* open his cupboard door to you. That may be more daunting for him than you imagine, since the mysteries of his soul may be mostly unconscious (meaning that he's even hidden them from *himself*). What's working in your favor, however, is that on some level he does want you to know the truth about him. That's why he keeps calling your attention to what he's hiding—by tossing out tantalizing hints from time to time, or "accidentally" leaving an intriguing little key out on the table.

Try these tactics to encourage him to open up:

Face the Secret in Yourself

By delving deeper into your own inner world, you may also gain new insights into his, since there's often an uncanny fit between the secrets lovers hug to themselves—as in the story of Bluebeard, where his dark fear was that no woman would ever want him, and his wife's secret was that she didn't love him, just his money.

Create an Atmosphere of Acceptance

Subtly reassure him that you wouldn't abandon him. Let him know that you love him and would try to understand—or help solve—the problem that's burdening him. Also tell him that it's worse *not* knowing, since that is what would be more likely to drive you away.

Be Alert for Clues, but Don't Actually Snoop

Remember that trust is a *major* issue with this man, so he may leave his diary or the key to his locked closet out as a test. Besides, stealing the information you want gives you his secret in reverse, since you're in a poor position to confront him with a love letter you found as you rummaged through his underwear drawer. If you do, it's almost certainly the death knell for the romance, as it was for Bluebeard and his wife, which is why you should save snooping as an absolute last resort. If you're ready to walk away anyway, finding a phone number for his parole officer in his Rolodex could be just the impetus you need to speed you on your way.

If, on the other hand, he drops an intriguing hint, as Donald did when he made an odd comment about "the horror show with Linda" to his new girlfriend, by all means follow up. After some not too subtle nudging, she's now learned all about Linda and her alleged crimes of the heart against Donald.

Reward Him When He Reveals Himself

Since confidences don't come easily to him, even a tiny revelation, like that he worries about how well he's doing at work, could make him feel vulnerable. Be an empathetic listener, and resist the temptation to offer your advice or tell him how he *should* feel, either of which could sound like put-downs, as you're implying there's something wrong with how he *does* feel. Instead, look for subtle ways to be loving to him, so he'll start to associate revealing things about himself with being treated compassionately when he feels most vulnerable. You might offer to take him out to dinner that night, or share an intriguing secret of your own—such as a sex fantasy he might be eager to act out with you! Positively reinforcing each of his revelations will cause him to open up more and more in spite of himself.

Share Insights You Have About Him Sparingly

Since secretive men hate to be analyzed, avoid pressing his buttons too hard—even if you think you've figured out where he's going wrong and want to offer a *helpful* insight. One woman noticed that after he lost his job, her boyfriend began to spend virtually every waking moment at Alcoholics Anonymous meetings—even though he hadn't had a drink for ten years. When she suggested he'd grown overly involved with helping other people with their problems to avoid facing his own, he went ballistic and shouted, "If you're saying I'm hiding out at AA, you're dead wrong!" Since then, he's refused to discuss the topic at all, but he did cut back on AA attendance and found a new job.

Never Use His Revelations Against Him

Even if his disclosure comes at an awkward time, such as when you're having a fight, don't use it as a weapon against him—or he'll barricade the door to more important secrets even tighter. Christine was storming around the house after a spat with her lover when he remarked that she reminded him of his mother, who also fumed around the home when he'd displeased her as a boy—or sometimes even walked out and left him alone for hours. Later, when Christine wasn't angry any more, she said calmly, "I'm glad you told me about your mother, and I'll try to control myself more in the future."

Prove that you're trustworthy by not telling his secrets to anyone else—even your best friend. For him, your opening his closet door to others would be the cruelest betrayal of all.

12

THE DRAMATIC DAREDEVIL

In a faraway land, there once lived a poor boy named Aladdin. One day as he was playing outside the one-room hut he and his mother shared, a stranger asked if he were the son of Mustapha, the tailor. "I am," the boy told him, "but my father died when I was very young."

"I am your uncle, your father's brother. You look just like him," said the stranger. He kissed Aladdin and promised to show him a wonderful thing, so the boy boldly set off with the man, who was actually an evil sorcerer. After many miles, the false uncle built a fire, and threw magic powders into it. The earth trembled, and a hole opened with stairs leading downward.

"Go down," the man commanded, "but do not touch anything until you pass through the doors at the bottom, or you'll die. The path will lead you to an orchard, in whose midst you'll see an oil lamp burning. Put out the lamp and bring it to me." Then the sorcerer gave him a ring from his finger and claimed that no harm would come to him.

Aladdin was soon back at the staircase with the lamp and some fruit he'd picked for his mother. The sorcerer, who knew *the lamp would make him the most powerful man alive, was waiting impatiently. "Quick, let me have the lamp, and I'll help you up," he said, planning to kill Aladdin when he obeyed. But the boy refused to hand the lamp to him, because he'd tucked it safely in his pants, underneath the fruit. The sorcerer cursed and the rocks closed above Aladdin's head.*

As he clawed at the rocks, he accidentally rubbed the ring the sorcerer had given him. A large figure emerged and said, "I am the Genie of the Ring. What is your wish?"

"I wish I were back home," Aladdin said, and instantly found himself there.

He told his mother of his adventure and showed her the lamp and the fruits, which actually were precious jewels. When he asked for food, his mother sadly answered that there was none. "I'll sell the lamp and buy some," she said. As it was very dirty, she rubbed the lamp so its worth would rise. Smoke poured from the spout in the form of a huge man. "I am the Genie of the Lamp," he said. "What is your wish?"

She fainted in fright, but Aladdin snatched the lamp and said, "Fetch us food." The Genie carefully stepped over her, and with a dramatic gesture, conjured up a flying carpet laden with many silver plates of delicacies. Aladdin patted his mother's cheek until she came to and joined him on the carpet for a feast.

"Whenever you need me, rub the lamp," the Genie said as he disappeared into the spout.

A few years later, the sultan ordered everyone to stay inside as his daughter went to the bath. Aladdin was consumed by a desire to see the princess, who was always veiled from head to toe, in the nude, and—naughty boy that he was!—hid behind a door in the bath where he'd spied on his mother more than once. After one peek at the lovely princess, he fell in love.

Aladdin's mother laughed when he told her to take the jeweled fruit to the sultan and convey a marriage proposal to his daughter, but she did as he asked. The sultan was enchanted by the gift, and promised to set a wedding date. But weeks later, Aladdin learned the princess was to be married that very night— to the vizier's son instead!

Asking his mother not to look, he got out his lamp and gave it a good rub. "Bring me the newly married couple as soon as they get into bed," he commanded the Genie. After they were brought to him, he ordered that the groom be put outside in the cold until dawn and then boldly climbed into bed with the princess. . . .

Is life with your fearless and flamboyant lover like careening down the road at a hundred miles an hour—a wild, unpredictable trip that is both terrifying and tantalizing? Coco compares her boyfriend to a carnival ride she loved—and hated—as a child. "You rode up and down on a magic carpet of canvas with rollers under it which tossed you all over the place. By the end, I'd be scraped up and bruised, and swear never to go on it again, but the next time we went to the carnival, I couldn't wait to get on the ride, which is exactly what happens with Michael. Every time I say I'm through with him, a few days later I miss the exciting, out-of-control feeling he gives me, and find myself back on that bumpy magic carpet ride again."

Whether it is a purely emotional roller coaster as with Coco's man—a rock singer who provokes melodramatic scenes and multiple breakups, followed by gloriously passionate reconciliations—or a physical one, like Phyllis's up-and-down love affair with a thrill seeker who is never happier than when he's hurtling off a cliff on his hang glider, flirting with danger can seem strangely seductive.

But what's the hidden hook that high adventure, or high drama, holds for these men, and why do we let ourselves be lured into high-risk romances with them? Here's a look at dramatic daredevils, and the reckless passions they can unleash in us.

His Telltale Traits

Like Aladdin, these free spirits are equally fearless as they make a death-defying plunge into the depths of the earth or boldly bed a shy princess. Their daring feats and flair for the dramatic give them an unmistakable and often very *erotic* aura of excitement that makes it hard for even the most cautious of women to resist a ride on their magic carpet.

To decide if *your* partner qualifies as one of these alluring adventurers, test him on these thrill-seeking traits:

Even as a Boy, He Was Addicted to Rebellious Excitement

Your man has never been one to play it safe. As a child, he was more likely to escape boredom by skateboarding down the freeway or by recklessly riding after the fire engine on his bike to see the blaze than by immersing himself in a good book. He may have some hair-raising boyhood exploits he loves to recount with great drama—perhaps he was almost arrested for spray-painting graffiti in the schoolyard or breaking into a deserted house that was supposedly haunted, or has a sexy scar on his thigh from tumbling out of a tree during a hurricane. Like Rosemary's boyfriend, he may have been a regular at the local emergency room after some adventures went sadly awry—but didn't hesitate to risk life and limb again the second he got the stitches out, or the cast off.

Early in life, your partner discovered that adventure can be *addictive*, partly because taking physical risks triggers a release of powerful brain chemicals that produce a delicious natural *high*. Researchers have also discovered an intriguing side effect of thrill seeking: sexual arousal. Teenage boys, for example, often get erections from scary activities like leaning over the edge of a cliff or fleeing from police. Risk has an erotic side for all of us, since making love and reacting to danger arouse us in similar ways: Our senses are greatly heightened, and our bodies flush with excitement as the experience builds to a climactic peak that's followed by exhilaration and a release of tension. It's no wonder your man flirts with danger—it's the ultimate *aphrodisiac*!

He Turns Ordinary Events into Adventures

Even if he's just going out for a sandwich or taking his clothes to the cleaners, an Aladdin will devise little ways to inject drama into these routine chores. He'll come back with a colorful story about how he took a shortcut down a dark alley, encountered a fascinating stranger, or discovered an odd little shop along the way. Nor does he follow a predictable routine—he may lounge in bed until noon one day, then get up at dawn the next to ride his mountain bike down a dangerous trail that he's just heard about. If he can avoid it, he'll never go to work the same way twice—he's always looking for interesting new routes, or trying to set a new speed record. Don't expect him to hold a nine-to-five job either—that's much too mundane for an adventure lover like your Aladdin!

Along with a constant craving for novelty, your mate also has an almost pathological dread of boredom. He likes to keep all his senses stimulated to near overload—he relishes loud music, exotic or spicy foods, bright colors, sensual fabrics and fragrances, and sexy massages. There is nothing subtle about his tastes—for him, the bolder, the better. He is quick to embrace the latest trend—whether it's a new dance, a risky sport, or even an illicit drug—and lives by the motto "I'll try anything once."

There's a Very Theatrical Quality to His Looks, Mannerisms, or Style of Dress

Isabel's boyfriend definitely doesn't believe in blending in with the crowd, she says. "I'll never forget when he came to see me at the very conservative bank where I work. We were all in pin-striped suits, when he showed up in oversized jeans that hung down to expose his underwear! I thought I'd die, I was so humiliated."

Dressing in a defiant or offbeat way isn't an occasional whim for a dramatic daredevil, it's his consistent pattern. Your lover uses his physical appearance to draw attention to himself—he will show up at a casual party in a black velvet cape and top hat, or a formal one in a zoot suit from the 1940s and sneakers. He adores clothes that make a memorable statement—it could be a motorcycle jacket he never takes off or a T-shirt reading SCREW YOU! Your man may adopt a distinctive hairstyle—like blond dreadlocks, or a crew cut with a lightning bolt shaved into it—or have exaggerated, stagy gestures he uses to dramatize his every utterance.

His Emotions Are Opulent and Exaggerated

Along with all of his theatrical flourishes and poses, your boyfriend may be almost embarrassingly emotional. He may fling his arms around some casual acquaintance and hail that person as a dear friend, or be moved to tears at only mildly sentimental moments. He'll express his feelings in the most melodramatic style. In a situation that might make you slightly annoyed, he will swear he is ready to tear his hair out—and may grab a handful of his tresses to illustrate what he means. Or, if you are a bit disappointed by something, your lover is sure to be utterly devastated, heartbroken, wounded to the quick—or so he'll claim as he clutches his chest in anguish.

What you'll quickly notice about your boyfriend is that he'll abruptly go from one seemingly deep emotion to another, making you feel like you're on a bumpy magic carpet ride. You may suspect he bounces from one emotional extreme to its exact opposite so easily because he's faking his feelings, but actually his passions aren't just pretense. The reason they flicker so briefly is that they're extremely shallow, and easily blown out by a gust of opposing feelings.

He Makes You Believe the Relationship Is More Intimate Than It Actually Is

It's easy to be taken in by the apparent potency of an Aladdin's feelings about you. Ginny, for example, says she once went to bed with one of these men an hour after meeting him. "I was on a bus, fumbling for exact change, when he stepped up to me and produced the right coins with a charming flourish. He was very good-looking, so when he started telling me that he'd fallen in love with me at first sight, I was all too happy to believe it. Six bus stops later, he'd convinced me to get off with him and go to a hotel.

"The sex was incredible, beyond anything I'd ever imagined—and since he kept telling me I was the love of his life, I thought it was the start of a glorious relationship. He made me feel that he'd never leave my side, but the next morning, he disappeared as dramatically as he'd come into my life, and gave me an out-of-town phone number that turned out to be a phony. I never saw him again."

Most of these bad boys aren't as bad as that, but be warned: Though your partner may promise his eternal love, "always" doesn't necessarily mean "forever" to a melodramatic male. It is just one of those strong, emotional expressions that comes so easily to his lips. At heart, your partner is an actor, so if the role he seems to be playing is Romeo to your Juliet, remember that your tale may end as *tragically*.

He's Fascinated by Romantic Challenges

Not only does your partner like testing the limits of his allure with a woman who is hard to get, but he may consider her even more appealing if she's involved with someone else. Secretly, he's intrigued by a love triangle, where he has to compete with another man for his lady's affections, as Aladdin does with the vizier's son (and later with the sorcerer). He's happy if he beats out a romantic rival to get you—or overcomes your initial reluctance—because winning you is proof of his prowess. A woman is a more dangerous challenge to him than any of his other feats.

He May Be Inappropriately Provocative or Sexually Seductive

Not surprising, a man who sees himself as a bold adventurer on the playing fields of life is not going to be shy about expressing himself sexually. Within minutes of meeting you, he may tell you that he'd love to "fuck your panties off"—a come-on you'd find hopelessly crude from any other man, but strangely *intriguing* when you hear it from him. There's a sultry air about him that makes you suspect he has probably fucked a lot of women's panties off—and is very, very good at it. Or he may be more subtle and just caress your fingers with his, or let his eyes send scorchingly sexy messages of desire.

Like those male strippers who know exactly how to arouse women without alarming them, your Aladdin goes right to the *edge* of being offensively sexual. He's likely to be very good-looking, and to dress in an overtly erotic way, with black leather jeans that ride low on his hips or a soft silk shirt you long to stroke. His provocative persona makes him magnetic to women, but a threat to other men, who understandably don't want him around *their* girlfriends (. . . in case you're wondering why he has so few male friends).

He Uses His Penis as a Magic Lamp to Grant Your Wishes—and His Own

Ever since your lover was a little boy, he's felt there is something magical about being male, because his upbringing has convinced him that having a penis gives him mysterious power over women, starting with his mother. It didn't take him long to find out that *rubbing* it produced marvelous thrills, which he associated with the daredevil exploits he found so sexually arousing as a teenager. That persuaded him his penis could perform great feats: Not only did it throb with pleasurable excitement when he defeated danger, but it gave him an aura of dangerous sexuality that helped him win women away from other men.

Like Aladdin, who lay in bed and rubbed his magic lamp to get everything he needed to seduce the sultan's daughter, your partner relies on the magic powers of his penis to captivate and keep you. By summoning his erotic genie, he can grant your wishes by giving you the best sex that you've ever had—a real magic carpet ride to rapture!

Flirting with Danger

What's the secret seduction that thrill seeking holds for your lover? Is he just addicted to the erotic carpet ride of adventure, or does he have a secret *death* wish? Actually, it's a bit of both: What draws him to daredevil feats is the intriguing mix of pleasure and potential *punishment* they offer. Putting himself at risk gives him exactly what his unconscious craves: sexual arousal that he may have to pay for with pain.

One man, for example, had an extremely revealing response

when an interviewer asked what drew him to his extraordinarily hazardous profession: wrestling alligators. He said he was intrigued when he saw a gruesome spectacle that would have scared away any sane soul: watching another man *lose* a battle with one of these beasts and get four of his fingers bitten off. Sounding strangely *disappointed* at having escaped a similar fate—at least so far—he added he's begun to find wrestling seven-foot alligators a bit dull, and despite the vehement objections of his fiancée, intends to switch to larger and more potentially lethal *crocodiles*.

An attraction to danger usually originates in a childhood like Aladdin's, where the future daredevil became *unusually* close to his mother because his father was physically or psychologically absent. Just as he reached the age when all young boys dream about seducing their mother, she rubbed his fantasies as Aladdin's mother did with his "dirty" magic lamp by turning him into a substitute for her missing husband. While she may not have been sexually *abusive*, her flirty manner as she hugged him tight and called him her little man created a household charged with an extremely inappropriate erotic tension.

Not only is this where your lover's sometimes inappropriately provocative or sexually seductive behavior stems from—it's how he was *taught* to relate to women—but it sparked his fascination with danger. He still feels guilty about the forbidden thrills he felt around his mother—as he peeked through the bathroom door she often left invitingly ajar as she took her bath, or looked at her bare breast as she leaned over his bed in her low-cut nightie—and believes he should be penalized for them.

Like Aladdin, your boyfriend may still be a bit of a voyeur at heart—and will delight in watching you undress, or better still, do a sexy striptease for him! (True voyeurism, incidentally, involves spying on couples who are having sex or on nude women, especially ones who resemble the man's mother. It's a sexual compulsion that often emerges at an unusually early age—about fifty percent of voyeurs start before age fifteen. The vast majority also enjoy normal sexual activities with their girlfriend or wife, but gain secret gratification from spying on unsuspecting strangers.)

The crime your lover accuses himself of—and expects to atone for through his high-risk antics—is *collusion*. Unconsciously, he knows the seduction was not entirely one-sided: He played along with his mother's flirty games, just as Aladdin does as he takes out his magic lamp in his mother's presence and teasingly tells her not to look as he rubs it. What he fails to understand, however, is that as a helpless boy, he was actually his overly stimulating mother's *victim*, not her willing accomplice.

What he secretly expects—and fears—is that an evil sorcerer (or angry father) will someday appear, intent on revenge, and take his magic lamp away. It's this childhood anxiety that a daredevil is acting out as he climbs in the pit to wrestle an alligator that may bite his fingers—or his penis—off. Not only is he driven to confront his deepest dread by repeatedly putting his "extremity" into the jaws of danger, but if nothing too terrible happens, he may up the ante and challenge a ferocious crocodile. It's a provocative *dare* to the evil sorcerer who looms so large in his mind.

Much the same motivations underlie your lover's attraction to romantic triangles—they're an even bolder way of taunting the sorcerer. Whenever he challenges another man—by trying to steal his woman—he is symbolically stealing the lamp away from its original owner, his father. That's exactly what he thinks he did as a child, when he wooed his mother in his imagination, and on some level, won her. Each time he puts his lamp on the line with some romantic rival, he re-creates his role in this forbidden contest, and offers his "father" an opportunity to get the ultimate revenge—if he can.

The greater your lover's sexual guilt, the more *dangerous* his exploits are likely to be. If he only blames himself a little, he may limit himself to more minor risks, as Emily's lover does. "He considers himself a daredevil when he runs a red light at night or does a back flip off the high diving board, but he never does anything that would put his safety in real jeopardy." Sasha's sweetheart, on the other hand, has yet to discover a sport he considers too risky—whether it's skydiving, free soloing up cliffs (climbs with no protective gear whatsoever), or bungee jumping.

Regardless of whether your boyfriend wrestles alligators or just runs red lights, the allure is much the same. Every time he risks the razor's edge, it is like playing Russian roulette for a stake he feels fits his childhood crime. If he escapes unscathed, it is an exhilarating release of his bottled-up anxiety and guilt. As the genie pours out of the magic lamp of his penis, he's powerfully reassured that if he feels this good, what he did as a child couldn't have been all *that* bad.

All too soon, however, the disturbing tensions return, and so does a gnawing, almost desperate need to put himself at risk again. Soon your lover is strapping on his hang glider and standing at the edge of the cliff. As he looks longingly into the terrifying abyss that calls so temptingly to him, he adjusts his wings, and wonders if he has the right stuff to survive one more ride. . . .

Playing with Fire

April says that the very trait that drew her to her lover, a motorcycle stunt rider, is now what most disturbs her about him—his relentless craving for kicks. "The first time I ever saw him, he was jumping through a ring of fire on his motorcycle. My pulse was pounding a million miles per hour, and I was even more excited when a friend introduced me to him after the show. It was lust at first sight—because I looked at him taking off his scorched fireproof suit, and thought he was hot, hot, hot!"

When they started dating, she thrived on the vicarious thrills she felt every time he revved up his engine and roared through the flames, April remembers. "It was almost as if I was on the back of the bike, being singed by the same heat. But now that I've fallen in love with him, this fantasy is more of a nightmare, because when I think of him risking it all on one wild leap, as the crowd cheers him on, it isn't exciting—it's scary. I'm getting to be a nervous wreck from living in constant terror that he'll be hurt—or killed. Even though I've begged him to stop, he won't."

As April has discovered, daredevils hold a complex attraction for us—they're fascinating, frightening, and ultimately frustrating. Often, they're easiest to admire from afar, just as we would a remote bonfire that sends seductive sparks our way, inflaming us to lusty infatuation. Watching from a safe distance as he exposes himself to risks we wouldn't *dare* take ourselves has a voyeuristic attraction that's a mirror image of his fascination with forbidden thrills. There's a part of him that secretly wants to fall in the fire and be punished, and a part of us that would secretly love to see it happen. After all, if jumping through flames was safe, who would pay to watch?

A man who goes to physical, emotional, and erotic extremes can be especially intriguing if you were a cautious child, or like the sultan's daughter, had overprotective parents who dressed you in a (psychological) veil to keep you sheltered from the world—and its sexual dangers. To escape from the smothering cocoon of their concern, you might turn to a daring lover who gives you permission to push past the limits that your parents imposed on you. It's an exhilarating exploit to finally defy them—and fly away to freedom on Aladdin's enchanted carpet.

Just how far into risk you're willing to ride with your lover depends on how powerful your need to rebel is. For some of us, it may be adventure enough to boldly rub his magic penis and command it to make all of our naughty sexual wishes come true. His erotic genie will gladly rise to the occasion and act out your fantasies with great melodramatic abandon. So adept is an Aladdin at giving you the ultimate in erotic thrills that it is easy to get sexually *addicted* to him. The high you get in bed with him might feel like no high you've ever had—in fact, you're very likely to mistake it for *love*, when it's really the magic of his lamp that you crave.

For other women, a swashbuckling sweetheart can arouse a lust for adventure that extends far beyond the bedroom. Felicity, for example, says her boyfriend talked her into flying a glider plane even though she is so terrified of heights she can't stand to look out a seventh-floor window. "When we got aboard this little plane, which looked like it was made out of styrofoam and Scotch tape, with the instructor, I thought I must be out of my mind. As the ground crew attached the plane to a truck for takeoff—these ultralight planes have no engines, and just float on hot air currents—I held my boyfriend's hand so tightly that I actually left a mark—that's how frightened I was.

"Once we got aloft, the plane was so silent it was eerie—not a sound except the breeze blowing gently across the wings. By the time the instructor told me to take the controls, I found I'd gone beyond my fear, and was unexpectedly thrilled. There I was at the helm of a plane, flying it through the sky—all by myself! I felt like the bravest person on earth!"

Even if you do let your boyfriend persuade you to try bungee jumping or piloting a glider plane, you could still be playing it safe in another way. Very often, a woman who is drawn to a daring lover is reluctant to risk her heart, and considers a relationship that's filled with melodramatic scenes, spine-tingling excitement, and flashy sex a reasonably convincing substitute for the intimacy she finds so terrifying. For her, a melodramatic madcap is like a scary fun house at the county fair: a great source of manufactured thrills at a relatively cheap price.

The problem, as April discovered with her fire-jumping lover, is that there's a hidden danger to dating a daredevil: Despite all your precautions, you may still get *burned*, by love. Suddenly you may hear an echo of your overprotective parents in your own voice, as you start to worry over him, and implore him to stop taking the risks that once made him so irresistibly seductive to you. That's when you realize going on a magic carpet ride can be a lot *riskier* than you ever imagined!

Can You Live Happily Ever After?

After an ecstatic night in Aladdin's arms, the princess begged her father to annul her marriage to the vizier's son so she could be Aladdin's bride. The sultan was reluctant to marry his daughter to someone so poor and demanded a price for her that he thought no man could pay—forty basins full of gold and precious jewels.

With a vigorous rub of the lamp, Aladdin arranged for a parade of richly dressed servants to take his mother and the gold and gems to the palace. Amazed, the sultan told her to hasten home and tell her son he was awaited with open arms. Aladdin was in no hurry and bid the genie to prepare an aromatic bath, and bring costly clothing and a horse surpassing the sultan's.

When the sultan saw Aladdin in all his magnificence, he

wanted to have the wedding that very day. The young man put him off so he could command the genie to erect a palace for his princess far finer than the sultan's, since he could not take her to live in the hut he shared with his mother. The next day, he and his mother arrived on the flying carpet to claim his bride.

The evil sorcerer heard of Aladdin's good fortune, and came up with a wicked scheme. When he saw the young man out riding his horse, he stood outside the castle and called, "New lamps for old," until the princess looked out. Not knowing the value of Aladdin's lamp, she traded it for a new one. At the sorcerer's command, the genie took him, the palace, and the princess off to a foreign land.

The furious sultan ordered the executioner to cut off Aladdin's head unless he could produce the missing princess. He quickly summoned the Genie of the Ring, whose limited powers only let him take Aladdin home to the palace. Peeping through a window, he saw the sorcerer pull out the lamp and try to seduce the princess with its magic.

Aladdin commanded the Genie of the Ring to bring him a certain powder, then called to his wife after the sorcerer finally left the room in frustration. After a joyful reunion, he told her to put on her prettiest gown and receive the sorcerer with smiles. "Tell him you agree to be his wife and want to drink a toast in celebration."

She did as he said, and secretly put the powder in the sorcerer's cup after he poured the wine. The sorcerer started to kiss her, but she said, "Let's drink first, and then you can do what you will." As the sorcerer drained the cup, the life drained out of him. The princess let Aladdin in, and he took the magic lamp out of the sorcerer's pocket and gave it one last rub.

"Take the palace and all that is in it back to where we belong," he said. After they got home, he locked the lamp safely away just in case he ever needed its magic again. But Aladdin never did have to rub his lamp again because he and his princess had everything they could wish for in one another.

Can your lover really grant all of your wishes with his magic lamp, or is his flying carpet headed for a crash, with *you* aboard?

Here is how to take some of the risk out of romance with your bold adventurer.

Be Very Sure That You're Not Mistaking Lust for Love

It's hard to keep sex in its proper perspective with this guy—because he rubs you just the right way in bed. But even the most sublime sex won't keep you ecstatic forever if other, even more essential ingredients of intimacy are absent. Is he somebody you sincerely *respect* because of his honesty, compassion, and good character—a man who you'd be proud to spend your life with—or are you just going along for the addictively erotic ride he gives you?

Before you insist that your partner is much more than a magic penis to you, examine just how crucial a role his compulsive quest for excitement plays in your relationship. Could you be hooked on the voyeuristic thrill of watching him take death-defying risks or hearing his dramatic tales of high adventure? Remember that he'll act as if the relationship is more intimate than it really is, and that your own fear of falling in love may make you all too willing to accept his opulent sexuality or his flashy—but shallow—passions as evidence he cares deeply for you.

Don't Get So Carried Away on His Magic Carpet Ride That You Put Yourself at Risk

It is a *dangerous* mistake to throw caution to the wind just because your lover does. If you're too timid to tell him to put on the brakes when he is roaring down the highway at a recklessly unsafe speed, you may *literally* die of embarrassment. Instead of worrying about looking like a wimp when you say no to an unacceptable risk he urges you to take, realize that sometimes it is the boldest move of all, because it takes true courage to find your voice and let him know that you respect your life more than he does his own.

Similarly, don't expose yourself to sexual risks to give him, or yourself, a momentary thrill. Sure, sex may seem sexier to you if you play birth control roulette—but consider the consequences if you get *caught*. Every year so many women lose the gamble that, in many parts of the world, including the United States, unplanned pregnancy is actually more common than planned pregnancy. Would you really want to risk conceiving an unwanted child just for kicks? And is *any* edge of excitement worth forgoing the protection of having him wear a condom, when it puts you at risk for AIDS or other sexually transmitted diseases?

Be an Anchor for His Emotional Ups and Downs

As your lover flies wildly off on an adventure, or is being buffeted by one melodramatic mood after another like a kite riding through a hurricane, the best thing you can do for your relationship is to be a calm, *safe* landing pad he can return to when he needs to refuel. Because you aren't the volatile risk taker he is, your sane, sensible approach to life will be a quiet source of *strength* to him when he feels he is exhausted from his physical and emotional flights of fancy.

It's vital, however, to find a balance that's comfortable for you between being a party pooper who refuses to participate at all in his thrill-seeking activities, and putting yourself at risk with mad abandon. If you say no to every adventure, no matter how tiny, he'll consider you a deadweight—not an anchor—and may fly off to find a partner who takes more pleasure in his magic carpet.

Stay Away from Probing Questions or Criticism of His Mother

She's a hot button for your boyfriend in more ways than one, so it is better not to press him too hard about any issue connected with her. He's filled with unresolved tensions and ambivalence toward her, and may vent his explosive feelings on *you* should you stray too far into this danger zone. Like Aladdin, who wants his mother's approval of his every romantic move—and brings her with him when he goes to claim his bride—your man feels it's important for the two key women in his life to get along. Be nice—and very respectful—of his mom, but don't expect to get close to her. Not only is she apt to be just as volatile as he is, but she is extremely *possessive* of her little man.

Help Him to Kill the Evil Sorcerer

Until your lover makes peace with his father, he'll never overcome the secret death wish that underlies his love of danger. If his father is still alive, gently encourage him to reestablish a connection, so positive new memories can extinguish the exaggerated fears and fantasies that he now associates with him. Or, if his father is dead, he might reexamine his childhood in therapy, and explore why he's turned his father into an evil, larger-than-life sorcerer who is plotting to steal his magic lamp.

If he resists this idea—as many daredevils will, since they rarely consider their compulsive risk taking as much of a problem as you do—another tactic to try is getting him involved in other activities that make him feel good about himself, such as mastering a *safer* sport, completing his education, putting his dramatic talents to use in a theater group, or taking a bold business risk and starting his own company. As he starts to value his own life more, he'll realize how much he has to lose by putting himself in foolish danger to appease an evil sorcerer who only exists in his imagination.

Don't Ever Throw Away His Magic Lamp— or Trade It in for a New One!

Since your lover lives in constant dread that someone will try to take his penis—and believes that he owes everything that he has, including you, to its magic power—he's exquisitely sensitive to sexual rejections. Consider how Maxine's boyfriend reacted when she gently extricated herself from his ardent embrace at dawn because she had to rush off to an early meeting. "While we were kissing, I could feel that he had an erection, but since he gets one *every* morning, I pretended not to notice so that I could leave to deal with the pressures of work. That insult to his manhood provoked him not to call for a week—and I finally had to apologize!"

He counts on his sexual prowess to keep you, and will suffer agonies of jealousy should he see you flirting with another man. It is like he's lost his lamp to an evil sorcerer—his worst fear come true. He'll summon the erotic genie at his command to get you back, but once he does, he will make you pay for the pain that you've caused him—probably by leaving you to wait and worry as he flies away on some mad escapade.

Don't Expect Him to Give Up Flying Carpets and Other Thrills

While you may be able to talk him out of recklessly exposing himself to every risk that comes his way, your melodramatic lover will always be a daredevil at heart. If you ever try to force him to choose between you and danger, he can't help but opt for the irresistible lure of adventure. What you can—and *should*—do, however, is express concern about him without turning it into an ultimatum. When you feel he may be going over the top, try saying, "I can't help worrying about you because I care about you. Please take more precautions."

Though he may act angry if he thinks you're interfering with his risk taking, part of him appreciates your efforts to keep him out of harm's way. This loving concern about his safety is something he never got from his mother as a child, and may be what he secretly craves when he tells you about some crazy new kick he is thinking of trying. It could be a test to see if you care enough to put his needs first, as his overly seductive mother never did, and protect him from his most dangerous desires.

Be aware of your own ambivalence about his adventurous side. While one part of you may be trying to tame your Aladdin, another part may be eagerly egging him on to even more daring exploits. You secretly realize that if you ever did succeed in turning him into an obedient little lapdog, he'd lose the very trait that attracted you: his hot aura of high excitement.

Free-falling adventures with your dramatic daredevil are scary, but falling in love with him can be even scarier. You need to decide if his magic carpet ride is worth it—since these bad boys are not for the fainthearted!

13

THE PRINCE OF
DARKNESS

eep in the vaults below a desolate castle in Transylvania was the lordly tomb of Count Dracula, the undead prince of the vampires who had been spawned hundreds of years ago by a witch and her demon lover. Inside, the air was heavy with the sickly smell of death as the Count shoveled graveyard dirt and coffin fragments into a large wooden box in preparation of his journey to England. He planned to finish before sunrise, since daylight made even the most powerful vampire vulnerable. Like a slash of blood across his extraordinarily pale face, his red mouth formed a malevolent smile—baring his sharp teeth—as he thought about the fresh prey that awaited him across the water.

A large black bat circled overhead as Lucy Westenra sat outside under a full moon several nights later and told her best friend, Mina, about the three marriage proposals she'd gotten that day. "Why can't a girl marry all the men who want her, so she could always have someone to save her from her fears? I feel unworthy of any of them—John Seward, the brilliant doctor who runs the lunatic asylum down the road; Quincey Morris, the brave

American who has had so many adventures; and especially the Honorable Arthur Holmwood, who visits us so often and of whom Mamma is very fond. He is now to be my husband."

Much later that night, Mina awoke and was alarmed to see her old friend sleepwalking, a habit that Lucy shared with her father, who often appeared by her bed in a trancelike state when she was young. Not wanting to wake Lucy's mother, who had long been afflicted with so weak a heart that the slightest shock could kill her, Mina hurried out the door after Lucy, but lost sight of her in the mist.

Then a ray of moonlight penetrated the fog and illuminated the virginal white of Lucy's nightgown. She lay languidly on a seat by the graveyard as a black figure with pointed batlike ears, a white face, and red, gleaming eyes leaned over her. Her full lips were parted, and she was breathing in deep, excited gasps. "Lucy!" Mina screamed in fright. The tall black figure raised its head, gave an angry snarl, and ran off into the night, leaving Lucy moaning and shuddering, but apparently unhurt—except for two tiny puncture marks on her neck.

The next day, Lucy seemed oddly invigorated, and urged Mina to keep her nocturnal adventure secret, to avoid upsetting her mother. Mina agreed, but took the precaution of locking Lucy in her room at bedtime to keep her safe. Twice her friend tried to get out, then complained in her sleep when she couldn't. The following evening, she asked Mina to go on a stroll with her. When they got near the graveyard and saw a black figure seated alone, a dreamy look came over Lucy's face as she murmured, "His red eyes! His red lips!"

A strange sound from Lucy's room woke Mina later in the night. She unlocked the door, and found her friend asleep with her neck on the sill of the open window bathed in moonlight. A large bat sat next to her, which to Mina's mounting horror, cast no reflection at all on the mirrorlike surface of the glass. Its mouth was dripping with fresh blood, and its fiery red eyes gave Mina a malevolent stare that seemed to say, "You're next!"

Are you entranced by a lover who seems predatorily passionate? Lily is both fascinated and a little frightened by the intensity of her new boyfriend's ardor. "The first time we went out, he told me at the end of the evening he'd fallen madly in love with me, and had never felt this way about a woman before. As he compared us to the great love stories of all time, I kept thinking, 'What's wrong with this picture?' because it seemed too good to be true. But since I was still getting over a man who had made me miserable with his thoughtlessness and lack of affection, I was thrilled to have such a sexy, gorgeous guy so hot for me."

From the start, she noticed something that troubled her about her partner, she adds. "He gets irrationally jealous of every man that I know, even the pimple-faced assistant who answers the phone at work. There are also some guys from the office I sometimes have a drink or a meal with, but now I almost hate to get together with them, because I know Evan is sure to give me the third degree about each second I spend with them. You'd think we were having an orgy, not a couple of burgers and a beer!"

This complaint sounds all too familiar to Carla, who has had a series of obsessive lovers. One called ten times a day and appeared unexpectedly at her office just to check up on her, while another actually broke into her apartment, convinced she was with another man. (She wasn't; Carla was so soundly asleep that she didn't hear the doorbell.) Scarier still was the ex-cop with a nasty temper—and a gun—who stalked her for months after they broke up, she recalls. "He'd sit outside my apartment in his car all night long, making me feel as if I was under house arrest. I was afraid to go out on a date, or even go to visit my friends, for fear of provoking a confrontation with him."

Why didn't she get a court order? She just shrugs, as if to imply that she's a helpless victim of her own allure, the kind of woman who drives men crazy with desire for her. When she finally got tired of the ex-cop's alarming attentions, she moved to a new city—and on to a new lover who is every bit as possessive as his predecessors.

His Telltale Traits

Are you dating a Dracula, a man whose overpowering attraction to you has a dark side? These characteristics suggest that the man in your life might have the markings of an obsessive lover—or even a sex-starved *stalker.*

He Comes On Very Strong at the Start of Your Relationship and Seduces His Way into Your Life

Like Lily's boyfriend, your lover may immediately overwhelm you with apparent devotion, and tell you he's never loved anybody as much as he loves you, a line that most of us lap up—even if we're secretly skeptical of such an intense, almost instantaneous ardor. So mesmerizing can this exciting vision of ultimate passion be that we hesitate to shatter it by scrutinizing his motives too closely. We love the flattering mirror he holds up that makes us appear more alluring than we'd ever imagined, and ignore the inner uneasiness we feel when we realize it reflects nothing at all about him.

Since these men are masters of whirlwind courtship, it is easy to get drawn into a full-blown relationship before we quite know what's hit us. Jody, for example, says her first date with her lover lasted three *weeks.* "We were both on vacation when we met, so there was no reason for me to leave his side—not that I would have wanted to. He did everything in his power to keep me with him. First we went to a romantic café on the beach, and then he kept me out dancing until dawn. We talked for hours, then spent whole *days* in bed, interrupted by an occasional meal he'd whip up for me. He makes love like a dream—I felt as if I'd discovered sex for the first time!"

He's Irrationally Jealous

The fuel that ignites his fiery passions is an overpowering desire to make you totally his. Not only may your mate start pressing very early in the relationship for you to commit exclusively to him, but if you do, far from being reassured of your fidelity, he'll become *increasingly* possessive. At first, it might just seem like the usual lover's jealousy, but it often escalates to suspicion—or even paranoia—about even the most insignificant interactions between you and other men. Give the mailman a pleasant smile in the morning, and he may see it as a sexual come-on. If you have to stay late at work, he may think you're sleeping with your supervisor, and perhaps the company president as well.

In some cases, this obsessive jealousy can even inspire your Prince of Darkness to stalk you, and see if he can catch you with another man. One particularly paranoid art dealer found he couldn't keep as close a watch on his girlfriend as he'd like because he was so busy at work, so he recruited her next-door neighbors as his spies. Although they reported nothing unusual when he called every night to check on her activities, he decided they weren't keeping close enough tabs on her—and hired a private eye to follow her around.

Though He Expects—and Demands—That You'll Be Faithful, He Has Sex with Other Women

Like Dracula, who stares at Mina with lustful red eyes while he's in the midst of giving Lucy his love bite, your boyfriend wants to have a harem at his beck and call. To him, monogamy is a one-way arrangement—it keep you in line, but does nothing to check *his* erotic urges. Even though he gets insanely jealous if you look at another man too long or show up five minutes late for a date with him, he expects you to ignore his flagrant infidelities. For him, having lots of ladies waiting in the wings is like an insurance policy: If you escape his control, he knows he won't be left starved for sex, or thirsting for love, very long.

He's Desperate to Own You

Since it's vital to your partner that you be available any time he wants you, your needs and plans are decidedly secondary to his. Leona's boyfriend would love it if she sat by the phone twenty-four hours a day in case he gets the urge to call her, she says. "It used to drive him crazy that he often couldn't reach me at work because I'm in sales, and spend most of the day seeing customers at their offices. Last week, he came up with what he thought was the perfect solution—he gave me a beeper for my birthday."

Along with constantly wanting to know your whereabouts so he can call you, a dominating Dracula may also interrogate you about how you spent every second you were away from him. Especially if you get home late, or aren't in the place that he expected you to be, he may grill you for hours about whom you saw, where you went, and exactly what you did.

Some men take their desire to dominate a few steps further, and try to isolate you from the outside world. A lover like this may encourage you to quit your job and let him support you, then limit your access to money, transportation, and the outside world, especially your family and friends. Your partner may try to hide his true agenda by claiming he can't afford two cars, then taking possession of the only vehicle so you can't go out without his knowing about it. Or he may insist the phone bill is too high, and restrict how many calls you can make. What he actually wants is for you to surrender to his hypnotic power and become totally dependent upon him.

He's a Definite Sexist

Don't expect your lover to endorse women's liberation: He knows it's politically incorrect to say he would like to keep you barefoot, pregnant, and in the kitchen, but he does believe in traditional sex roles. He loves to know that you are at home in makeup, high heels, and sexy underwear awaiting his next command. To him, it's the natural order of life for men to rule, while women, in his opinion, are there to serve and obey him—and bring beer when he's watching football.

He's Emotionally Volatile, with a Hair-Trigger Temper

Are you often on edge around your partner because you never know when some trifling incident might set off his explosive rage? Kerry's boyfriend has such a low boiling point that he frequently gets in screaming fights with total strangers, she finds. "Yesterday was typical. We were coming back from seeing a romantic film, and he was in a terrific, loving mood—until another car cut in front of him as we pulled up to the tollbooth. He was absolutely furious, and even though I begged him not to, he jumped out of the car and started cursing the other driver out. I was terrified, thinking 'What if this guy has a gun?' Luckily, all he did was give my boyfriend the finger and roar off—but my whole night was ruined."

Your boyfriend's feelings about you can abruptly swing from love to hate, and back again—a pattern that's very characteristic of a passionately possessive man. There is a constant battle between devotion and hostility in his mind, and since his rage is so intense, hostility usually wins. He sees the world in black-and-white terms, with no shades of gray in between, so for him, everybody—including you—is either all good or all bad. One minute he may idealize you as the best thing that ever happened to him, and the next feel that you're worthless and put you down with ugly names or other verbal abuse. It doesn't take much provocation for him to see red. Dee's lover once woke her in the middle of the night because he was furious about something she'd said a *month* ago, and spent an hour ranting and raving about it until she broke down in tears.

There May Be a Physically Abusive Side to Him

At certain times, the anger that's constantly smoldering just below the surface in these men can erupt into an intense rage toward you that is potentially violent. This occurs when your Prince of Darkness fears he's losing control over you—or losing you altogether. During these sudden furies, some of them may puff themselves up in a very scary way and make intimidating threats like "I'll break your neck," then, after they calm down, say they didn't really mean them. Others will actually hurt you—especially when threats *fail*—with anything from a slap across the face to an angry shove to full-fledged battering. Your possessions can also become the target during one of these explosive outbursts, as he vents his rage by smashing every dish in the house, or trashing your car. The more vulnerable and helpless he feels inside, the more menacing he tries to appear.

He Acts Out Self-Damaging Impulses

Your partner's rage may at times be directed toward *himself*. Some obsessive lovers manipulate their partners through threats of suicide, or make self-destructive *gestures*, such as swallowing aspirin or sleeping pills just before their girlfriend is due to arrive at their apartment, or slashing their wrist superficially with a razor. Theo's wife, for example, says that she's all too familiar with bloody razors and empty pill bottles. "I feel as if I'm being bludgeoned into giving in to his every demand, but I'm also terrified to leave—for fear he'll finally *succeed* in what he's so often threatened, and actually kill himself."

More often, your partner hurts himself in less overtly suicidal ways. He may act out his self-loathing through reckless driving, out-of-control spending, heavy drinking or using illegal drugs, unsafe sex, or even episodes of binge eating. What sets off these self-damaging impulses is the same switch that makes him fly into a fury with you: an extreme sensitivity to real or imagined slights and rejections.

He Has a Strong Sexual Charisma, and Is Often Rather Rough in Bed

The trait that's most likely to draw you—and other women— to a voracious vampire is his intriguing blend of courtly, almost old-fashioned charm and potent animal magnetism. He's the type to hold the elevator door for you or pull out the chair for you at dinner, then take you in the bedroom and ravish you like a wild beast. He may also enjoy a "playful" use of erotic force—

restraining your wrists as he makes passionate love to you, or tossing you on the rug for some down-and-dirty sex.

Like Dracula, he has a ravenous, almost *violent* appetite for sex, and may delight in giving you love bites—either on your neck or all over your body! That's a form of erotic aggression many of us enjoy—we may wear his hickey as a badge of honor to show everyone that we're so sexy we drive our man wild with passion. It's a visible sign of his intense ardor that fills us with a slight self-consciousness, a mild shame even. We're ambivalent about it, unsure whether to cover up the evidence that we've indulged in animalistic sex, or to flaunt it. There's also a delicious threat inherent in the vivid red mark on our neck—it signals both danger and a lust that could spin alarmingly out of control.

From playful wrestling matches or lover's bites, however, sex with this man tends to grow increasingly rough as the relationship progresses. He may bruise your breasts with painful pinches, grab your hair as he climaxes, or force your head down to his penis for oral sex. One woman says her ex-husband would often announce in a domineering tone over dinner, "I expect sex tonight." Later, he'd skip all foreplay—even a kiss or two—and enter her forcefully. What was his wife's reaction to this brutality? "The sex was pretty good," she insists. "Imagine, even though we were married for years, he still couldn't stop himself from turning into an animal in bed," she says, smiling with a misplaced sense of pride.

His Ruling Passions

What's behind your partner's passionate need to dominate and erotically overpower women? One reason why he often seems so hot with rage is that he viewed his parents, like Dracula's, as two very powerful, *evil* figures when he was a boy. He may have grown up in a home where he was a victim of physical, psychological, or sexual cruelty—or watched his mother being maltreated by his father or other men. To your lover, his chronically angry, possibly abusive father seemed like a demon—a terrifying inhuman monster—while he blamed his mother for failing to protect him, and thought her "as cold as a witch's tit."

Most significantly, your vampire lover is acting out intense anger toward his mother because she abandoned him in some way when he was young, such as by giving him up for adoption, putting him in a foster home, neglecting him, or favoring another child over him. Intriguingly, O. J. Simpson's mother testified at his double murder trial that as a baby, he was literally replaced at her breast by a child who was born very soon after he was—and developed such a serious vitamin deficiency that his bones were deformed for years, and continued to cause him pain throughout his adult life. One look at the horrific photos of his ex-wife Nicole's battered face reveals how violent his *jealousy* of the sibling who stole his life-giving milk from him and his *rage* at the mother whose neglect wounded him to the bone, must be.

Though your lover's milk supply probably didn't literally dry up when he was a baby, as O. J.'s did, in a psychological sense, he felt starved and rejected as a baby—and is still furious at Mommy for not filling him up with food and pleasurable feelings. That's left him with an overpowering oral aggression toward women. Like Dracula, he thirsts to possess you completely—so he'll never lose his source of emotional and erotic nourishment again—but has such a voracious appetite that he drains you with his never-ending demands. There's more than an edge of hostility in his lust to dominate—deep down, he's raging at the breast when he tries to swallow you up and suck the lifeblood right out of you.

Ironically, considering all of your partner's macho posturing and domineering ways, he feels chronically insecure and vulnerable inside. He has a batlike radar that alerts him to the slightest insult or hint he's being rejected, and flies into a fury. That's another legacy from his deprived childhood, when his mother never acted as a loving mirror to him, or gave him a sense he was valued or even noticed by her. As an adult, your partner may have such a shaky sense of himself that he feels much as Dracula does: *that he casts no reflection in life.* Any slight, whether real or imagined, big or small, is shattering because it makes him feel other people view him as nothing at all—just as he believes his mother did.

This explains your man's powerful need to make an impression—perhaps literally, by leaving a love bite on your neck, or sucking your nipples until they're bruised. Whether he's being "playfully" rough with you in bed or physically violent during an argument, he wants you to feel the force of his presence, and yield to him. He wants to control your mind and your body as fiercely as he can, so you can't ignore or desert him.

Paradoxically, what your partner may consider his most potent hold over you—his commanding, compelling sexuality—is one of his most powerful sources of *anxiety*. Because he never consumed his fill of food or oral pleasure as a child, he craves sex as the grown-up substitute for these needs, but secretly fears the effect his hot-blooded lovemaking may have on *you*, especially if he's your first lover or the only one of any significance. Just as Dracula woke the virginal Lucy with his vampire kiss and turned her into a passionate woman, your man may fear he'll arouse an animal lust in you as voracious as his own, and won't be able to hold on to you.

Margot says that's just what concerned the man who deflowered her at nineteen: "When he saw how much I loved sleeping with him, he was afraid he had created a monster. Now that he'd gotten me over the hump, so to speak, he thought I'd become a shameless slut who would cheat on him whenever I got the chance. When other men looked at me, he'd glare menacingly at them."

An Overpowering Attraction

Is it a dark, erotic spell that keeps Sandra in thrall to one passionately possessive man after another—even though she has had to change her job, address, and telephone number several times to escape their smothering devotion? "It's not that I have a sick need to be stalked, threatened, and terrorized by men I date; it's just that these guys always seem to find *me*," she claims. "I feel like I'm walking through life with a sign that says, 'Make me your love victim.' I guess I'm too gullible, and get swept up in their seductive ardor until it starts to turn *scary*."

Her childhood, however, offers an intriguing clue as to what the unconscious attraction could be. "My father was a successful doctor who had what amounted to a harem of ex-wives. All of them were just like my mother—beautiful, but completely helpless. My mother could barely drive a car: She was so intimidated by traffic that she probably used the Mercedes Dad gave her once a year—and had him do all her shopping, even long after they were divorced. Between her and the other three, Dad was always out changing some ex-wife's lightbulbs, delivering her groceries, or bringing over some money to bail her out of her latest financial jam."

Perhaps you, like Sandra, consider a man who won't leave you alone the best antidote to a father who was never around when you were growing up, or showed little or no interest in your welfare. You could unintentionally set yourself up to be a "victim of love" out of an understandable desire for a happy ending with a man so devoted he'd never neglect or ignore you— or physically, sexually, or emotionally abuse you, as your father may have done during your childhood. The problem is that, like Lucy, you sleepwalk into the very situation that you most want to escape: a relationship with a man who mistreats and hurts you.

Logically, you don't want to be abused, but it feels familiar to you, so once you've let a Dracula into your life, it's hard for you to resist when he bares his fangs for a drink of blood. What makes you so susceptible to your emotional vampire's dark spell is the same unconscious compulsion to re-create a traumatic childhood situation that impels Lucy to replace a father who came to her bed inappropriately at night with a lover who stalks her as she sleeps. This is also why some women stay with violent lovers: They know they should get out the first time their boyfriend hurts them, but the spell of this early emotional programming overpowers logic, and holds them in an abusive relationship.

A dangerously passionate man whose red eyes radiate both lust and rage might also attract you if you were raised in an extremely religious or sexually repressive household. To avoid the guilt of acting on forbidden erotic impulses, you may solve the problem the same way Lucy does—by wandering though the alluring darkness in a chaste white nightgown until you're overtaken by a hot-blooded man who has his way with you. Surrendering to Dracula's love bites is like acting out a rape fantasy—you can't be held responsible if a forceful lover *compels* you to enjoy sex. It's a way of having the best of both worlds: You can still see yourself as a chaste woman, while your partner is the bad boy who overpowers your inhibitions and opens you up to erotic ecstasy.

Because there's both pleasure and pain in his rough ravishing of you, it may have a *darker* draw as well—by echoing sexual abuse you experienced as a girl. You could be using the relationship to atone for the secret *guilt* you felt each time you were victimized: Unconsciously, you blamed yourself for having stimulated inappropriate sexual desires in your father or another man, and felt you'd somehow attracted him to fondle or molest you. In your innocence, you may have had a sense of excitement while sharing this secret with your father, or felt special because he singled you out among your siblings as the target of his abusive attentions—both very *normal* reactions for a traumatized child who is struggling to deal with a sick parent who forces himself on her.

If it was not you but your mother who was physically, sexually, or emotionally violated by your father, or a series of lovers, you may have absorbed an entirely different message: that this is what is to be expected in a relationship. You may feel you're supposed to be subservient, and put up with it when a boyfriend hits you or hurls harsh words at you. Having a mother who had so little self-respect that she'd go with any man—no matter how badly he treated her—could have convinced you that it's better to accept anything from a man, and hold on to him, than to walk away and be alone.

Regardless of which of these scenarios occurred when you were growing up, it's left you with such low self-esteem that you feel like nothing without a man, even if he mistreats you. That makes you extremely vulnerable to a Dracula, since you mistake his rage to possess you and his jealousy for love. You're mesmerized by his apparent aura of power as he swirls his black cape and commands you to be his, not realizing that it's a cover for his extreme insecurity and dread of rejection. Because you weren't well loved as a child, you crave the security he seems to offer when he swears that he can't live without you—and collapse helplessly into his arms so he can sink his sharp teeth into your neck.

Can You Live Happily Ever After?

Mina ran to get her husband, Jonathan. When they returned, the bat was gone, and Lucy was limp and deathly pale. Feeling a weak pulse, Jonathan sent for Dr. Seward, then blanched when he saw the deep wounds on her neck. "No common bat made that bite!" he cried. "It was that fiend from Transylvania!"

"Do you mean Count Dracula?" Mina asked, remembering that months ago her husband had come back from the Count's castle very ill with brain fever, and in his delirium had shouted incoherently about wolves, bats, and women who were dead, but somehow undead.

Just then, Dr. Seward arrived, accompanied by Lucy's fiancé, Arthur; Quincey; and their mentor, wise old Dr. Van Helsing. As he examined the woman the other three men loved, Professor Van Helsing looked grave as he said, "I've read of this, but I never saw such a case until now. Lucy has been attacked by a vampire!"

"Can you cure her?" Mina asked, hovering over her friend with motherly concern as Jonathan told the men about the Count.

"First, we must protect her by surrounding her with a wreath of garlic and religious amulets," the professor replied. "Unless we find Dracula quickly, and drive a stake into his heart, Lucy will change into a vampire, and be his undead bride for all eternity." Lucy languidly awakened and Dr. Van Helsing attended to her, warning her not to open any door or windows at night, as a vampire can only enter a house if he's invited in.

The men spent days searching for Count Dracula, and discovered a foreign aristocrat had rented a house nearby. Mean-

while, Mina began having restless nights in which she dreamed of a dark figure bending over her in the moonlight. Finally, one night she took a sleeping draft and was too drowsy to flee when she felt a strong presence in the room—a man in a black cape who had materialized from a strange mist. So mesmerizing was the devilish passion in his hot red eyes that Mina couldn't resist. Murmuring seductively, "I want to suck your blood," he tore her gown open, and sank his fangs into her neck.

Swooning, she fell onto the bed by her husband, who slept undisturbed. Just then the Count ripped his shirt open, slashed his breast with his long, sharp nails, and forced her lips to the wound. Suddenly, she felt a hot spurt of blood in her mouth that tasted both bitter and oddly sweet. She swallowed, and let out a wild shriek. The three suitors burst into the room, waking up Jonathan. Dracula sneered at them as he was evaporating, and said, "All the women you love are mine—forever!"

Their search for Dracula led them back to Transylvania, where, as the sun was sinking, they found him asleep in his makeshift tomb, bloated with Mina's blood. His eyes were red with hellish rage as they plunged a stake through his heart, and cut off his head. A look of almost unimaginable peace came over his face as he crumbled into dust.

Should you put a stake through your lover's heart, and call it quits—before his voracious demands, compulsion to own you, and jealous rages drive you *batty*? Are you wondering if there's any risk that his obsessive devotion to you could be *dangerous*? Before going any further with the romance, stay out of a full moon . . . and reflect carefully upon this advice.

The Safest and Smartest Move Is Not to Invite Him in to Start with

A relationship with a possessive predator is usually extremely volatile, so there is a good chance that it could explode into psychological, sexual, or physical mistreatment. Even if you don't fall prey to any of these perils, you may get hurt in another way, because a dominating Dracula is best at flashy beginnings—and agonizing endings—not sustaining a *mutually* gratifying love affair over the long term. His emotional extremes are likely to make your man too unstable to ever be the caring, protective partner you have craved all of your life.

Don't Let Him Suck Your Lifeblood and Make You Weak

Should you choose to stay with this man, never surrender any of the things that make you strong and potentially independent of him: your car, your job, your money, and your hobbies. The more sources of power you have outside this relationship, the more escape routes you'll have if being with him becomes too confining, frightening, or painful. Having many enjoyable ways to enrich your life helps keep you from becoming so dependent on your possessive partner that you are forced to become his obedient zombie.

Make Certain to Surround Yourself with a Protective Circle of Psychological Garlic at All Times

Along with hanging on to a car and cash, resist your boyfriend's attempts to isolate you from your friends and family. You need a circle of caring people who you can count on to help in a crisis—because with this partner, you may be calling them sooner than you think. Or, if your original family is more poisonous than protective, turn to a surrogate family, such as a support group, a psychotherapist, or a religious adviser. Knowing that somebody besides your boyfriend is sincerely concerned about your well-being and happiness can enhance your self-esteem so much that you won't need to put up with an intimidating man just because he swears no one else could love you more. Set firm limits in advance—so he knows you won't tolerate *any* abuse.

Insist He Get Therapy, Preferably from a Psychiatrist

It isn't just *your* problem if an obsessive man is making you miserable or frightened, it's his. As the only mental health specialist with medical training, a psychiatrist is best qualified to diagnose all the causes of his mood swings or rage, and what the best treatment is. There could be a *physical* component to his explosive temper, since research shows that many men who are violent toward women have had some history of head injury; or a *biochemical* one that medication might be able to bring under control.

A psychiatrist can also evaluate what kinds of therapy might be most appropriate to deal with your partner's emotional instability. Drug or alcohol abuse can be playing more of a role in his behavior than you may imagine; or he may need group or individual therapy focusing on what the causes of his volatile emotions are, and what he can do to bring them under better control.

Be Extremely Cautious About Leaving Him Alone with Children

If you have children with him, or from an earlier relationship, be warned: Studies report that two-thirds of woman-abusers also harm children in the home. If your lover has ever been physically or sexually violent toward you—or you feel there's *any* possibility he might be in the future—play it safe by not putting vulnerable youngsters under his supervision. And consider this: If you feel at all unsafe with him yourself, or even mildly uneasy about having him take care of your kids by himself, is this *really* the home environment that you want your family to grow up in? Why not leave now, and spare yourself—and your kids—further trauma?

Don't Collude in His Obsession
to Get Emotional Reassurance

Watch out for ways you may be *provoking* his paranoia and jealousy, such as flirting with another man when he's around or taunting him by being *maddeningly* vague when he presses you about how you spent an evening away from him. This may seem like a gratifying game to you because each time he gets insanely jealous, it's evidence that he cares, but you risk setting off an explosion that blows up right in your *face*!

Don't Let It Become a Fatal Attraction

Don't think that if you love him more, you will save your man from his demons. What a possessive predator feels toward you is not some grand, ultimate passion that the rest of the world is missing out on—it's abuse. While you read this section, don't close your eyes and deny that you could be in any danger. Before you assert that it couldn't happen to you, realize that it *could*—and has, to millions of women, who all thought that it couldn't happen to them either.

Here are nine red flags to watch for, and three compelling reasons to leave right now, while you still can. If you do, realize that it may not be enough just to walk away: Since these men are potential stalkers or batterers, protect yourself by getting a court order to bar him from further contact if you're at all frightened of him—as you should be. And take steps to thwart his attempts to contact or find you, from changing your phone number to changing your address—possibly to a woman's shelter.

Nine Warning Signs That You Are in Grave Danger

1. Your lover has a history of battering women, or has abused even one previous partner.

2. He has shown any inclination at all to stalk you—such as often showing up unexpectedly to check on you, driving by your home to see if you're in, spying on you through

your window, or pursuing you in other ways with unwanted intensity.

3. His dominance of you has escalated to the point where
   you feel cut off from the world, and at his constant beck
   and call.

4. He's threatened you with bodily harm, either verbally or
   by menacing you with a gun or other weapon.

5. Sex with him is getting increasingly rough.

6. He abuses drugs or alcohol, which decrease his control of
   his emotions—including rage.

7. His explosions of rage are getting more powerful, and
   more frequent.

8. You're constantly anxious around him, or feel so drained
   by the relationship that you're losing your grasp on life.

9. You're pregnant—and remind him of how furious he is at
   his mother, and any baby who replaces him at the breast.

Three Reasons to Leave Now

You Realize He Has a Harem

Why let yourself be locked up in the chastity belt of his
obsessive jealousy while he's sleeping with every woman who
opens up her door to him? Along with the obvious *health* risks
his promiscuous passions may expose you to, accepting your
partner's infidelities can encourage him to mistreat you in other
ways—because you're letting him know that you have so little
respect for yourself that you'd put up with *anything* to keep him.
That creates a climate that can actually invite abuse.

He's Been Violent Toward You at Least Once

Physical abuse doesn't only mean being beaten to within an
inch of your life. It means any cruelty he inflicts that makes you
go, "Ouch!" Whether it be black eyes to broken bones or slaps

to stab wounds, get out the *very first time*! Don't be sucked in by his abject apologies and his promises never to do it again, as Gerrie was. After her husband gave her a black eye during a dispute, she went home to her parents, who encouraged her to get a divorce. When her husband called every night in tears, sent gifts and letters, and swore he would never lay a hand on her again, she started to downplay the damage. "It's only a black eye," she said, "and he's so sorry about it." She went back—and got beaten up so badly she was hospitalized with internal injuries.

He Has Sexually Abused or Raped You

While some degree of rough sex may be acceptable between *consenting* adults, a lover who won't take no for an answer, or coerces you into sexual activities that only *he* enjoys, isn't being erotic—he's invading and abusing you. Don't rationalize unwanted violations of your body as a result of your man's overly passionate nature. He's controlling you by *not* controlling himself sexually, and showing you that his need to be in complete possession of you is so selfish and extreme that he's willing to degrade you in the most intimate way imaginable. It's not just time to walk away—it's time to *run*!

14

THE LETHAL LOVER

There was once a miller who told himself, "When the right suitor comes along and asks for my daughter, I shall give her to him." So eager was he to have his daughter leave home that he was actually willing to marry her off to just about anybody. When a suitor who appeared to be wealthy came soon after and asked for her, the miller immediately promised his daughter to the stranger. The maiden, however, didn't love this man as a bride ought to love her bridegroom, nor did she trust him. Whenever she looked at him or thought of him, her heart shuddered with dread.

One day he said to her, "We're engaged to be married, but you have never visited me. You must come and see me without fail this Sunday." The maiden replied hesitantly that she didn't know where his house was.

"I live in the dark depths of the forest," he told her. When she tried again to make an excuse and said she didn't know how to get there, he added, "I'll strew a path of ashes to guide you."

When Sunday came, the maiden felt strangely frightened as she started following the ashes. To be sure of getting back safely, she left a trail of lentils behind her. Night was falling when she finally saw a solitary house in the midst of the forest. It was so dark and desolate, it terrified her.

When she went inside, not a soul was to be seen, and the place was deathly silent. Suddenly a bird in a cage began to sing:

"Turn back, turn back, you bride-to-be.
Leave this house of death and fly free."

Ignoring the bird, she went from one empty room to the next, until she finally saw an old woman in the cellar. "Is this where my bridegroom lives?" she asked breathlessly.

"Alas, poor child, you don't know where you are," answered the woman. "This is a murderer's den, and if you stay with your robber bridegroom, death will be your marriage. He's a cannibal and has told me to put this kettle of water on the fire to boil. When he has you in his power, he'll kill you without remorse, then cook and eat you. Unless I find it in my heart to save you, you'll be lost forever!"

Just then the two women heard the bridegroom outside, laughing drunkenly as he dragged a shrieking woman into the house. "Quick," the old woman said. "Hide behind this barrel or all will be over."

The bride watched from her hiding place as he forced the other maiden to drink glass after glass of wine until her heart burst. He was unmoved as the girl wept and begged for her life—instead, he coldly threw her body onto the table once she was dead and started stripping it of valuables. Unable to get her gold ring off, he took an axe and chopped the finger off.

The severed finger flew through the air and landed in the lap of the bride. She trembled in terror as she heard her groom strike a match to light a candle and start to walk over to the barrel that hid her. . . .

Clara still shudders when she thinks of a man that she met on a recent trip to Italy. "I had just arrived in Brindisi on my way to board a ship to Greece when this guy started hitting on me. At first, I didn't want to talk to him because there was something really frightening about him—he had a scar on his face that made him look like a pirate—but there was also something mesmerizing about him. Anyway, he persisted until he got my attention. I could tell he was out for sex, but I thought that I could handle him, and agreed to go sight-seeing with him.

"Wherever we went—restaurants, stores, on the street, at the beach—people kept looking panic-stricken, clearing a path, and acting as if they were trying to give me a signal. Some even said things like, 'Do you know who you're with?' But I just wasn't getting it, except to feel like I was with someone important. Eventually, we wound up in a disgustingly dirty bathroom in the back of his house, and he told me to take off my clothes. He didn't physically force me, but his manner was so menacing I didn't feel I *could* say no. I was terrified and turned on at the same time when he started thrusting inside me without any pre-liminaries. After he'd finally satisfied himself, I looked around at this filthy scene, and felt degraded, and sick to my stomach—an all-time low, yet strangely an all-time high. . . .

"I was incredibly relieved when he let me leave afterward—it was like escaping from a prison or something—and even more relieved when I finally made it to my ship. The crew gave me the story on this guy: He was notorious for terrorizing his enemies by shooting them in the kneecaps or firebombing their homes. I could hardly believe it—I always thought these things happen to somebody else, not that *I'd* ever end up in a bathtub in Brindisi having sex with a madman."

Loretta says she's also drawn to men with a dark aura of sex and violence. Her lineup of previous lovers reads like a police "Most Wanted" list. One was a paroled bank robber with a long rap sheet and a live-in girlfriend; another was a John Travolta look-alike with Mafia ties; and a third was a very charming con man who ran her credit cards up to the limit, then abruptly left town—in *her* car. "I describe it as the 'desperado syndrome,' because the men that I'm attracted to have an outlaw edge of danger. They're guys that walk on the wild side, and don't give a damn about what anyone else thinks."

Shelley's boyfriend has a scary side she downplays as merely a love of mischief. "He's very charismatic, which is why he's so successful as a financier, but if anyone tries to cross him he'll pull a boyish prank to retaliate. One time, he was furious at an attorney who was threatening to sue him, so he drove by the guy's house at night—with me in the car—and shot out his front window with a gun. I was terrified that we'd be arrested, but Ted found this adventure *arousing*, and stopped the car a few blocks away so we could have sex. It was just a quickie on the backseat, but it was unbelievably thrilling—I've never felt him that *hard* before!"

His Telltale Traits

Do you, like the miller's daughter, find your lover makes you shudder with delicious dread? That aura of menace which surrounds your man may thrill and chill you, but it can also signal that you are hooked up with the *scariest* bad boy of them all—a deceptively seductive sociopath whose love might well be *lethal*.

He Has a Very Chilly Charm

At first you can't believe how nice he is—and you shouldn't. After you start going out, you'll soon notice that the more he tries to please you and says, "Whatever you want, darling," the more nervous you feel. Later on you realize that there's a catch—his pattern of "accidentally" doing things that wound you, such as making little jokes about you that embarrass you in front of your friends. What is worse is how your lover does these things so cleverly *you* end up feeling somehow at fault.

No male trait is as frustrating to women as this combination of chilly charisma and masterful manipulation. In a love affair, you can easily drive yourself to distraction trying to guess what his inner thoughts might be, or why your man might want to punish you with these passive-aggressive ploys. Compounding the problem is the fact that these coldhearted Casanovas typically deny they have some hidden agenda—or negative feelings of any kind. Jan's boyfriend, for example, claims he's never in a bad mood, yet acts oddly hostile.

There's a Hint of Madness in His Eyes

Though your man may not be conventionally handsome, he is likely to have a rugged sex appeal or an intriguing air of danger. Like Angela's boyfriend, he may sport a crudely drawn gang tattoo on his shapely biceps, or have a nose that was badly set after some barroom brawl. He acts quintessentially cool, but his eyes warn of the dark depths that lie just below his aloof exterior. His gaze is almost hypnotic—a combination of cold, barely suppressed fury; fearlessness; and an utter lack of restraint. It sends shivers down our spine, but can also make us tingle with wild excitement. One look into his eyes tells us this is a man who puts no limits at all on how far he'll go or what he might do.

He Has a History of Criminal Behavior

Has your lover ever run afoul of the law—whether it was being arrested for shoplifting as a teenager; being jailed overnight for drunken driving; or being convicted of a more serious crime, like arson or murder? Or are you involved with somebody who is *currently* behind bars, as Ellie is? She met her boyfriend, who is serving time for armed robbery, through a personal ad in the paper—and is now carrying on a love affair through the mail, and brief visits to his maximum-security prison. "My family thinks I'm crazy, but he's a wonderful person who just got into trouble because he was poor and didn't have all the opportunities I did."

Actually, you should be very concerned if your boyfriend has any past or present criminal involvement—even if he's never been *caught* at it—because he's showing the antisocial attitude that's very characteristic of psychopaths. Their most *dangerous* trait is a complete lack of conscience that lets them lie, cheat, steal, or even kill without feeling any guilt or remorse. There's a strong affinity between these amoral rogues and the criminal underworld, because at heart, they are con men who inflict harm on others for fun and profit.

He Wants People to Know That
He's Armed and Dangerous

The more powerless your man feels on the inside, the bigger his gun—or gun collection—is apt to be. Polly's boyfriend, for example, is a wiry man with a droopy mustache who doesn't look like he's got much of a pistol in *his* pants, but he made up for it with his memorable come-on line, she says. "Instead of asking if I wanted to come up and see his etchings, Rob asked if I'd like to come up and see his AK-47. I thought he was kidding, but actually he has a whole *room* full of guns, as well as some ninja knives and other exotic weapons." After they started to date, Polly soon realized that Rob was more attached to his weapons than he'd ever be to her.

Some desperadoes can do without a home arsenal, because they have turned their whole body into a lethal weapon. Kelly's lover is six and a half feet of solid intimidation. "You could walk on the meanest street on earth with him, and everybody would get out of his way, even if they didn't know he has a black belt in karate—because everything about him says, 'I'm one bad motherfucker, and you'd better not mess with me!' "

He's Obsessed with Violence and Pornography

Don't expect him to take you to a tender romantic comedy— he'd rather watch a movie where sexy coeds get stabbed in the shower. Anything with lots of blood and gore—or an X rating— will fascinate this man, though he may consider soft-core porn a little too tame for his lurid taste. His interests can span the entire spectrum of sex-oriented entertainment: raunchy videos, dirty books, peep shows, strip joints, watching nude women mud wrestle or perform live sex acts. What he drools over most of all, however, are pictures or videos that *combine* sex and violence— he is enthralled by images of women being tied up, beaten, raped, or butchered.

Your partner may be equally preoccupied with real-life acts of violence, and immerse himself in books or movies about famous serial killers or horrific true crimes. Kelly's intimidating

boyfriend, for example, subscribes to a variety of violent maga-
zines, and often regales her with grisly stories he's read about.
"The other day he was talking about some martial arts guru who
could rip the living heart out of a bull with his bare hands," she
says. "He's also fascinated with horror movies—and probably
has seen every *Friday the Thirteenth* sequel ever made a dozen
times."

Most of the Time, He's Cool, Calm, and Collected, but If He Gets Mad, Watch Out!

Not only do these men like violent movies; they're often violent themselves. Because your lover has little control over the
aggressive impulses that constantly simmer just below his seemingly unemotional exterior, it is easy for them to suddenly boil
up into explosive fury that appears to come out of nowhere.
(Substance abuse can intensify this trait by lowering his inhibitions—not that he has that many to start with.) Your lover's violent temper may lead him to get into fistfights with strangers
who look at him the wrong way on the street, or to become
physically abusive toward you.

Don't delude yourself into believing that your bad-tempered
beau would never hurt *you* because he loves you so much. What
makes the true sociopath so scary is that, like the robber bridegroom, he is capable of almost anything—assault, rape, possibly
even murder. Just about the only thing he *can't* do is care deeply
about another person, or fall truly in love with you.

He's a Loner—and a Drifter

Like the robber bridegroom, your man lives alone in the
dark woods, and never forms any deep attachment to people or
places that he passes along the way. He has few or no friends
and probably has never had a monogamous love affair that
lasted more than a year. He prefers solitary activities, such as
hunting, fishing, or playing pool—by himself. Because he's often
rather paranoid, and very suspicious of strangers—and to this
guy, *everybody* is a stranger—he has always got his psychological

guns drawn. It's part of his Wild West mentality: He believes it's smarter to shoot first, and ask questions later.

Understandably, in view of his attitude toward authority, a desperado is usually a problem employee—if he has a legitimate job at all. Odds are that your man has been fired several times, for such offenses as stealing company supplies, chronic absenteeism, or showing up drunk. (He's likely to be a substance abuser, either of alcohol, or of drugs like heroin or crack.) Or he may impulsively quit jobs—perhaps after losing his temper and punching his boss out. Off the job, he may be equally restless, and move from one location to another frequently or have no fixed address.

Fire Holds an Unusual Fascination for Him

While this trait is not always as obvious as the other characteristics listed here—unless he strews a trail of ashes for you to follow, as the robber bridegroom does—you may notice your lover enjoys lighting matches and watching them burn, setting bits of paper ablaze in an ashtray, or building bonfires at the beach. Perhaps he perks up when a fire engine roars by, or listens for fire alarms on a shortwave scanner, and drives over to look at the blaze. If you smoke, he may make an elaborate ritual out of lighting your cigarettes—or flicking a Bic that's set to a torch-like flame. Or, if he ever invites you over for dinner, don't be surprised to find him cooking meat on the barbecue!

Sexually, He's into S and M—with You as the M

This doesn't necessarily mean that your boyfriend gets out the whips and chains as a prelude to sex, since there can be a wide variety of ways he may express this interest. On the mildest level, he may just get himself hot by *fantasizing* about erotic domination and submission, while making love to you in a relatively normal manner. Or your man may find it arousing to demean you in bed—perhaps by calling you a whore or a cunt—or enjoy frightening you, maybe by putting his hands around your neck and asking what you'd do if he started to *squeeze*.

Some sadistic men like to act out scenes of *simulated* erotic cruelty, where they might tie you up with your silk scarves and pretend to be raping you; or have you play a fantasy role, such as sexual slave. Others can only have an orgasm by inflicting actual pain. (Be wary if your partner isn't able to ejaculate inside you—this could be the *first* sign he has sadistic fantasies he'll soon want to act on.) Erotic aggression can range from practices that hurt or humiliate you, such as forceful anal sex, all the way up to whipping, bondage, or even torture. No matter what level your lover starts with, he's likely to *escalate* to increasingly brutal or demeaning acts, just as an addict needs ever larger amounts of his preferred drug to get the same high.

Whether or not *he* acts on his sadistic urges, your boyfriend may sometimes ask *you* to hurt or humiliate him in bed. Actually, this isn't as much of a role reversal as you might think, because he dominates you into dominating *him*. It's a turn-on to have you spank or degrade him, because deep down your partner feels like a very naughty boy who needs to be thoroughly chastised.

What Lights His Fire

What's the origin of your outlaw's wary, emotionless outlook and his chillingly *cruel* streak? Ironically, it's likely to stem from a childhood in which he was brutally mistreated, but never felt that he was properly *punished*. Like the fictional Huck Finn, who cons people, tells whopper lies, steals things, and runs away, your coldhearted charmer may have had no mother in the home as he was growing up, and an alcoholic or emotionally disturbed father who alternately ignored him and beat him for no apparent reason. Or, if his family was intact, his home was filled with chaos and violent discord. Deprived of maternal love by a mother who was absent, or more commonly, sadistic and rejecting, he never formed the deep attachment to her that's normally the model for later love relationships.

That's why your man feels nothing now. There's no heart— or soul—to be found in his bleak psychological house because he was raised by emotionally impoverished parents who gave him no warmth, nurture, or human connections of any kind—other than physical abuse that may have had sexual overtones. Guilt and remorse are meaningless concepts to your partner, since his mother didn't care enough about him to supervise him when he was young, set limits, or offer appropriate discipline. Though your lover received plenty of harsh punishments, they were given very erratically, and rarely fit his crimes. The result is that he's never internalized a sense of right and wrong, and can commit violent or antisocial acts without being troubled by pangs of conscience.

This upbringing can create a well-known triad of symptoms in childhood that are predictors of a future sociopath: bed-wetting, cruelty to animals, and fire setting. Your boyfriend's childhood behavioral problems also may have included truancy from school, lying, running away from home, vandalism, and assault (possibly using a weapon).

While all of his antisocial acts, as a child or an adult, are sparked by the burning rage he feels toward his sadistically rejecting parents, pyromania illustrates it best. One convicted arsonist told the *Los Angeles Times Magazine* he dealt with disturbing memories of the tortures his mother inflicted on him by lighting a match and saying, "This is for you," when he set something ablaze. "I could build a fire [and] if I was mad at my mother, I could destroy her without touching her."

Arson can also be ignited by sexual compulsions from early overstimulation, such as sexual abuse. Firefighters say it's not unusual to find sexual emissions at the scene of a blaze, or for them to catch the culprit masturbating nearby, as he watches the hot flames rise and fall as though the fire were a porno flick.

Before you insist that *your* lover doesn't show any of these scary symptoms, it is important to realize that he may hide them under a veneer of charm. Rowena's boyfriend, for example, seems relatively normal, yet has several sociopathic traits. Not only did he spend two months in prison for assaulting a previous girlfriend—a charge he claims was fabricated by a scorned woman—but he supports himself by a series of scams. Along with being large and physically intimidating, he also enjoys telling "jokes" that make people nervous, she says. "When a friend of mine complained her apartment was infested with cockroaches, he told her a tactic he'd found effective was to set some of them on fire to scare off the others. You should have seen the look on her face!"

Regardless of *how* your lover acts out his rage and contempt for society's rules, the underlying drive is an intense lust for power. He's felt impotent and frustrated all his life because he never got his mother to feel anything for him. By setting fires, hurting women in bed, or cheating people out of money, he forces other people to feel very *big* emotions. Since your partner is so emotionally impervious that he's even detached from his own icy fury, it's very arousing for him to make other people angry, sad, or scared with his predatory, exploitative actions—it's almost as good as having strong feelings himself, instead of the ashes of dead emotions.

Not only is your partner's cruelty a way to gain vicarious revenge against his cruel parents; it also protects him from becoming the *victim* of other people's sadistic impulses, as he was during childhood. Frightening and dominating others—or you—is how he shows he's armed, and so dangerous that no one should even think about taking his pistol (or penis) away, a fear triggered by his mother's ferocity toward him (which explains why he may be afraid of ejaculating inside you—it makes him feel too vulnerable).

Why then would your man have even an *occasional* interest in masochism? Submitting to you sexually from time to time doesn't pose any real threat to him because he retains the upper hand by telling you *exactly* how he wants you to hurt, degrade, or dominate him. To your boyfriend, there's a paradoxical pleasure in being punished—having you spank him and tell him what a bad boy he is makes him feel *loved*. That's both because the only attention he got from his parents was sadistic abuse—which he may have found sexually stimulating—and because he secretly longs for a mother who is devoted enough to provide the loving discipline that he's lacked all of his life. Basically, he wants someone to whip him into shape—an impossible task, since he's too wary to allow you, or anyone, close enough to have any real impact on him.

Fantasies of Fixing His Fatal Flaws

Is it an erotic aura of danger that draws you to an emotionless but *fatally* charming outlaw, or do you relish the sense of power you get from having the baddest boy of them all under your spell? Actually, it's a bit of both, since a psychopath can seem like the *ultimate* Mr. Excitement: a man who goes to the furthest extremes of sex and violence.

There's an intoxication some women find in flirting with the forbidden: You may be drawn to a desperado like a moth to a flame because you unconsciously *want* to be burned. Your gnawing need for punishment drives you into the arms of a lethal lover—who wants you to play masochist to his sadist—since your overpowering guilt about your erotic urges makes you secretly believe the only orgasm you deserve is *death*.

Having a father who was violent, cruelly rejecting (like the miller who was willing to marry his daughter off to anyone, even a cannibal), or overly sexual around you could be what has branded a twisted association between sex and aggression into your brain. You may still blame yourself for being physically or sexually victimized when you were young, feel worthless because your father didn't value you, or have irrational guilt about not being able to stop his violence toward your mother or other women—and believe you should be punished for what you view as your childhood crimes.

Another way you (and your lethal lover) may have been traumatized as you were growing up was by repeatedly seeing your parents being sexual with each other, or with other partners—a frightening experience to a child, who may think Daddy is injuring and invading Mommy with his forceful thrusts and rough caresses. The more one witnesses this "primal scene," the more an alarmed youngster concludes that sex is savage, animalistic, and very painful.

There is a voyeuristic thrill that a violent, or potentially violent, lover may give you. Like the miller's daughter, who was callously discarded by her unfeeling father, then peeped out from behind a barrel as her groom robbed and killed another woman, you might *identify* with your outlaw's cold-blooded rage more than you realize. You may get vicarious pleasure out of watching him hurt others because deep down you'd like to get even with somebody who hurt you, such as an abusive father or a cruel, rejecting mother. Unconsciously, you might admire an outlaw for doing what you only dream of: lashing out at a society (and parents) that wronged you, and made you feel like an unloved outcast.

Taken to its furthest extremes, this sense of identification explains why some women are drawn to dangerous criminals, or even serial killers, who can seem like the biggest studs of all. One of these women, Eva, appeared on TV a few years ago to proclaim her love for Richard Ramirez, the "Night Stalker" who tortured thirteen women to death. To her, the allure is that "he broke away from the system. The world is overpopulated, so the murders don't matter. The women were going to die anyway." Her bond with Ramirez, who is now behind bars, is that she grew up as a virtual prisoner herself, raised by parents who kept her apart from other kids by schooling her at home; and she shares his pathological hatred of women (who remind her of her singularly depriving mother).

Like Eva, who revels in Ramirez's crimes—but also sends him poems in an effort to rehabilitate him—you may find that part of you applauds your lover's antisocial acts, and another part longs to *rescue* him from his dark side. What you're expressing is both impotent anger about being raised in a chaotic and loveless home, and your own wish to have been rescued from parents who left you, like the miller's daughter, to walk alone and unprotected through the dark, frightening woods of life. Since you felt so helpless as a child, the idea of taming a dangerous lover may be very seductive to you because if you succeed in taking the thorn out of your tiger's paw, you'll be even more powerful than he is.

While this fantasy plays a role in every bad-boy relationship, it's particularly potent for women who get involved with prisoners. Whether they're drawn to a celebrity serial killer or a run-of-the-mill robber, what often attracts them to a boyfriend who is behind bars is that he can't escape from *them*—or their help. Deep down, they feel so unlovable that they fear a free man wouldn't want them, or that a convicted criminal—the baddest of the bad—is all that they deserve. A lover who is in jail—and dependent on them for gifts, letters, money, and love—offers a satisfying illusion of *ultimate* control. He may be bad, dangerous, or even deadly, but right now, he's at their mercy—at least until he gets out.

Whether your man is a prisoner, or one of the many predators who still walk among us, your fantasies of fixing his fatal flaws are just that—fantasies, or even potentially *deadly* delusions. Trying to turn this man-eating tiger into your tame tabby won't give you the power and self-esteem that eluded you in childhood—it simply puts you at risk for becoming his next *prey*!

Can You Live Happily Ever After?

As the robber bridegroom staggered drunkenly toward the barrel the miller's daughter was hiding behind, the old woman called out to him. "Come back to dinner. You can look for the finger later. It's not going anywhere." When he sat down, she poured him wine she'd laced with a sleeping potion.

He soon collapsed on the floor and started snoring lustily. The bride crept from her hiding place and stepped cautiously over the sleeping robber to escape. Outside, she saw that the path of ashes had blown away, but the lentils had sprouted and were pointing her in the right direction.

When she got home, she told her father what had happened, but he shrugged and did nothing. On the date set for the wedding, the robber bridegroom appeared, along with the miller's friends and relatives. Soon the guests were making merry and telling stories, but the maiden was silent until her groom said, "Come, my love, can't you think of anything? Don't you have a tale for us?"

"I'll tell you about a dream that I had," she replied. "I was walking alone in a dark woods when I came to a solitary house where not a soul was to be seen. A bird in a cage sang,

'Turn back, turn back, you bride-to-be.
Leave this house of death and fly free.'

"This was only a dream, my love! Then I met an old woman who told me I was in a murderer's den, and that my bridegroom would cut me to pieces and eat me. She hid me behind a barrel when we heard him come home, dragging a screaming maiden with him. This was just a dream, of course!

"He made her drink wine until her heart burst, and she fell down dead. It was only a dream, my love! He robbed her corpse, then chopped off her finger to take her gold ring. This was just a dream, my love! The finger flew through the air, landed in my lap . . . and here it is!"

The bridegroom, who turned as pale as ashes when she produced the finger, tried to flee, but the guests grabbed him and handed him over to a magistrate to be executed for his crimes.

Is something warning you there could be a house of horrors at the end of *your* partner's path of ashes? Listen carefully to that caged bird, because the only way you'll live happily ever after is to get out of this relationship while you're still alive. There's no way to turn this frog into a prince, because what you're living isn't a fairy tale, it's a slasher movie! Don't wait for more red flags—if you recognize the telltale traits of a sociopath in your lover, fly free, while you still can! Here's how:

Avoid Confronting Him Alone

Notice how the fairy-tale bride waits until it's completely safe before she gives her lethal lover the finger—both literally and figuratively? That's just what you should do, except that it's smarter not to reject your partner in person, even if there are other people around. Instead, write him a good-bye note that clearly ends the relationship, and don't go back for anything—to talk things over, get belongings you may have left at his home, or even to collect money that he owes you.

That was the near-fatal mistake model Marla Hansen made. She spurned her sociopathic landlord's romantic advances and moved out, but saw no harm in meeting him at a crowded bar to collect her rent deposit. Tragically, he then lured her outside, where a hired thug repeatedly slashed her pretty face with a

razor, and scarred her for life. Don't risk *your* life—or looks—
for money or belongings. If need be, hire somebody to collect
your stuff—preferably when he isn't home.

Disappear

Move, disconnect your phone, leave no forwarding address,
change jobs—and then increase your security in your new location by installing lots of sturdy locks or, better yet, an alarm
system. Or, if this is not financially feasible, consider seeking
refuge with friends or family members in another state. Tell no
one where you live or what your new phone number is—he
could charm or threaten it out of the people you know.

The good news—if you can call it that—is that you won't
have to take these precautions forever. Unlike the passionately
possessive lover who can turn into a stalker, this man will ultimately *stop* looking for you, because he's only capable of
shallow, short-lived attachments. He'll lose interest once he has
fresh *prey* in his sights, and then you'll be safe.

Stop Him—Before He Dates Again

Another good way to protect yourself—and other women
who might fall for his fatal charm—is to tip off authorities to
any criminal behavior of your partner's that you are aware of.
Let the police know about his weapon collection, drug dealing,
or any other indication of how dangerous he is to society. Hopefully they'll find a good reason to lock up this bird of prey in the
cage where he belongs—at least until he can get the proper psychiatric treatment. Some of these men may be able to be partially
rehabilitated through years of intense psychotherapy, medication, or treatment for an underlying neurological condition. But
don't wait for miracles—they may not come in your lifetime.

Finally, Untwist Yourself Through Therapy

Once you get this man completely out of your life, get help to construct strong psychological defenses that will keep you from letting any other lethal lover in. You urgently need to build up your self-esteem, and understand why you would get involved with somebody who has such a frightening potential to harm or even kill you. You should also get treatment for other forms of self-destructive behavior that you've slipped into, such as alcohol or drug addictions. Expect to spend at least a year unraveling the knots in your psyche before you'll be ready to fly on to a healthy, *life-enhancing* love affair!

15

$\mathcal{L}$IVING HAPPILY
EVER AFTER

$\mathcal{W}$hat can fairy tales teach us about romance in the real world? Like dreams, they speak to us about our deepest desires, warn us of dangers, and help us better understand ourselves and our attraction to bad boys. Not only do they encourage us to believe, as children do, that we have hidden powers within us—if we're just bold enough to use them—but these stirring stories of enchantment also hold magical secrets that can guide us to getting the relationship we yearn for. Here's a look at the lessons about living—and loving—happily ever after we can learn from fairy tales.

Keep Your Eyes Wide Open
When You Look for the Prince of Your Dreams

It's easy to sabotage yourself—so you don't get the love you yearn for—by looking at a relationship through emerald-colored glasses. Even a wizard who spins dreams and only *pretends* to grant wishes can seem magical if you view him through the flattering lens of your fantasies—until he floats off in a balloon filled with his own hot air. It's natural to idealize the man you love, even if he is a bad boy; but if you listen only to your romantic reveries, and ignore the reality of his hurtful behavior, you risk being lost and abandoned in the illusory world of Oz.

If you're involved with a married man, avoid the temptation to make the Little Mermaid's fatal mistake. So focused was she on her daydreams of a happy ending that existed only in her mind that she refused to face the unpleasant truth: The prince that she loved had pledged his heart to another. Similarly, Janetta over-romanticizes her married lover's every utterance, and turns it into a commitment to a future together. As he caresses her body with hot kisses and says, "I love being with you," she forgets about his wife and kids, and hears, "I'd love to be with you *always*." Like the Mermaid, she is setting herself up for a broken heart, as her inflated illusions are sure to collide with reality eventually—and burst like so many bubbles in the cold sea.

Intriguingly, *men* rarely have this problem—you don't hear of male "mistresses" lingering in relationships with married women for years, hoping that these women will eventually get a divorce. Instead, guys quickly feel queasy in the subservient role of "other man" and press for an exclusive commitment early on. If they don't get it, their practical, self-protective side tells them to end the affair and move on to a more promising romantic prospect. We women would do well to show the same emotional respect for ourselves, and flee from the pain of a futile attraction, instead of romanticizing it into a great love story.

While some of us let our fantasies lure us into relationships that are wrong for us, others allow an overly rosy view of romance to keep them from fully appreciating a lover who is right for them. Lucy sleepwalks her way into the dangerous arms of Dracula because she mistakes his intense rage to possess her for ultimate passion; while Beauty spends night after night dreaming of a perfect prince, unaware she has already found him in the Beast. What these tales show is that love is not always what we imagine it to be—we must look at every attraction *realistically*; otherwise, our dream lover may turn out to be a nightmare.

Trust Your Animal Instincts—
You Know If He's Mr. Wrong

In the first moments after meeting a man, you have all the clues you need to tell if he's right for you. Even though he appears to have all the outer trappings that you are looking for—he's gorgeous, sexy, and crazy about *you*—if you feel there is something off about him, there probably is. Your internal Toto may be exposing your wizard as an imposter; or a cautious canary inside you may be singing a warning to run for your life—because he's a lethal lover.

If something about your man is setting off alarm bells, don't let him sweet-talk you out of your initial uneasiness, as Patsy did. "When I met Roger at a party, I was a bit tipsy and began flirting outrageously with him. Instead of being thrilled the next morning when he called at eight a.m. dying for a date with me, I had a yucky feeling—'Oh no, what have I done?'—but let him talk me into going out with him that night. By the end of the evening he was whispering that he was madly in love with me, while I was wondering if this was just a line. Still, I was flattered and had what I thought was a hot and heavy romance with him for months—until I found out he was cheating on me with every woman who fell for his act."

Don't Assume That Your Lover Has More Magical Power Than You Do Just Because He's a Man

When the Little Mermaid cuts off her tongue to catch a mortal, Cinderella's stepsisters mutilate their feet to fit the prince's glass slipper, and Dorothy woos her Wizard by assuring him that even though she wears magical silver slippers, she is meek and unthreatening, they're all making the classic feminine mistake: giving up their power to get a man, or keep him. This strategy can seem seductive when you are attracted to a bad boy, because you may be afraid that you'll drive him away if you voice too many demands. Instead, show him you can stand on your own two feet, or present yourself as his equal.

Cutting off parts of yourself that your lover may not like—or refusing to recognize the power that's inside you—can also reflect an underlying sense that there's something unlovable about you. It may stem from a childhood in which you were mistreated or made to feel that you deserve to be punished. This secret guilt may be what you are unconsciously acting out when you wound yourself—or let your boyfriend know it's okay for *him* to wound you too. What you need to remember, however, is an ironic lesson of these fairy tales: The more you dance on knives to please your prince, the more likely you are to create the very result you most fear—being rejected by him.

Instead of making yourself weak—and dangerously vulnerable to the predatory bad boys of this world—try another, wiser fairy-tale tactic: Keep your partner from overpowering you by cutting *him* down to size if he's asking for it or deserves it, as the Blue Fairy did when Pinocchio's lies and attempts to manipulate her made his nose grow ludicrously long, or when he made a complete ass of himself on Pleasure Island. Don't let your fear of losing your man keep you from speaking up when you see he's going too far, or you'll only encourage him to continue to take advantage of you. Instead, find a balance of power that you're both comfortable with.

Wave Your Own Magic Wand and Make Love Happen

Wouldn't you love to have a fairy godmother who could magically change you into the belle of the ball? Part of what makes fairy tales so alluring to children is that we rejoice when characters like Cinderella and Aladdin are lifted out of their bleak, depressing circumstances by magical helpers who show them the way to get their heart's desire: a love that solves all of their problems and makes them happy ever after. Even as adults, we yearn to believe some guardian angel is watching out for us, and will ultimately guide us to romantic joy.

What keeps us from exploring the magic that really is in the universe, however, is our misconception that it's a force we can't tap into on our own. Instead, we feel that all we can do is wait helplessly for the magic person or magic ingredient that will make our relationships work. "If only I were prettier, smarter, richer, or more lovable, then I'd meet the right man," we tell ourselves, not realizing that all of us *already* have the power within us to grant our own wishes. By believing we're worthy of happiness and finding our inner magic, we can be our *own* fairy godmothers and wave the wand that brings enchantment and delight into our love life. Then we and the men in our lives can work real magic together . . . the magic of love.

Make Sure Your Prince Has Found His Inner Treasures

Before a man is ready for an intimate relationship with you, he needs to explore the deep recesses of his unconscious, and discover the hidden treasures he has to offer a partner. Like Aladdin, who woos the sultan's daughter with magic from the lamp he found underground, a commitment-minded lover will share the insights he's gleaned from looking beyond the surface into himself. And just as the Beast finally wins his Beauty by letting her see him lying defenselessly in his cave, the right lover should be willing to reveal his true self and most profound feelings to you.

Watch for this sign because it will tell you if your man is psychologically receptive to having a rich, meaningful relationship. It's not until the Frog emerges from his well that he hops over to the princess eager to begin a romantic involvement. Remember, however, that just being in touch with himself is not enough— your prince should have genuine *treasures* to offer. Dracula, for example, understands *his* needs very well and emerges from his underground realm to search for a woman who can satisfy them, but can only give *you* an undead counterfeit of love because he brings his dirt-filled tomb with him. Since his unconscious is a graveyard of primitive sexual and aggressive instincts, he has no riches to share—which is the kiss of death to a love affair.

Don't Be So Hungry for Love That
You Let Your Lover's Hunger Deplete You

Notice how ravenous male characters are in fairy tales? They're lurking in the woods looking for little girls, or grannies, to gobble up; croaking at the door to dine from a princess's plate; or flying through the moonlight in search of a soft female neck to sink their fangs in. What this symbolizes is the extreme neediness and insatiable demands that are typical of bad boys. This feeling of inner emptiness springs from never having gotten enough love and nurturing as children. They're still angry about being deprived by their mothers, and greedily turn to the women they get involved with to fill the bottomless pit inside them.

Although a hungry guy can seem very appetizing to some women—because it's flattering to feel so urgently needed—ultimately, he can leave you dangerously drained. Remember the self-sacrificing Blue Fairy who lavished so much love and attention on Pinocchio that she starved herself? It's better to be alone for a while, if necessary, than to let your lover devour you or leave you emotionally bankrupt. Always nourish yourself *first*—don't look for a man to fill you up. Hunger and neediness shouldn't be the basis for a relationship.

Look in the Mirror, Mirror on the Wall,
and Tell Yourself That You Deserve
to Be Treated Like a Princess

When you look at yourself, do you focus only on your flaws—the ten pounds you need to lose, the way that you let men walk all over you, or the mistakes you've made in the past? If you feel more like Cinderella in her sooty rags—or the mud-covered damsel in distress from "The Princess and the Pea" who stands wet and stammering at the prince's door—than like someone who merits *royal* treatment, low self-esteem may be playing a bigger role in your attraction to heels than you admit. Perhaps the real reason why you're so willing to settle for a frog is that you don't feel entitled to a prince.

Feeling down on yourself can lead to a self-defeating cycle

because every time you let a man treat you poorly, it ratchets your self-respect down another notch—and makes it harder to stand up for yourself next time he tries to treat you like dirt. To escape this self-defeating rut—and get the relationship you want—look into the mirror every morning with loving eyes. Even if you do have a few flaws—and who doesn't?—affirm to yourself that at heart you are a *real* princess, and deserve the very best that a man has to offer. While it may take time for these positive messages to take hold and replace the negative ones you're carrying around now, learning to admire and appreciate yourself is the key to finding a mate who will put you on a throne.

Notice what your man's relationship to *his* mirror is—it tells you how he sees himself. Is he a self-absorbed Pinocchio who is in love with his looking-glass image; an enigmatic Bluebeard who hides behind mirrors that keep the focus on you—and away from his secrets; or a vampire who feels he casts no reflection in life? Observe whether he takes good care of himself—if he dresses sloppily or abuses his body with alcohol, he's definitely not going to treat *you* with respect—and be especially attentive to what he says about himself. Since bad boys often like to flaunt their wicked ways, he may tell you exactly what his flaws are. Don't downplay the importance of these remarks, which he may make in a lighthearted or offhand manner: If your lover reveals something negative he sees in his looking glass, listen and be warned!

In real life no one is perfect—not even princes or princesses. You need to learn which flaws to correct and which to accept in yourself and in him.

Be Aware of Your Lover's Hidden Tests—and Be Wary If He Has a Locked Closet Full of Secrets

Is it just men in fairy tales who leave a mysterious key or magic lamp around to learn if their woman can be trusted with it; put a pea under her mattress to find out if she's the princess she claims to be; or refuse to make a commitment until they've checked to see if her foot is a perfect fit for their glass slipper?

Not at all. The rogues of the real world are often equally reluctant to get deeply involved in a relationship—or risk their heart at all—so they protect themselves by setting up secret tests to see if they can trust you.

Most women don't recognize these little ploys, or realize how often men use them to learn how their girlfriends really feel about them. Heather, for example, was hurt when her new flame, a basketball coach, abruptly broke a date with her so he could schedule an extra team practice, and paid little attention to his assurance that he would have more time for her in the spring. What she didn't grasp was that he was subtly asking if she'd still be there for him then. Like a boy who deliberately misbehaves and then runs to his mother to see if she still loves him, your partner may pull some annoying stunt to find out how much he can get away with—and still be forgiven.

Why does your partner feel such a need to reassure himself of your love? Ironically, in many fairy stories, it's the male characters who turn out to be unreliable, deceptive, and dangerous, while their female counterparts are honest and loyal. First the Wolf tricks Little Red Riding Hood into wandering off the path, and then he disguises himself as her grandmother to get her into bed with him. Similarly, Pinocchio lies repeatedly to the ever forgiving Blue Fairy. This gives an intriguing insight into a romantic scoundrel's psychology—he's suspicious of the women in his life because he unconsciously projects his *own* untrustworthiness on them. Since he knows he puts himself first, lies when it suits him, and doesn't always care if he hurts his girlfriend, he expects that if given the chance, she'll do the same to him. His wariness might go back to his very first male-female relationship—with his mother—as he may have been hurt and deceived by her as a child and has learned to guard his heart very carefully as an adult.

What your man needs to learn, and you should remember as well, is that love has compromises, but it can't flourish in a climate of deceit, tricks, and manipulative deals. Be sincere about your own feelings—and doubts—and encourage your partner to speak seriously and openly to you about his. Don't let the relationship advance to the next stage until you've moved beyond these games, and forged an intimate bond of trust—and truth.

Love Is a Journey, Not a Destination

Are you so caught up in your desire to live happily ever after with the prince of your dreams that you don't allow yourself to enjoy the here and now of your relationship? Many of us are in such a hurry to be in love, and be loved deeply in return, that we act like impatient kids on a long car trip who ignore the spectacular scenery along the way, because they're so busy asking, "When are we going to get there?" Instead of savoring the early stages of a romance to the fullest, we want to rush down the road to *instant* commitment. "I don't want to waste time with the wrong person," we tell ourselves. "I need to know right now if he's *the one*. Either it's love or it isn't, so when are we going to get there and find out for sure?"

It's easy to feel lost and frightened traveling through the woods of the unknown, like Little Red Riding Hood, Beauty, and the Robber Bridegroom's bride-to-be. But when you focus only on the journey's end—and wish there was a Lear jet to love that would transport you past all the scary or uncomfortable parts of getting to know another person and letting him discover the real you—you're missing the whole point of romance. It should be more like a graceful ride in a gilded coach or a meandering magic carpet ride that *slowly* carries the two of you toward intimacy. Don't let fear of flying into the unknown or fear of falling in love keep you from embarking on this journey to discovery with your man. The more you are willing to explore his mysteries—and reveal your own—the sooner you could find yourself in that enchanted place where both of you feel truly loved and appreciated by the other.

Your Kiss Can't Turn Every Frog into a Prince

Before you smugly believe you can transform your Pinocchio into a real live boy, break the spell that makes your brooding poet act like a beast, or swim your drowning prince to safety through the storm-tossed sea, examine your self-sacrificing impulses and ask yourself *whose* problems you are really trying to fix—his or your *own*? Paradoxically, women who feel impelled to rush to the rescue whenever they see a male in distress, no matter how hurtful and destructive his bad habits are to them, are often expressing an urgent desire to be rescued from their own pain. So compelling is this need to be healed that it can often drive you to the very men who are worst for you.

This rescue fantasy—the belief that you're powerful enough to save a man from his inner demons—can spring from a childhood longing to rescue your father from an unhappy marriage, business failures, mental or physical illness, addictions, or other woes. If only you could free him from his onerous burdens, you thought, then he'd finally love you as you wanted to be loved. Since you never succeeded in being your father's savior, you now hope that rescuing your Beast from *his* burden will change him into an ever grateful prince who will give you the love you lacked as a child. Sadly, however, you'll often discover that despite all your consoling kisses and unselfish help, a lover like this will never turn into the devoted Daddy you're searching for; instead, he just keeps hopping from one crisis to another, just like your real father did.

Whether you gravitate toward frogs in desperate need of a fix or power-mad princes who want you to play Cinderella so they can repair *you*, what's hooking you on heels is a gnawing need to be saved from *something*. You may be drawn to darkly erotic Draculas because their eyes promise to release you from your sexual inhibitions; to dramatic daredevils who vow to take you away from your humdrum life onto a nonstop roller coaster of wild exhilaration; or a wolf who offers an escape from Mother's rules. Whichever of these scenarios best fit you, it's crucial to think about what's lacking in your life, because once you know your heart's desire, you can begin to rescue yourself. Then you may want to kiss your Frog good-bye and move on to a man who doesn't need rescuing.

Obsession Does Not Equal Love

Are you ever frightened by the intensity of your lover's passion for you—or yours for him? Before you dismiss this problem as a case of loving a little too *much*, you should realize there's an important difference between love and obsession. Obsession typically begins when one partner feels the other's love slipping *away*, and becomes so desperate to recapture it that he or she starts doing things which ultimately undermine what's left of the romance, such as snooping, spying, or stalking the other person. As the relationship deteriorates further, the rejected partner's compulsion to pursue and possess usually *escalates*, which can lead to harassment, abuse, or even violence.

Though you may feel none of this applies to you or your man, be warned: The combustible ingredients of potential obsession are present in *every* bad-boy romance—and can put you *both* at risk of becoming impassioned pursuers, for two key reasons. The first is that when you choose a rogue as a lover, you're picking a man who is and always will be elusive. That's because all bad boys are unavailable in some important way—whether they are married, wary of intimacy because they have so many skeletons hidden in their closet, too in love with themselves to be open to a deep relationship with you, or on a never-ending quest for the perfect princess who fits their slipper or passes their pea test.

Not only is this part of the unconscious allure a heel holds for you—since you're probably just as phobic about commitment as he is and secretly *prefer* a lover who can't be caught—but it can set you up to become obsessed with him. It may sound paradoxical to pick an unavailable man, and then get desperately engaged in a futile effort to capture him, but immersing yourself in the chase gives you the illusion that you're avidly seeking a relationship, while protecting you from the anxieties that actually finding one would arouse in you. Very often, women who run after rogues grow addicted to the thrill of the hunt—even though they don't really want the guy—and intensify their chase to the point of obsession when he remains maddeningly elusive.

The Little Mermaid fits this pattern perfectly. Even though she spies on her prince from afar and invades his world uninvited, she fails to make the one move that would secure the relationship she claims to want so desperately. When he's lying on the beach, vulnerable and clearly available, instead of telling him that she was the one who saved his life, she hides behind a rock until she hears him commit his heart to another woman. As soon as she sees he's safely unavailable, she instantly resumes the chase. Do *you* also unconsciously sabotage your relationships by hiding when you have a real chance of romantic success, and pursue only when failure is assured? If so, think of the heart-broken mermaid and ask yourself why you're drawn to *doomed* love affairs.

If all bad boys are slippery and anxious to escape intimacy, why would they be in any danger of getting obsessed with a woman? If your man is an Aladdin, he could be after the for-bidden pleasure that peeking at you provides. The overpowering need that a love-starved guy—whether he's a wolf, vampire, or some other type of rogue—has for you is not necessarily *per-sonal*. Far from showing that your beau can't live without *you*, his obsessive pursuit may indicate that he's so desperate to be loved that no one could possibly be available *enough* for him—even if she'd let him devour her totally or bleed her dry. So a Dracula or wolf always feels you are holding out on him, which can start him on an obsessive prowl for more—and more, and *more*.

Don't Get Burned by the Flames of Dangerous Passion

Yes, bad boys have a hot sexual aura that's very seductive—otherwise, why would we put up with their hurtful habits?—but it's only half of their attraction. It is easy to be blinded by the incandescent erotic skyrockets these men set off in us, and not notice the dark thread of danger—or even violence—that runs through these relationships. This could be a bigger part of your wild stallion's allure than you realize, since women often become *addicted* to the extreme excitement risky romances seem to offer.

It's okay to crave passion, because a relationship without fire would soon flicker out, but fairy tales remind us that it can take two dramatically opposite forms. There's the smoldering rage that blazes in Dracula's hot, red eyes—and the Robber Bride-groom's brutal barbecue—or there's the enduring glow of love that Beauty experiences as she accepts the Beast's marriage proposal and looks up to see millions of fireflies lighting the night sky in ecstasy. Make sure your man knows how to channel his fire, unlike the Wizard, whose hot air blows him away from you. And flee from the alluring—but potentially lethal—lover who wants to lead you down a path of ashes to your incineration. Find a man who has enough spark and warmth to light your fire—but not enough to burn you.

Risk Your Tender Heart—but Don't Toss It Away on Every Wolf Who Skulks By

If you've been hurt in your past love affairs, you may be tempted to follow the example of the princess who falls for a frog because he gives her back her golden heart to show he won't break it the way her previous lovers did. Being overprotective of *your* heart however, can make you so afraid of falling in love—and risking another rejection—that you refuse to pursue the prince of your dreams, and find yourself sharing your golden plate—and your soft, silken bed—with a frog you feel is far beneath you.

Going to the opposite extreme, however, and being so eager to be in a relationship that you toss your love away on a man who has no heart, and will never love you in return, is equally hazardous. But what are the warning signs to watch for? Be careful of men whose heart is taken or you can end up like the Mermaid who felt hers break. Be wary of heartless Pinocchios who ignore your needs as they pursue only their own pleasure. But the most heart-stopping men of all are dominating Draculas who drain you of your lifeblood if you make the mistake of confusing their possessiveness with love; and ruthless robbers who take relentless advantage of women until their heart bursts.

What if you've already been wounded by a bad boy? Take heart: All isn't lost if you have made some romantic mistakes in the past. A broken heart, like a broken bone, can heal even stronger than it was before. Instead of being hard on yourself, or feeling foolish for having fallen for the wrong man—or men— look for lessons in each failed relationship that will help you to love more wisely the next time. Refuse to become bitter, or let your scars prevent you from exploring glorious new possibilities. You're more discerning now and your heart is more resilient than you think, so follow it and take a *reasoned* risk on romance!

Break the Spell of Your Childhood Instead of Repeating It Endlessly in Your Relationships

Have you mythologized your parents into wicked witches, demons, or scheming sorcerers who still have a dark power in your adult life? This can create an unconscious compulsion to replace your evil parent with a bad boy and replay your old traumas in a new relationship—perhaps by picking a man who is just like Dad, as Beauty does when she goes from her wounded father to an even more wounded Beast; or one who is his exact opposite, as Cinderella does when she chooses her power-mad prince as an antidote to the wimpy, ineffectual father who let himself be overruled by her cruel, dominating stepmother.

You may also be susceptible to the spell of a scoundrel for the same reason that some fairy-tale heroines are: You felt abandoned or unprotected by your mother. Perhaps she was absent entirely, as is the case for Dorothy and the Little Mermaid; or put you in danger the way Lucy's mother did when she closed her eyes to her husband's habit of sleepwalking into her daughter's bed. Either of these scenarios can leave you stuck in a childhood stage where you're struggling with two powerful, opposing wishes: your desire to capture the first prince in your life—Daddy—and your unsatisfied need to have your mother protect you from a father who is too available, and takes advantage of you emotionally, physically, or sexually. This is the spell that makes bad boys so seductive to you—because they're available and unavailable at the same time, they encourage you to reenact this script, by giving you the hope that you can finally figure out a way to make the story end *happily*.

Remind yourself of this fairy-tale wisdom: *There is no spell that can't be broken,* whether it's an attraction to men who cause you pain, or the unresolved childhood conflicts that are fueling these frustrating love affairs. You're not the helpless prisoner of a scoundrel's sorcery; if you find him enchantingly desirable, it's because you've *chosen* to let him charm you. He may speak to you in your dreams, as Beast does to Beauty; rub his magic lamp to get you into bed with him; or entrance you with his hypnotic gaze; but if his wicked ways are making you miserable, you already have all the ingredients you need inside you to make a magic potion of your own—and free yourself of whatever hold he has over you.

If you have a *pattern* of three or more bad-boy relationships, are involved with a Dracula or Lethal Lover right now, or are having trouble extricating yourself from any destructive passion, get professional help. A good psychotherapist may be the Dr. Van Helsing you need to help you drive a stake through the heart of a lover who is doing you harm—and finally bury the past!

True Love Feels Like You're Home at Last

Like Dorothy, who keeps wishing—futilely—that the Wizard would magically transport her back to Kansas, a lot of us look for a lover we can truly feel at home with, then discover to our distress that the "home" we've found with him is the very one that made us so unhappy as children. To keep from finding yourself back in the desolate gray farmhouse where you grew up, you need a man who makes you feel that you have finally found the home you've longed for—a cozy, *safe* place where there's always a warm fire burning in the hearth, tasty food on the table, and a loving man who wants to embrace you forever.

Before you can get to this idyllic place, however, you have to believe it exists—and that *you* belong there. Often women who were raised in a dysfunctional home don't expect to find anything better as adults because their upbringing has imprinted them with the idea that they are fundamentally unlovable. This feeling—or a fear of re-creating your hurtful childhood home if you let yourself get too close to a man—can leave you standing in the doorway of the palace you've yearned for, because you refuse to let your prince carry you over the threshold. Like the Little Mermaid, you may hide from the happiness that should be yours, because you feel like a fish out of water as soon as that perfect Hallmark card home is actually within your grasp—and swim off in a panic.

When deciding if you've found Mr. Right, take a close look at what kind of home he can provide for you—literally and psychologically. Renata, for example, was very taken with a musician who had all the trappings of success—a glamorous career, a BMW, and an expensively decorated apartment—until she noticed one discordant note: There was no food in his refrigerator. "At first, it didn't bother me because we were spending blissful hours together in his bedroom, not hanging around the kitchen; but later on, after we'd broken up, I felt it was symbolic of everything that was wrong with the relationship. Keith put up a great front, but underneath he had nothing to nourish me—or any woman—with."

It can also be a danger sign if you feel your lover is like a famished frog, wicked wolf, or voracious vampire who *invades* your home. While you may just be scared of intimacy—and worry that if you let a man into the secure fortress you have built for yourself you may get hurt—a *strong* sense of violation indicates that you've hooked up with a heel who is genuinely intrusive, and will try to move in on you. If so, barricade your door with garlic and protective amulets, and only open it again after you've replaced him with a boyfriend who, like Aladdin, wants to build a nest where the two of you can find safe refuge from the world's woes in each other's arms. That's when you will agree that home really is where the heart is!

Real-life Happy Endings

There are a few things fairy tales *don't* tell us about how to achieve a successful relationship in the real world. Finding a man who loves you isn't enough to make you live happily ever after, as many women fantasize when they tell themselves that the entire key to their happiness is meeting and capturing the right guy. The problem with this way of thinking, however, is that it encourages you to passively accept your fate in romance. Instead of putting your life on hold as you wait for a prince to come along and make you the princess of his heart—or for a frog that you hope to change into a prince with your kisses—why not put a tiara on your own head and start making yourself happy now?

Since most tales end with the prince and princess going blissfully off into the sunset, they prime us to believe there's only one happy ending to a relationship. That leaves us wishing we could be in Cinderella's shoes, find the pea that proves we're the princess our man is looking for, or learn the secret kiss that will turn our beast of a bad boy into a handsome prince. But there are two other endings to a romance that could *ultimately* bring us joy. Like Little Red Riding Hood—or Mina—we might find that with the help and support of friends (or a trusted therapist), we can emerge safely from a dangerous or destructive attraction, and be free to find a healthier love with someone else. Or, even better, like Dorothy, we may discover we have the power to rescue ourselves or make magic when we click our own heels—instead of waiting for a Wizard to fly us home.

Of course you want to fall in love—and *yes*, it *would* give you the greatest joy of all to be loved in return—but you need to love *yourself* first. No man can make you feel like a princess until you believe that you are one already. Too many of us want to turn ourselves over to any lover who tells us that his magic carpet can fly us away from all our problems, then discover that he's just another bad boy who has *new* ways of making us miserable. What we should do is stop rescuing rogues, and start rescuing ourselves, because once we've nourished ourselves with love, self-esteem, and belief in our own magical powers, we're finally ready to make all our fairy-tale fantasies of love come true. That is when we'll find the prince we deserve, and embark on the exhilarating adventure of living happily ever after!

A LETTER TO THE READER

Is your "Bad Boy" the most seductive heartbreaker of them all? Did he have an affair—and charge it to your credit card? Is he the type who may or may not show up on your birthday, and if he does, he's the only gift—warts and all? Did he take off to Mexico in your car and then call you weeks later at 3:00 A.M. expecting you to invite him over for sex? Is he on the lam from the law—or his ex?

Share your story with us—and if we include it in a future book, you'll get a free autographed copy, along with the knowledge that you're helping other women with similar problems. Tell us about your man's wicked, wicked ways, and send your story to:

Dr. Carole Lieberman and Lisa Collier Cool
Bad Boy Contest
c/o Dutton Signet
375 Hudson Street
New York, NY 10014-3657

NOTES

The following books of fairy tales were consulted in preparing this book:

The Adventures of Pinocchio, Carlo Collodi, trans. Fritz Kredel. New York: Grosset and Dunlap, 1946.

Andersen's Fairy Tales, Hans Christian Andersen; "The Mermaid" and "The Real Princess." Stamford, Connecticut: Longmeadow Press, 1988.

Andersen's Fairy Tales, Hans Christian Andersen; "The Princess and the Pea" and "The Little Mermaid." New York: Signet Classics, 1987.

Andrew Lang Fairy Tale Treasury; "Cinderella," "Beauty and the Beast," and "Blue Beard." New York: Avenel Books, 1979.

The Arabian Nights Entertainment, Andrew Lang, ed.; "Aladdin and the Wonderful Lamp." New York: Dover Publications, 1969.

Cinderella and Other Tales from Perrault, Charles Perrault; "Cinderella, or The Little Glass Slipper," "Little Red Riding Hood," and "Blue Beard." New York: Henry Holt and Company, 1989.

The Complete Fairy Tales of the Brothers Grimm, trans. Jack Zipes; "The Frog King"; "Cinderella"; Little Red Riding Hood"; and "The Robber Bridegroom." New York: Bantam Books, 1987.

The Complete Grimm's Fairy Tales, trans. Margaret Hunt and James Stern; "The Frog King," "Cinderella," "Little Red Cap," and "The Robber Bridegroom." New York: Random House, 1972.

The Complete Hans Christian Andersen Fairy Tales, Lily Owens, ed.; "The Little Mermaid" and "The Princess and the Pea." New York: Avenel Books, 1981.

Dracula, Bram Stoker. New York: Signet Classics, 1965.

The Family Treasury of Children's Stories, Pauline Rush Evans, ed.; "Cinderella." New York: Doubleday, 1956.

Jack Kent's Hokus Pokus Bedtime Book; "The Frog Prince" and "Aladdin and the Wonderful Lamp." New York: Random House, 1979.

Pinocchio, Carlo Collodi. New York: Puffin Classics, 1974.

The Wizard of Oz, L. Frank Baum. New York: Del Rey Books, 1956. New York: Waldman and Son, 1977.

The Wonderful Wizard of Oz, L. Frank Baum. New York: Signet Classics, 1984.